Photoshop® and Illustrator Synergy Studio Secrets™

JENNIFER ALSPACH

PHOTOSHOP® AND ILLUSTRATOR SYNERGY STUDIO SECRETS™

IDG BOOKS WORLDWIDE, INC.

AN INTERNATIONAL DATA GROUP COMPANY

Foster City, CA ▲ Chicago, IL ◆ Indianapolis, IN ▼ Southlake, TX

Photoshop® and Illustrator Synergy Studio Secrets™

Published by

IDG Books Worldwide, Inc.

An International Data Group Company

919 E. Hillsdale Blvd., Suite 400

Foster City, CA 94404

www.idgbooks.com (IDG Books Worldwide Web site)

Library of Congress Catalog Card Number: 97-078213

ISBN: 0-7645-3134-4

Printed in the United States of America

10 9 8 7 6 5 4 3 2

1K/QT/QT/ZY/FC

Distributed in the United States by IDG Books Worldwide, Inc.

Distributed by Macmillan Canada for Canada; by Transworld Publishers Limited in the United Kingdom; by IDG Norge Books for Norway; by IDG Sweden Books for Sweden; by Woodslane Pty. Ltd. for Australia; by Woodslane Enterprises Ltd. for New Zealand; by Longman Singapore Publishers Ltd. for Singapore, Malaysia, Thailand, and Indonesia; by Simron Pty. Ltd. for South Africa; by Toppan Company Ltd. for Japan; by Distribuidora Cuspide for Argentina; by Livraria Cultura for Brazil; by Ediciencia S.A. for Ecuador; by Addison-Wesley Publishing Company for Korea; by Ediciones ZETA S.C.R. Ltda. for Peru; by WS Computer Publishing Corporation, Inc., for the Philippines; by Unalis Corporation for Taiwan; by Contemporanea de Ediciones for Venezuela; by Computer Book & Magazine Store for Puerto Rico; by Express Computer Distributors for the Caribbean and West Indies. Authorized Sales Agent: Anthony Rudkin Associates for the Middle East and North Africa.

For general information on IDG Books Worldwide's books in the U.S., please call our Consumer Customer Service department at 800-762-2974. For reseller information, including discounts and premium sales, please call our Reseller Customer Service department at 800-434-3422.

For information on where to purchase IDG Books Worldwide's books outside the U.S., please contact our International Sales department at 650-655-3200 or fax 650-655-3295.

For information on foreign language translations, please contact our Foreign & Subsidiary Rights department at 650-655-3021 or fax 650-655-3281.

For sales inquiries and special prices for bulk quantities, please contact our Sales department at 650-655-3200 or write to the address above.

For information on using IDG Books Worldwide's books in the classroom or for ordering examination copies, please contact our Educational Sales department at 800-434-2086 or fax 817-251-8174.

For press review copies, author interviews, or other publicity information, please contact our Public Relations department at 650-655-3000 or fax 650-655-3299.

For authorization to photocopy items for corporate, personal, or educational use, please contact Copyright Clearance Center, 222 Rosewood Drive, Danvers, MA 01923, or fax 978-750-4470.

ABOUT IDG BOOKS WORLDWIDE

Welcome to the world of IDG Books Worldwide.

IDG Books Worldwide, Inc., is a subsidiary of International Data Group, the world's largest publisher of computer-related information and the leading global provider of information services on information technology. IDG was founded more than 25 years ago and now employs more than 8,500 people worldwide. IDG publishes more than 275 computer publications in over 75 countries (see listing below). More than 60 million people read one or more IDG publications each month.

Launched in 1990, IDG Books Worldwide is today the #1 publisher of best-selling computer books in the United States. We are proud to have received eight awards from the Computer Press Association in recognition of editorial excellence and three from *Computer Currents'* First Annual Readers' Choice Awards. Our best-selling *...For Dummies®* series has more than 30 million copies in print with translations in 30 languages. IDG Books Worldwide, through a joint venture with IDG's Hi-Tech Beijing, became the first U.S. publisher to publish a computer book in the People's Republic of China. In record time, IDG Books Worldwide has become the first choice for millions of readers around the world who want to learn how to better manage their businesses.

Our mission is simple: Every one of our books is designed to bring extra value and skill-building instructions to the reader. Our books are written by experts who understand and care about our readers. The knowledge base of our editorial staff comes from years of experience in publishing, education, and journalism — experience we use to produce books for the '90s. In short, we care about books, so we attract the best people. We devote special attention to details such as audience, interior design, use of icons, and illustrations. And because we use an efficient process of authoring, editing, and desktop publishing our books electronically, we can spend more time ensuring superior content and spend less time on the technicalities of making books.

You can count on our commitment to deliver high-quality books at competitive prices on topics you want to read about. At IDG Books Worldwide, we continue in the IDG tradition of delivering quality for more than 25 years. You'll find no better book on a subject than one from IDG Books Worldwide.

John Kilcullen
CEO
IDG Books Worldwide, Inc.

Steven Berkowitz
President and Publisher
IDG Books Worldwide, Inc.

*Eighth Annual
Computer Press
Awards ≥1992*

*Ninth Annual
Computer Press
Awards ≥1993*

*Tenth Annual
Computer Press
Awards ≥1994*

*Eleventh Annual
Computer Press
Awards ≥1995*

IDG Books Worldwide, Inc., is a subsidiary of International Data Group, the world's largest publisher of computer-related information and the leading global provider of information services on information technology. International Data Group publishes over 275 computer publications in over 75 countries. Sixty million people read one or more International Data Group publications each month. International Data Group's publications include: **ARGENTINA:** Buyer's Guide, Computerworld Argentina, PC World Argentina; **AUSTRALIA:** Australian Macworld, Australian PC World, Australian Reseller News, Computerworld, IT Casebook, Network World, Publish, Webmaster; **AUSTRIA:** Computerwelt Osterreich, Networks Austria, PC Tip Austria; **BANGLADESH:** PC World Bangladesh; **BELARUS:** PC World Belarus; **BELGIUM:** Data News; **BRAZIL:** Annuário de Informática, Computerworld, Connections, Macworld, PC Player, PC World, Publish, Reseller News, Supergamepower; **BULGARIA:** Computerworld Bulgaria, Network World Bulgaria, PC & MacWorld Bulgaria; **CANADA:** CIO Canada, Client/Server World, ComputerWorld Canada, InfoWorld Canada, NetworkWorld Canada, WebWorld; **CHILE:** Computerworld Chile, PC World Chile; **COLOMBIA:** Computerworld Colombia, PC World Colombia; **COSTA RICA:** PC World Centro America; **THE CZECH AND SLOVAK REPUBLICS:** Computerworld Czechoslovakia, Macworld Czech Republic, PC World Czechoslovakia; **DENMARK:** Communications World Danmark, Computerworld Danmark, Macworld Danmark, PC World Danmark, Techworld Denmark; **DOMINICAN REPUBLIC:** PC World Republica Dominicana; **ECUADOR:** PC World Ecuador; **EGYPT:** Computerworld Middle East, PC World Middle East; **EL SALVADOR:** PC World Centro America; **FINLAND:** MikroPC, Tietoverkko, Tietoviikko; **FRANCE:** Distributique, Hebdo, Info PC, Le Monde Informatique, Macworld, Reseaux & Telecoms, WebMaster France; **GERMANY:** Computer Partner, Computerwoche, Computerwoche Extra, Computerwoche FOCUS, Global Online, Macwelt, PC Welt; **GREECE:** Amiga Computing, GamePro Greece, Multimedia World; **GUATEMALA:** PC World Centro America; **HONDURAS:** PC World Centro America; **HONG KONG:** Computerworld Hong Kong, PC World Hong Kong, Publish in Asia; **HUNGARY:** ABCD CD-ROM, Computerworld Szamitastechnika, Internetto online Magazine, PC World Hungary, PC-X Magazin Hungary; **ICELAND:** Tolvuheimur PC World Island; **INDIA:** Information Communications World, Information Systems Computerworld, PC World India, Publish in Asia; **INDONESIA:** InfoKomputer PC World, Komputek Computerworld, Publish in Asia; **IRELAND:** ComputerScope, PC Live!; **ISRAEL:** Macworld Israel, People & Computers/Computerworld; **ITALY:** Computerworld Italia, Macworld Italia, Networking Italia, PC World Italia; **JAPAN:** DTP World, Macworld Japan, Nikkei Personal Computing, OS/2 World Japan, SunWorld Japan, Windows NT World, Windows World Japan; **KENYA:** PC World East African; **KOREA:** Hi-Tech Information, Macworld Korea, PC World Korea; **MACEDONIA:** PC World Macedonia; **MALAYSIA:** Computerworld Malaysia, PC World Malaysia, Publish in Asia; **MALTA:** PC World Malta; **MEXICO:** Computerworld Mexico, PC World Mexico; **MYANMAR:** PC World Myanmar; **NETHERLANDS:** Computer! Totaal, LAN Internetworking Magazine, LAN World Buyers Guide, Macworld Netherlands, Net, WebWereld; **NEW ZEALAND:** Absolute Beginners Guide and Plain & Simple Series, Computer Buyer, Computer Industry Directory, Computerworld New Zealand, MTB, Network World, PC World New Zealand; **NICARAGUA:** PC World Centro America; **NORWAY:** Computerworld Norge, CW Rapport, Datamagasinet, Financial Rapport, Kursguide Norge, Macworld Norge, Multimediaworld Norge, PC World Ekspress Norge, PC World Nettverk, PC World Norge, PC World ProduktGuide Norge; **PAKISTAN:** Computerworld Pakistan; **PANAMA:** PC World Panama; **PEOPLE'S REPUBLIC OF CHINA:** China Computer Users, China Computerworld, China InfoWorld, China Telecom World Weekly, Computer & Communication, Electronic Design China, Electronics Today, Electronics Weekly, Game Software, PC World China, Popular Computer Week, Software Weekly, Software World, Telecom World; **PERU:** Computerworld Peru, PC World Profesional Peru, PC World Puerto Rico, PC World SoHo Peru; **PHILIPPINES:** Click!, Computerworld Philippines, PC World Philippines, Publish in Asia; **POLAND:** Computerworld Poland, Computerworld Special Report Poland, Cyber, Macworld Poland, Networld Poland, PC World Komputer; **PORTUGAL:** Cerebro/PC World, Computerworld/Correio Informático, Dealer World Portugal, Mac*In/PC*In Portugal, Multimedia World; **PUERTO RICO:** PC World Puerto Rico; **ROMANIA:** Computerworld Romania, PC World Romania, Telecom Romania; **RUSSIA:** Computerworld Russia, Mir PK, Publish, Seti; **SINGAPORE:** Computerworld Singapore, PC World Singapore, Publish in Asia; **SLOVENIA:** Monitor; **SOUTH AFRICA:** Computing SA, Network World SA, Software World SA; **SPAIN:** Communicaciones World España, Computerworld España, Dealer World España, Macworld España, PC World España, PC World Communications; **SRI LANKA:** Infolink PC World; **SWEDEN:** CAP&Design, Computer Sweden, Corporate Computing Sweden, Internetworld Sweden, it.branschen, Macworld Sweden, MaxiData Sweden, MikroDatorn, Natverk & Kommunikation, PC World Sweden, PCaktiv, Windows World Sweden; **SWITZERLAND:** Computerworld Schweiz, Macworld Schweiz, PCtip; **TAIWAN:** Computerworld Taiwan, Macworld Taiwan, PC World Taiwan, Windows World Taiwan; **THAILAND:** Publish in Asia, Thai Computerworld; **TURKEY:** Computerworld Turkiye, Macworld Turkiye, Network World Turkiye, PC World Turkiye; **UKRAINE:** Computerworld Kiev, Multimedia World Ukraine, PC World Ukraine; **UNITED KINGDOM:** Acorn User UK, Amiga Action UK, Amiga Computing UK, Apple Talk UK, Computing, Macworld, Parents and Computers UK, PC Advisor, PC Home, PSX Pro, The WEB; **UNITED STATES:** Cable in the Classroom, CIO Magazine, Computerworld, DOS World, Federal Computer Week, GamePro Magazine, InfoWorld, I-Way, Macworld, Network World, PC Games, PC World, Publish, Video Event, THE WEB Magazine, and WebMaster; online webzines: JavaWorld, NetscapeWorld, and SunWorld Online; **URUGUAY:** InfoWorld Uruguay; **VENEZUELA:** Computerworld Venezuela, PC World Venezuela; and **VIETNAM:** PC World Vietnam. 3/24/97

To my parents, for their unconditional love and unwavering support. Without their guidance and amazing genes, this book would not have been possible.

FOREWORD

WELCOME TO A NEW WAY OF WORKING

You may have noticed on the cover of this book is a *Publish* magazine logo and the words "authorized and approved." For those of you familiar with our magazine, and for those not, I'd like to explain what that phrase means and to tell you how particularly excited we are to add our endorsement to this great title. This book is, in fact, a great example of what *Publish* stands for and what we do each month to help our readers master the sometimes difficult software contained in the artist's toolbox of today.

If you've worked with Adobe Photoshop or Adobe Illustrator for any length of time, you already know what powerful tools these are. And, likewise, you have probably discovered that increasingly no digital artist can practice his or her craft in only one software program. At both *Publish* and IDG Books, we've recognized for some time that the key to creative success is no longer just the mastery of individual software titles. The only way a computer screen can be considered a truly blank canvas is when you have the option of creating in both vector and pixel modes—the digital equivalent of mixing watercolor with pen and ink.

We have all come to accept Adobe Photoshop as the standard pixel editing and creation program. And there is arguably no better vector-drawing companion tool than Adobe Illustrator. With Version 4.0 of Photoshop, and Version 7.0 of Illustrator, Adobe has turned these two individual software tools into a synergistic duo that delivers common interface designs and work methods. In fact, the editors at *Publish* handed Adobe one of their prized Impact Awards last year for designing products that work even better together than they do individually. In this book, you'll discover how many of today's leading digital artists leverage the power of both Adobe Photoshop and Adobe Illustrator, along with other powerful tools, such as Macromedia Freehand, Painter, and Bryce, to complete their creative visions. And therein lies another similarity with *Publish* magazine.

Like Jennifer Alspach, we believe one of the best ways to learn is from watching how others have mastered their craft. Since we began publishing in 1986, we continually find that the most popular sections of our magazine are the ones that show, step-by-step, how contemporary artists achieved great results. The lineup of individuals covered in this book reads like a who's who of digital artistry. If you read *Publish*, it's likely you've seen many of their works before—we've both covered and used much of the talent you'll read about in the following pages. And if you are not familiar with *Publish*, we hope the quality and helpfulness of this book will make you want to discover why we have become the number one magazine for electronic publishing professionals.

Everyone involved in this series of books is truly committed to excellence and creativity. Our mission at *Publish* and at IDG Books is constantly to present you with new learning opportunities and to help cut through the glut of information available on computer technology. By bringing a unique focus to creative subjects, like looking at the synergy between programs instead of just the individual features, we are trying to understand and be sensitive to the way you work.

Much of the power yet to be unleashed by technology has more to do with work methods and workflow than with new features and gimmicks.

I hope you enjoy this title and that it helps you think in new and creative ways about two of the most important tools on your desktop. And, please, if you have any thoughts or suggestions about how we can improve this series, please let me know. You can visit the *Publish* magazine Web site, Publish RGB, at `www.publish.com`. You can send e-mail to me at `ggable@publish.com`. We'd be delighted to hear how you've tapped the capabilities of Photoshop, Illustrator, and other great applications to extend your creative vision.

Gene Gable
President/Publisher
Publish magazine
San Francisco

PREFACE

"Cool image, man, did you use Photoshop to do that?"

"Well, I drew the basic shapes in Illustrator and imported the file into Expression. In Expression, I painted in the shapes except for the person, which I finished in Illustrator. Then I rasterized the image in Photoshop and used KPT Noise for texture and adjusted the Hue/Saturation. On a copy, I pointillized the background to create a transparent effect. . . ."

As you can see, achieving an amazing image is no longer done in just one program. Many artists use a variety of programs to create their images. This multiple program usage was my inspiration to write *Photoshop and Illustrator Synergy Studio Secrets*. While many books are in the market for specific programs, none addressed the secrets—and problems—of working between programs as this one does.

Coming up with a title for a book of this stature posed another problem. The name *Photoshop, Illustrator, FreeHand, Dimensions, Painter, Bryce, Goo, Soap, PhotoTools, VectorTools, MaskPro, Eye Candy, QuarkXPress, PageMaker, and the Web Synergy* seemed a bit lengthy. In talking to IDG Books Worldwide, we finally came up with a much shorter and more suitable name: *Photoshop and Illustrator Synergy Studio Secrets*. While the title only mentions Illustrator with Photoshop, you'll soon see those two programs go hand in hand and blend well with other programs.

In writing this book, I contacted many artists whose images now grace its pages. I found many artists use Illustrator and Photoshop first, and then turn to other programs to create unheard-of effects. Without the support and ingenious techniques of these artists, this book would not have been possible. Their insights are invaluable, and the step-by-step images along the way really give you an idea of how to create an image similar to theirs.

WHO SHOULD READ THIS BOOK

This book is aimed at all artists, graphic designers, and anyone else who likes to play around with images. It is also for the curious-minded who always want to know how something was done. From the basic illustrator to the advanced professional, this book targets all levels of image creation.

COFFEE TABLE BOOK OR GALLERY SHOWCASE?

With all the amazing color images, *Photoshop and Illustrator Synergy Studio Secrets* would make a great coffee table book, but you'll probably want to use it as a reference and learning tool. This book is broken into two parts. Part I is called "Product Secrets." The secrets you'll find in the first part relate to the problems, issues, and results of working between programs. From file types to using only pieces of an image, this book will show you the best ways to achieve your desired effect. If you are working in 2D, 3D, or for the Web, this book has it all. You'll learn secrets of 3D software, painting software, page layout, and many other programs.

Part II, aptly called "Studio Secrets," is packed full of images to amaze the mind and boggle the soul. It is filled with eye-popping art and techniques from the artists themselves. Some art even comes with step-by-step images to show you how it was truly created. The topics covered range from purely artistic, text and textures, realism and logos, advertisements, 3D effects, and finishing touches.

CD-ROM OR NOSE RING

In the back of this book, you'll find a CD-ROM filled to the brim with secretive information. Actually, it is crammed full of galleries of art from the book, demo software, and exclusive—FREE—plug-ins! Last, but certainly not least, is the exclusive filters provided by Extensis Corporation. The filters you'll get with this book are PhotoShadow, PhotoGlow, Phototips, and Intellihance Lite. In addition to the exclusive filters, you'll get demo versions of many third-party products from Extensis' full range of product demos, including Alien Skin's Eye Candy, Painter 5, and more.

READ THIS BOOK OR ELSE . . .

. . . get lost in the shuffle of mediocre art creations. I have always searched for a book to cover the topics of multiple programs. Now the search is over. This book is guaranteed to be a hit at parties, social gatherings, and a great gift idea to the artist in all of us. If you would like to contribute to the next edition of *Photoshop and Illustrator Synergy Studio Secrets*, send me your submissions and insights to `Jen@bezier.com`. Prepare yourself to enter a journey to enlighten your artistic soul.

ACKNOWLEDGMENTS

I'd like to thank all the artists who contributed to this book. (To see the full list of artists, check the artist's index in the back of the book.) If you see art you like or you are interested in using some of the art you see in your next project, drop the artist a note, e-mail, or fax. The art you'll see is widely diversified and uses Photoshop and Illustrator in some way of their creation process.

A special thanks goes to Mike Roney whose prodding and pushing led to this wonderful book. Mike's insights on the products helped mold this book into a fantastic reference. I also want to thank Katharine Dvorak, Stephan Grünwedel, Marcia Baker, Tom Debolski, Andy Schueller, and the rest of the production staff of IDG Books Worldwide.

The CD-ROM is more than a funky hair accessory, thanks to the help of Mark Mehall, Sioux Fleming, and Diana Smedley, all of Extensis. Thanks also goes to Kevin Hurst, Craig Barns, and the rest of the Extensis team.

Many thanks to my parents, Carolyn and James Garling. Without them, this book wouldn't have been possible. Their constant encouragement and support taught me I can do anything. Thanks also goes to my husband, Ted. His love and encouragement were essential to me in finishing this book. And a very special thanks goes to Gage Alspach, who made me complete this book on time.

CONTENTS AT A GLANCE

CONTENTS

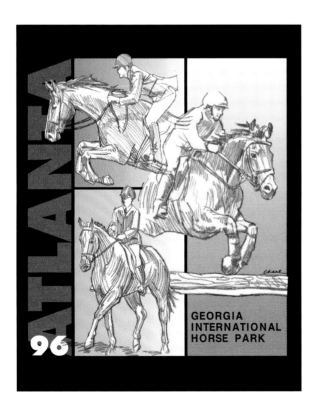

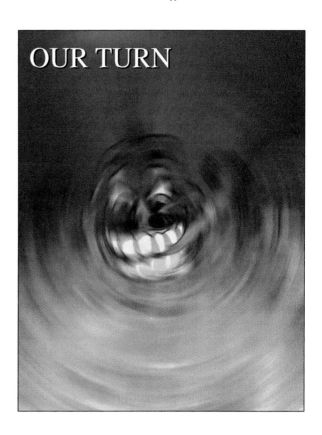

CHAPTER 4

PIXELS TO VECTORS AND
BACK AGAIN   61

CHAPTER 5
PHOTOSHOP AND ILLUSTRATOR WITH THIRD-PARTY PLUG-INS   75

CHAPTER 6
PHOTOSHOP AND ILLUSTRATOR WITH OTHER APPLICATIONS   113

PART II: STUDIO SECRETS   127

CHAPTER 7
TRACING PHOTOS AND USING HAND-DRAWN SKETCHES   129

CHAPTER 8
LOGOS, TYPE, AND IMAGES   141

CHAPTER 9

REALISM AND FINE ARTS   157

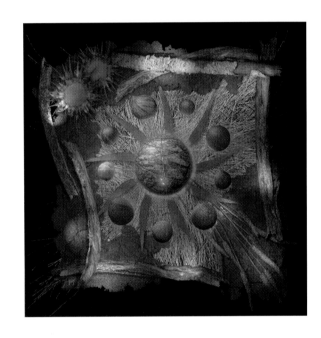

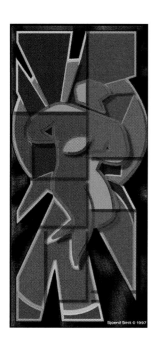

PART I
PRODUCT SECRETS

CHAPTER 1
PHOTOSHOP TO ILLUSTRATOR TECHNIQUES

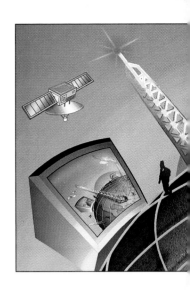

Using only one application to finish a project isn't enough anymore. With the ease and compatibility of file exchange between programs, more and more artists are using multiple programs to complete a project. The main link between the multiple programs is Adobe Photoshop. Its versatility enables users to enhance their images and save them in a format to be used in other applications. Third-party plug-in vendors like Extensis Corporation, KPT products, and Alien Skin have extended Photoshop's and Illustrator's editing ability beyond belief.

Moving a Photoshop image into Illustrator is done for a few reasons. One reason to take a Photoshop image into Illustrator is to trace over the image to create vector-based art. Many artists first sketch an idea, and then scan the sketch into Photoshop. In Photoshop, that sketch is cleaned up and saved to be placed or parsed into Illustrator for tracing. After tracing the image in Illustrator, you can then add color, text, and effects.

Another reason for taking a Photoshop image into Illustrator is to add type. While Photoshop has a type feature, it is pretty limited because you can't edit the type. The type in Photoshop also tends to look rough compared to type in Illustrator, which prints out smoothly. Placing or parsing an image into Illustrator is common to finish out the layout and type because Illustrator does a better job. Photoshop can create anti-aliased type and print out fine, but the type is uneditable.

What we see depends mainly on what we are looking for.

JOE JONES

PLACED OR PARSED, EPS OR TIFF—WHICH IS RIGHT FOR YOU?

The only way to get a Photoshop image into Illustrator is to open the file as a parsed image or to place the file in the document. Much confusion exists about whether placing or parsing a Photoshop image into Illustrator is better. After deciding which you want to do, you then must decide what file format from Photoshop will work best for your final image.

With all the choices in a Photoshop file, how can you determine which one is right for you? The File menu enables you to place or parse a Photoshop image. That image can be any form of a saved Photoshop file. In Illustrator 7, you can place or parse any Photoshop-saved format. A parsed image reads, interprets, and displays an EPS file. You cannot parse any other Photoshop file formats. You need to open the other Photoshop file formats. You can also simply open a Photoshop file, rather than place or import the image. Of course, not all formats print as the high quality you want. In addition, the placed image will have an *X* through the box and display the preview, the parsed image will not (1.1).

To parse an image, choose File ➢ Open; to place an image, choose File ➢ Place.

FILE TYPES

Adobe Illustrator 7 accepts all Photoshop file formats. Of course, all file formats don't have the same end results. Typically, you would choose to use a TIFF or an EPS file to place or parse into Illustrator. The TIFF can be embedded or link itself into the Illustrator file. The EPS would have to accompany the file along to the printer. The EPS file also can be embedded or linked, but the advantage of an EPS file is the DCS saving format. *DCS* is the acronym for *Desktop Color Separations*. The DCS saving format saves the four plates individually, as well as a fifth file for preview only. The four plates include the cyan, magenta, yellow, and black plates. The fifth file saved is a combination of all plates for a preview only. This is the preferred method when using high resolution files from Photoshop. The drawback is the file size is larger than the TIFF.

If you choose to place your image, your file is considered linked. This means the original TIFF or EPS must accompany the final file for output. The placed file can only be transformed (scaled, rotated, reflected, or sheared). You cannot apply any of the Photoshop filters or Gallery Effects filters to the placed image.

A parsed file imbeds the file into the Illustrator format, so the original needn't accompany the file for output. Many people prefer a parsed file because of this embedding. Another great reason for using a parsed file is you can apply any Photoshop filter or Gallery Effects filter to the parsed image, as well as any transformation.

Parsed

1.1A

Placed

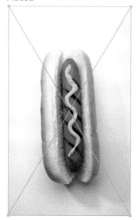

1.1B

RESOLUTION

When using any Photoshop file, the resolution of that file is important. In Illustrator, you needn't worry about resolution of vector-based images, but when you start placing or parsing Photoshop images you must consider the resolution of those images. The Drag-and-Drop feature of Adobe's products can be quite handy. But when you drag a Photoshop image into Illustrator, the resolution is limited to screen or 72 dpi (dots per inch). Figure 1.2 shows the difference between a parsed image and the same image dragged-and-dropped (1.2).

An Illustrator file is resolution independent. This means it will print to the resolution of your printer. Photoshop files need to have the resolution set before you print. If you are using a Photoshop image in

Parsed image

1.2A

Dragged-and-dropped image

1.2B

Illustrator, you must make sure the resolution of the Photoshop file will print at the quality you want. To get a high-quality printed image, you must determine what line screen values your printer can handle. You set the value of the line screen. A low line screen value will result in a rougher quality print because the dots are placed farther apart. A high line screen value creates a smoother quality print because the dots are placed closer together. The resolution of your Photoshop image can be determined by the line screen to which you are going to print. A good formula to follow is to double the line screen value to get your image's resolution in dots per inch. This way, you can scan in your photo at the right resolution from the beginning, before putting the image into Illustrator. Even though Illustrator is resolution independent, if you put a low-quality Photoshop image in the Illustrator file, the Photoshop image will print out as a low quality.

A common mistake is to scan in everything at a high resolution, regardless of how the file will be printed. This results in a darker, denser colored image because too many pixels are being used unnecessarily.

GETTING YOUR IMAGES INTO ILLUSTRATOR

Many ways exist to get a file from Photoshop into Illustrator. The most common way is to open the file. The typical way the power users of Photoshop and Illustrator get a file into Illustrator is to copy and paste. Copy and paste will preserve the resolution or dpi of the Photoshop file. You have been able to drag-and-drop files between the programs since Illustrator 6.0 and Photoshop 3.0.4.

DRAG-AND-DROP

Drag-and-Drop is now the easiest way to copy a file from page-to-page and from program-to-program. Drag-and-Drop works between the Adobe programs like Photoshop, Illustrator, and PageMaker. The concept is simple: To drag-and-drop an image or vector, select the part(s) you want to drag, and then hold the mouse button down on the image and drag to your Illustrator or Photoshop document (1.3). The

difference between this and copy and paste is when you copy an image, it must go to the clipboard. More time is taken to perform this function because a copy remains on the clipboard until you copy something else. The only drawback to Drag-and-Drop is, when you drag a section from a Photoshop image to drop into Illustrator or PageMaker, the resolution changes to Screen or 72 dpi.

COPY AND PASTE

Copy and paste is probably the most common way to get a selection from one page or program into another. Copy and paste works with most, if not all, software programs. Consider copy and paste the universal way to copy your images to another area. To copy a piece or pieces of an image from Photoshop to Illustrator, select the piece(s) you want to copy, and then select Copy from the Edit menu. In Illustrator, select Paste from the Edit menu to paste the object you just copied. Unlike Drag-and-Drop, when you copy a pixel image from Photoshop, it will retain that image's resolution.

USING PIECES OF PHOTOSHOP FILES

The images from Photoshop aren't the only things you can use from Photoshop. You can use any path drawn in Photoshop as well. By using your selection tools, you can select a section of an image and use only that section.

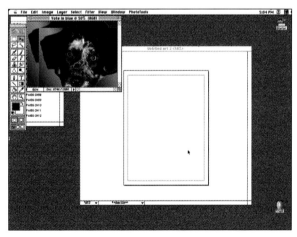

1.3

CLIPPING PATHS

A *clipping path* is a path drawn in Photoshop that clips the image within the path without actually cropping the file. What this means is the image will only be seen within the path's boundaries. A clipping path is a way of masking out the pieces you don't want and only viewing the pieces you do want. You can save a clipping path in Photoshop. Most people think of using a Clipping path for QuarkXPress or PageMaker, but few know you can use a Clipping path saved as an EPS file in Illustrator. Figure 1.4 shows a parsed image with and without a clipping path applied (1.4).

USING COLOR FROM THE PHOTOSHOP IMAGE

You can select color from your placed or parsed image from Photoshop in Illustrator. The eyedropper Tool in Illustrator can "suck" up the color attributes of any placed or parsed image (1.5). This feature may not sound that astounding, but it is a great ability for the artist to match a color in the rasterized image.

PATHS AND SELECTIONS FROM PHOTOSHOP

Any vector path drawn in Photoshop can be used in Illustrator by simply copying and pasting the path into Illustrator. The Drag-and-Drop feature doesn't work with a path so you have to copy and paste. What's nice about using a path is you can get an exact outline of an image you want to draw in Illustrator. If you are trying to draw the perfect horse head, you can select the background, select Inverse, and then let that selection be created as a path in Photoshop. You can then copy and paste that path into Illustrator. This saves you from having to trace a path in Photoshop or Illustrator (1.6). In a sense, this is quicker than scanning and tracing over a photo. You already have the outline, now just fill in the vector art with blends, gradients, or patterns.

Selections can easily be copied and pasted into Illustrator. Rather than using the whole image, you can select only the section you want and drag-and-drop the image into Illustrator. By dragging-and-dropping, you get only the selection, not the box with the whole image. When you use a clipping path, you

EPS image

1.4A

EPS image with clipping path

1.4B

get the whole image, but only the one section is masked. The file size will be larger when you save with a clipping path because it saves the whole image, rather than only the section you want to see.

USING NATIVE PHOTOSHOP AND ILLUSTRATOR FILTERS

Illustrator has a standard set of plug-ins or filters. These filters can be applied to your vector images, as well as your raster ones. Not every Illustrator filter can be applied to your rastered object, but many do apply. Most Photoshop filters can be applied to bitmaps right from Illustrator, as described in the following section.

APPLYING ILLUSTRATOR FILTERS

A little-known and seldom used area of Illustrator is the use of native Illustrator filters on rasterized objects. A placed or parsed image can have some filters applied directly to the image. Most of the Color

filters can easily be applied to your rasterized image. You can Adjust Colors, Convert to CMYK, Convert to Grayscale, Convert to RGB, Invert Colors, Merge Spot Colors, or Saturate (Desaturate) your rasterized image from the Color Filter menu. You can also Create and Object Mosaic or Create Trim Marks.

The Color filters are quite useful in tweaking your image without going back into Photoshop. You can easily adjust the colors to add or take away Cyan, Magenta, Yellow, or Black (1.7). Maybe your image is a little dull. Use Saturate to flood more color in the raster. If you need to show a negative of your raster, simply choose Filter ➤ Colors ➤ Invert (1.8).

The Object Mosaic filter is the only way to make your rasterized image into a vector image with Illustrator. The Object Mosaic filter works with any placed image. Object Mosaic created tiny squares of color to recreate the rasterized image. The more tiles you specify, the more detail you'll get. The catch (of course there's always a catch!) is the more tiles you use, the longer it will take to create the Object Mosaic version of your image.

1.5

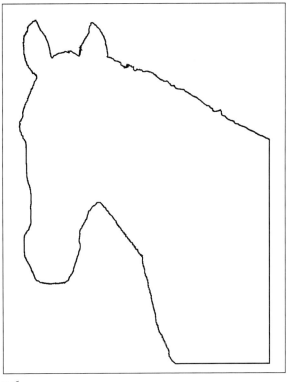

1.6

To create an Object Mosaic, follow these steps:

STEP 1 Select your placed image and choose Filter ➢ Create ➢ Object Mosaic (1.9).

STEP 2 In the Object Mosaic Dialog box (1.10), adjust your settings to your preference.

STEP 3 Press OK and you'll see your rasterized image turn into little squares of color (1.11).

STEP 4 Apply Transform to each of the tiles to get some spectacular results (1.12).

USING PHOTOSHOP FILTERS IN ILLUSTRATOR

One area you may not know you can use from Photoshop is Photoshop filters. You can copy Photoshop filters from Photoshop into the Illustrator Plug-Ins folder. Your parsed Photoshop images can now have Photoshop filters applied to them from within Illustrator. You have been able to use native Photoshop filters right from Illustrator since Illustrator 6.0. Copy or make an alias of the filters

Original

1.7A

Original

1.8A

Adjust Colors applied

1.7B

Inverted Colors

1.8B

and put them in your Illustrator Plug-Ins folder. (You must quit and relaunch Illustrator to activate these filters.) The easiest way to do this on a Macintosh is either to duplicate or make an alias of the Photoshop Plug-Ins folder and put them in the Illustrator Plug-Ins folder. On a Windows system, you copy or make a shortcut of the folder. This way, you needn't guess which filter will work. The ones that will work in Illustrator will be available under the Filter menu in Illustrator. By putting these filters in Illustrator you save yourself from having to jump back and forth between Photoshop and Illustrator to achieve these effects. The filters you can access are illustrated on the following pages (1.13 A – F).

1.9

1.11

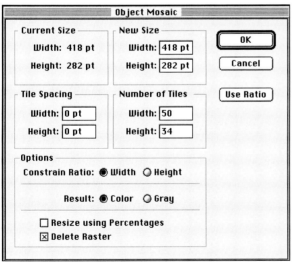

1.10

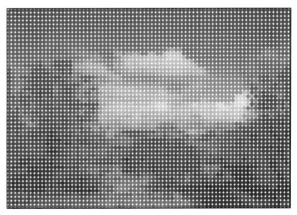

1.12

Artistic Filters

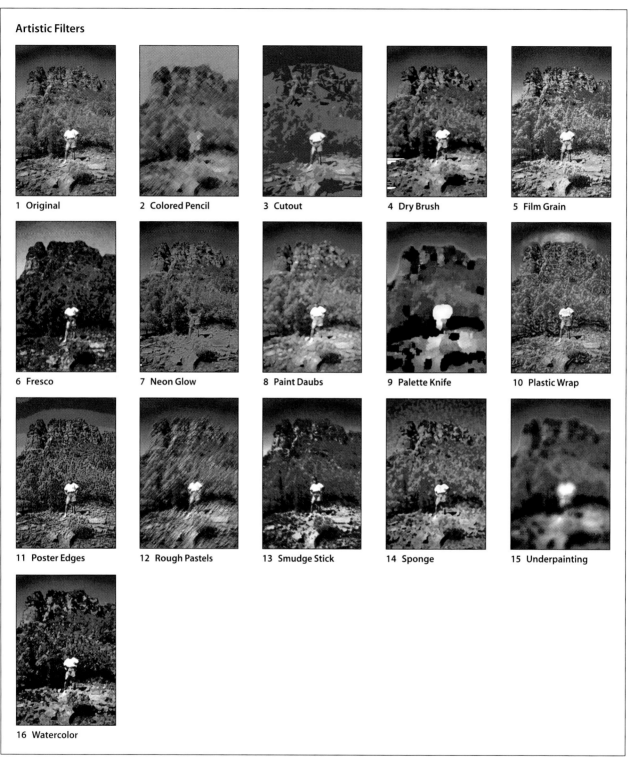

1 Original

2 Colored Pencil

3 Cutout

4 Dry Brush

5 Film Grain

6 Fresco

7 Neon Glow

8 Paint Daubs

9 Palette Knife

10 Plastic Wrap

11 Poster Edges

12 Rough Pastels

13 Smudge Stick

14 Sponge

15 Underpainting

16 Watercolor

1.13A

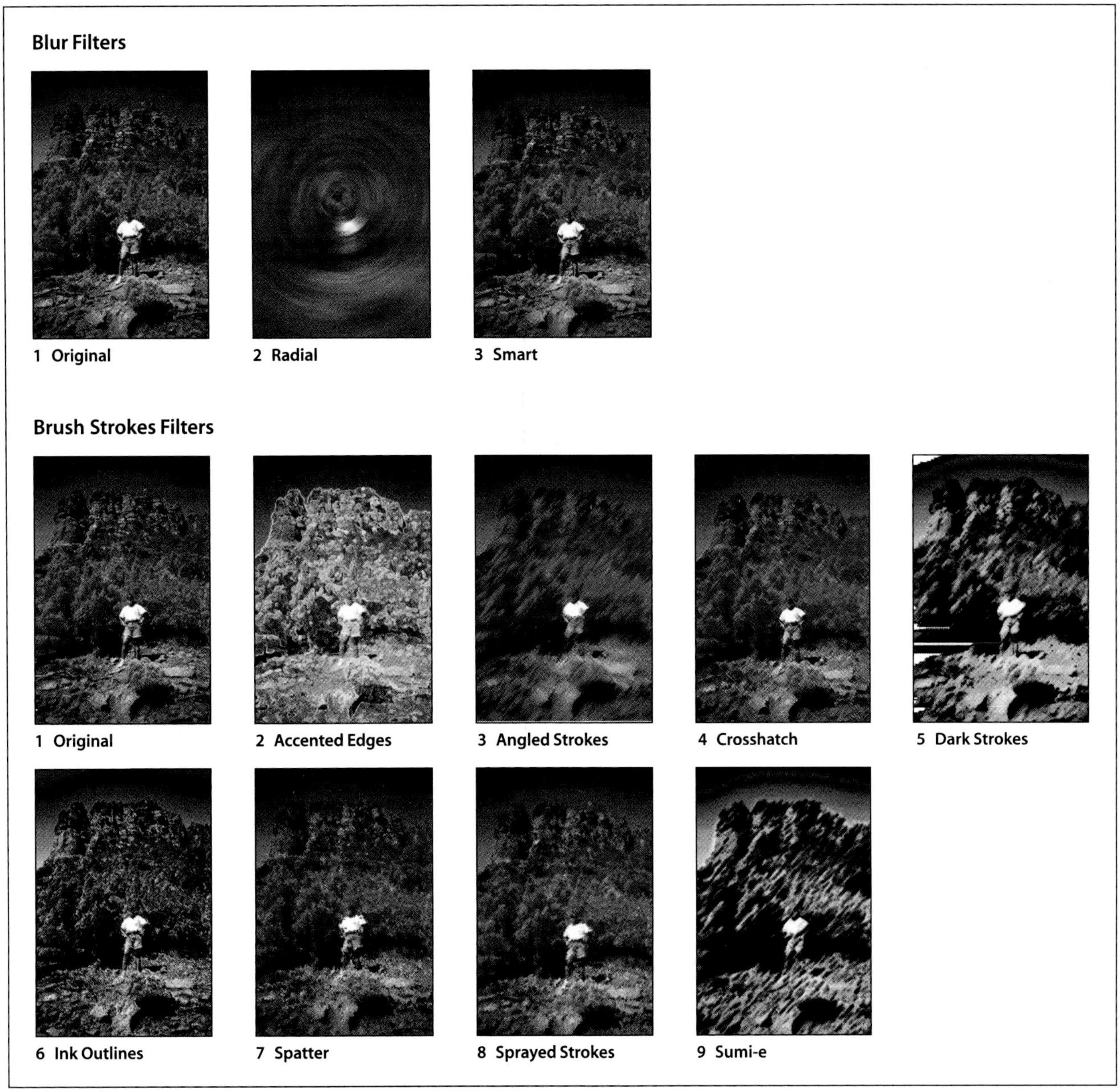

Blur Filters

1 Original

2 Radial

3 Smart

Brush Strokes Filters

1 Original

2 Accented Edges

3 Angled Strokes

4 Crosshatch

5 Dark Strokes

6 Ink Outlines

7 Spatter

8 Sprayed Strokes

9 Sumi-e

1.13B

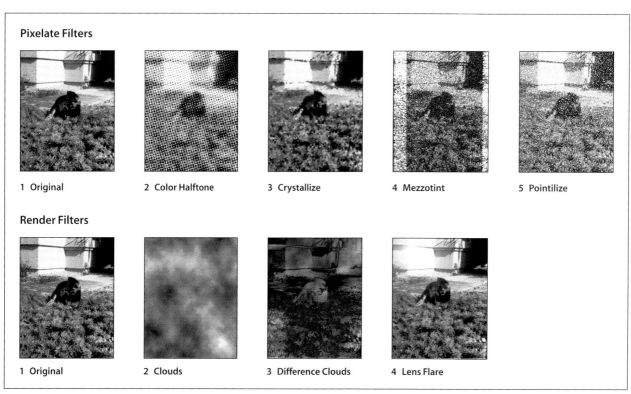

Distort Filters

1 Original 2 Diffuse Glow 3 Glass 4 Ocean Ripple
5 Pinch 6 Polar Coordinates 7 Ripple 8 Shear
9 Spherize 10 Twirl 11 Wave 12 Zig Zag

1.13C

Pixelate Filters

1 Original 2 Color Halftone 3 Crystallize 4 Mezzotint 5 Pointilize

Render Filters

1 Original 2 Clouds 3 Difference Clouds 4 Lens Flare

1.13D

Sketch Filters

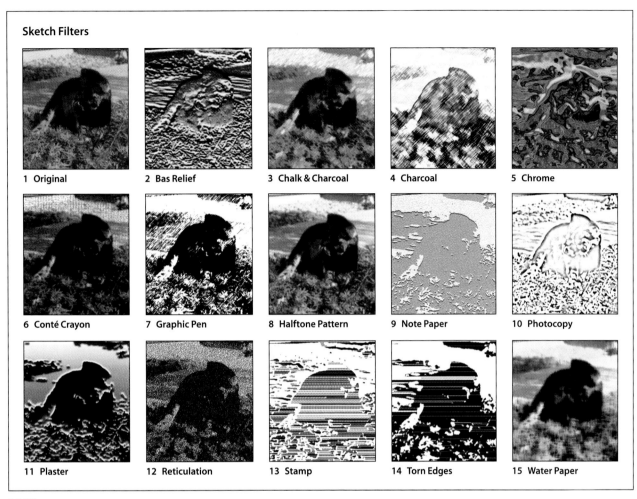

1 Original   2 Bas Relief   3 Chalk & Charcoal   4 Charcoal   5 Chrome

6 Conté Crayon   7 Graphic Pen   8 Halftone Pattern   9 Note Paper   10 Photocopy

11 Plaster   12 Reticulation   13 Stamp   14 Torn Edges   15 Water Paper

1.13E

Stylize Filters

1 Original

2 Exclude

3 Glowing Edges

4 Solarize

5 Tiles

6 Wind

Texture Filters

7 Texture

8 Craquelure

9 Grain

10 Mosaic Tiles

11 Patchwork

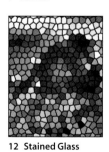

12 Stained Glass

13 Texturizer

1.13F

USING ILLUSTRATOR WITH PHOTOSHOP FILES

The main reasons artists use Illustrator with their Photoshop files are to build a sketch to enhance in Photoshop or to add type in Illustrator to their rasterized art. A rasterized image from Photoshop that needs type must be done in Illustrator, or another vector-based program, so you can edit that type again. Type also prints better from Illustrator because the file is printed in a Postscript form—Photoshop type comes out pixelized.

You can create some amazing effects with type in Illustrator for your rasterized image, as Pat Cheal did with this equestrian shirt she designed (1.14).

1.14

Printing the separations for this screenprint art for black shirts can be pretty tricky, and usually requires the printer to make several camera shots of the art. Pat has come up with a method that enables her to print the spot color separations in one step, fairly easily, using Adobe Illustrator. The tricky part is not having black print in the design, thereby eliminating another separation. The design calls for the black of the T-shirt to show through the other ink colors. Pat used the Pen tool to create solid white shapes behind the sketches. (Scanned pencil sketches, converted from grayscale to dithered bitmaps, saved as EPS files with transparent whites.) Then, to print the white separation, she used the invert command in page setup to change the black dots you see here to white, knocking out the background.

You can use Photoshop to create images, which you then add labels to in Illustrator (1.15). You could also create cover art using Illustrator for text and art, and use Photoshop to soften and add light and shadow. You can create magazine articles incorporating Photoshop and Illustrator, as well. (For more ideas on text, see Chapter 8 and Chapter 10.) The following steps show you how to create a cover page for an article incorporating Photoshop and Illustrator.

STEP 1   Open your original image in Photoshop (1.16).

STEP 2   Select the area on which you want to start the text with your Rectangular Marquee (1.17) and choose Levels under the Adjust submenu of the Image menu.

STEP 3   Drag the black Output levels slider (at the bottom of the dialog box) toward the right. With the preview box checked, you can see how much lighter the image will be (1.18). This is the area over which you will put type, so be sure to make it light enough so you can read the type.

STEP 4   Save the file and Open the file in Illustrator as a parsed image.

STEP 5   Using the Type tool, drag a rectangle over the lighter area.

STEP 6   Type in the information for your article (1.19).

Going from Photoshop to Illustator is done quite often, but not as often as going from Illustrator to Photoshop. Illustrator completes Photoshop in the area of text where Photoshop is lacking. An illustration done in Illustrator can be enhanced by using Photoshop, and then brought back into Illustrator for type. For more information on going from pixels to vectors and back again, see Chapter 5.

1.15

1.16

1.17

1.19

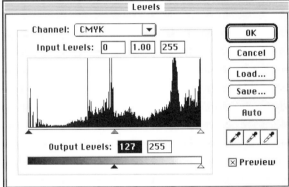

1.18

CHAPTER 2
ILLUSTRATOR TO PHOTOSHOP TECHNIQUES

Chapter 1 discussed the techniques of taking an image from Photoshop to Illustrator. The more common way to go, however, is from Illustrator to Photoshop. Illustrator provides the rough sketch and Photoshop finishes off the image with light, texture, and shadow. Illustrator creates the skeleton of an image and Photoshop adds a touch of realism.

Technical art done in Illustrator benefits from the capabilities of Photoshop by softening the harsh edges and adding textures using Photoshop's filters and adjustments. Photoshop can add the texture and depth Illustrator lacks. For example, Robert Forsbach's *Trojan* (2.1) shows the use of Photoshop for texture in the trees. The clouds also benefit from Photoshop's ability to smooth out blends from Illustrator. *Bugs* (2.2) shows how you can use the transparency effects of Photoshop to achieve the appearance of movement in the molecules. The ends of the twisted cords are enhanced by adding Noise to create texture.

In addition, text and logos can be taken to the next level in Photoshop. With Photoshop's native filters, you can add depth, embossing, texture, and much more. Illustrator is used many times to get text with different typefaces and sizes into Photoshop. Figure 2.3 shows different typefaces and sizes that were created in Illustrator and spruced up in Photoshop (2.3). Photoshop was used to add texture, bevels, and lighting effects. While Photoshop can do many things, text isn't a strong point. You can create text in Photoshop, but you are limited to one size and one

When in doubt, make it symmetrical.

ROBERT FORSBACH

2.1

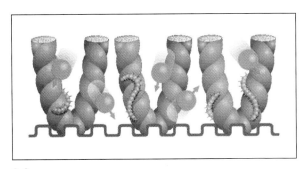

2.2

TROJAN
Robert Forsbach

19

typeface per text entry. This leaves the artist to use other programs, such as Illustrator, to create text effects and Photoshop to add the depth, shadow, and texture.

USING ILLUSTRATOR FILES IN PHOTOSHOP

It is much easier to take Illustrator files into Photoshop than to take Photoshop images into Illustrator. First, you have less to think about. There are only three choices of how to save your Illustrator file: Acrobat PDF, Illustrator, and Illustrator EPS. Second, because Illustrator is vector based, the resolution of the rasterized image will depend on the Photoshop file into which you are taking it. You can drag-and-drop, copy and paste, or just open the Illustrator file in Photoshop.

FILE TYPES

Photoshop can open any form of an Illustrator document. You can save your file as Acrobat PDF, Illustrator, or Illustrator EPS, and Photoshop will be able to open it. When you open an Illustrator file in Photoshop, you will get the Rasterize Generic EPS Format dialog box. In this dialog box you choose the size, resolution, and mode of the generic EPS file you are opening.

> **TIP**
>
> When using type from Illustrator, be sure to use the spelling checker on all type you'll take into Photoshop. Once the type is in Photoshop, it can't be edited to correct any typographical errors.

2.3

RESOLUTION

If you are opening an Illustrator file in Photoshop, the Rasterize Generic EPS Format dialog box will appear (2.4). In this dialog box, you can set the size of the image, as well as the resolution and mode. You can also choose to have the image anti-aliased and the proportions constrained. What this means for you in terms of resolution is you set the resolution in the Rasterize dialog box. Going from Photoshop to Illustrator, you need to set the right resolution to print out from the Illustrator document. Going the other way, you can set it before it goes into Photoshop.

Illustrator is vector based and the files print at the resolution of the output device. As a plain Illustrator file, the resolution is determined by the Postscript printer to which you are printing. This means if you print to a 600 dpi printer for proofing purposes, the file will be printed at the 600 dpi. That same file when sent to a high-end printer for a dpi of 2540 will print at 2540 dpi. Illustrator prints at the resolution of the printer selected. In Photoshop, however, a rasterized Illustrator file will adapt to the resolution you choose.

GETTING YOUR FILES INTO PHOTOSHOP

Getting an Illustrator file into Photoshop can be done three ways. The most common way to get an Illustrator file into Photoshop is to copy the Illustrator selections and paste them into Photoshop. With Illustrator 6.0 and Photoshop 4.0 you have the ability to drag-and-drop between the programs. Unlike when you drag-and-drop a Photoshop file into

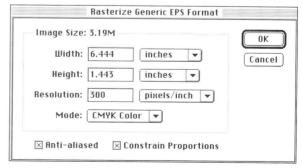

2.4

Illustrator, you aren't limited to a 72 dpi image when you drag-and-drop an Illustrator file into Photoshop.

The last way to get an Illustrator file into Photoshop is actually to open the Illustrator file in Photoshop. To do this, go to Photoshop's File menu, choose Open, and select your Illustrator file. This will bring up the Rasterize dialog box. In this dialog box, choose the width and height of the image you are opening. You also choose the resolution you want the file to be. The other options are Anti-alias and Constrain Proportions. The Anti-alias checkbox is usually checked to minimize the jagged edges to your lines.

The Constrain Proportions checkbox will bring in the Illustrator image at the size you want, keeping the height and width in proportion. If you uncheck this option, you can change the size of the art as well as the proportions.

DRAG-AND-DROP

You can also choose to drag-and-drop only a specific selection rather than the whole image. This way you can add pieces to an existing Photoshop image easily.

It helps if you have the windows resized, so you can see both documents easily. Then you can be sure you have centered the Illustrator selections on the Photoshop document. Figure 2.6 uses only the bird and the one banner from the Illustrator image *Bird Banner* (2.6, 2.7). The bird and the one banner from the Illustrator image were dragged-and-dropped into

> **TIP**
>
> When Opening black-and-white line art, you may want to uncheck the Anti-aliasing button. This will open the file without adding that one gray pixel to smooth out the jagged edge. This way, you get a clean black-and-white line art opened in Photoshop. See Figure 2.5 for the difference between a file that has been anti-aliased and one that hasn't been anti-aliased (2.5). Many artists choose not to anti-alias even though the edges look smoother. It is easier to select the black-and-white areas cleanly without the in-between anti-aliasing pixel.

Anti-aliased button checked

2.5A

Anti-aliased button not checked

2.5B

2.6

Photoshop. Since Photoshop 4.0, all dragged, dropped, and pasted images are automatically put into their own layer. This great new feature of 4.0 makes transforming pasted objects so much easier. The bird in Figure 2.7 was easily rotated and the pieces of the bird I didn't want to keep were selected and deleted. The dragged-and-dropped Illustrator image was then pasted into its own transparent layer. When you delete a section of that layer, the bottom layer shows through.

TIP

If you happen to drag-and-drop to your desktop, a PICT image of your selection will show up as a picture clipping on your desktop. Illustrator will display three messages as it is making this picture clipping. The three messages are: Converting dragged items to EPS (AICB) format, Converting dragged items to EPS format, and Rendering to PICT format. (The acronym *AICB* stands for *Adobe Illustrator Clip Board*.) With a Picture clipping you can use this in any program that takes PICT images.

2.7

COPY AND PASTE

Copying and pasting is probably the most thorough way to get an image from one program or document into another. It has become almost second nature to hit ⌘/Ctrl+C and ⌘/Ctrl+P to copy and paste. Copying a whole image or just a selection of an image takes only a few steps. First, select the piece(s) you want to copy from Illustrator and choose Edit ➤ Copy. In Photoshop, choose Edit ➤ Paste. The piece(s) you copy from Illustrator will become imported at the resolution of the Photoshop file into which you are pasting.

USING PIECES FROM ILLUSTRATOR

In Photoshop, you aren't limited to using only vector-based images from Illustrator. Type, for instance, is a common element artists copy from Illustrator into Photoshop. You can use a whole vector image or just a section of the image in Photoshop. If you have created any cool masks, those can be used in Photoshop as well. When you paste a copied element from Illustrator, you'll get a dialog box asking whether you want to paste in as paths or pixels. If you choose the paths option, you get the outline of the elements only. If you choose pixels, you get the full rendered image.

MASKS

A *mask* is an Illustrator and Photoshop element. The Mask feature in Illustrator creates a cut-out over the top of your selected image. Masks are relatively easy to create and a great way to cut out the parts of your vector art or raster art you don't necessarily want to view.

Here's how to create a mask in Illustrator:

STEP 1 Create a vector image or a raster image from which you want to cut a section (2.8).

STEP 2 Create your mask or cut-out shape by moving the mask shape on top of your vector/raster image where you want it to be cut out (2.9). The stroke or fill color of this mask doesn't matter, because as soon as you create a mask, the stroke and fill of the topmost object will become None. Be sure the object you want to do the cutting out is on top. I created the type TWIRL and converted the type to outlines by choosing Type ➢ Create Outlines.

STEP 3 Select all pieces of the type and create a compound path by choosing Object ➢ Compound Path ➢ Make. This will enable all pieces of outlined type to become a mask. You can also think of it as a multiple mask because you use multiple objects to create your mask.

STEP 4 Select all pieces and choose Object ➢ Masks ➢ Make (2.10).

After creating the mask, you can Select All and copy and paste into Photoshop as pixels. I pasted the mask into an already existing document so I could enhance both images. Using Photoshop's Adjust Layers option, I adjusted the background layer to rotate the color's hue and lighten. I then used the Pointilize filter on the background to add some texture. In the text/mask layer, I added a drop shadow and increased the intensity of the colors (2.11).

If you want to create a bunch of cutouts on one image in Illustrator, you can do it with multiple masks. Multiple masks can also be created in Illustrator, just like regular masks, but with one additional step. After creating your initial mask shapes, you need to select all the masks and make certain they are on top of the image you are masking. Then, while they are still selected, make them a compound path.

2.8

2.10

2.9

2.11

Follow these steps to create a multiple mask in Illustrator:

STEP 1 Create the initial object you want to mask (2.12).

STEP 2 Create the multiple objects you are using to cut out the initial shape (2.13).

STEP 3 Select all the objects to be used for cutouts and choose Object ➢ Compound Path ➢ Make.

STEP 4 Select the cutout objects and the shape you want to mask and choose Object ➢ Mask ➢ Make (2.14).

This creates a multiple mask on one object with ease. You can also create a multiple mask without creating a compound path, but it takes many more steps and creates a larger file size.

2.12

TIP

I converted the type to curves to save problems with sending the correct fonts to the printer. When using type in this way, you should make all the type pieces a compound path so they can be handled as one object. To make the outlined type pieces a compound path, select all the pieces of type and choose Object ➢ Compound Path ➢ Make. This way, the mask will use all the type and not just the last letter of type. The outlined type is actually a bunch of paths, as if you drew them with the Pen tool. Because you want to use multiple shapes as a mask, you must make all the shapes one compound path. Multiple masks need one compound path so Illustrator can mask all shapes properly.

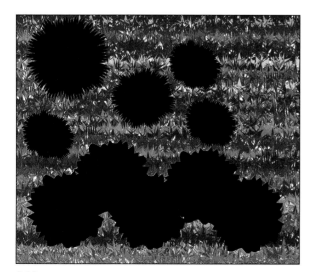

2.13

2.14

TYPE FROM ILLUSTRATOR

Creating cool effects with type is probably the most fun you can have in Photoshop. While Photoshop 4 has improved the Type tool slightly, it still has a way to go. In Photoshop, you are limited to only using one typeface and one type size per type entry. Many users turn to Illustrator for bringing type into Photoshop. Importing type from Illustrator is done by copying and pasting or dragging-and-dropping or, if the whole document is used, by opening the file.

In Illustrator, you can also assign a different color for each letter of type. You can have each letter be a different typeface and size. The possibilities are endless. Once you create your type, copy and paste or drag-and-drop it into Photoshop to add jazzy touches. Figure 2.15 shows the use of different type-faces, sizes, and patterns or colors from Illustrator. The figure was then taken into Photoshop to add texture and light (2.15).

To create a textured type, as shown in Figure 2.15, follow these steps:

STEP 1   In Illustrator, create some type with your Type tool. Assign a different typeface to each letter of type and vary the horizontal scale (2.16).

STEP 2   Change the type to outlines by choosing Type ➤ Create Outlines.

STEP 3   Give each letter a different color or pattern (2.17).

STEP 4   Select all the letters and choose Edit ➤ Copy.

STEP 5   In Photoshop, create a new document about 6 inches wide × 4 inches tall with a resolution of 266. Change the image to RGB color and give it a white background (2.18).

STEP 6   Choose Edit ➤ Paste. You have the choice to paste as pixels or to paste as paths. Your type will come in on its own layer. Move the type as needed to center. You can also scale the type larger by choosing Layer ➤ Transform > Scale (2.19).

STEP 7   Select one letter using the lasso tool. Under the Filter menu, choose a filter to apply to this letter. I chose Extensis' PhotoTools PhotoEmboss for the first letter. The next letter, I chose Alien Skin's Eye Candy Fur filter. For the letter *U*, I used Photoshop's Pixelate ➤ Mezzotint.

2.15

2.16

2.17

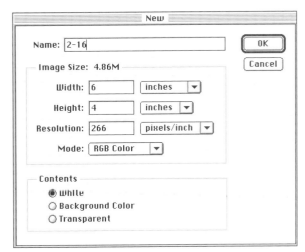

2.18

For the letter *G*, I used KPT 3.0 Texture Explorer. Finally, for the letter *H*, I used Extensis' PhotoTools Slope Bevel (2.20).

STEP 8 The next step to finish off this image is adding a drop shadow. I selected the type on the type layer and created a new layer between the background (white) and the type. I then created a shadow to give the type a 3D look (2.21).

STEP 9 To make the background more interesting, I filled the background layer with black. I then applied Photoshop's Texturizer filter with a brick pattern. Next, I scaled the pattern up and applied the Noise filter to add more texture (2.22).

New to Illustrator 7 is the capability to create vertical type. In the toolbox, the pop-up menu from the Type tool shows you the new cursor for vertical type. The vertical type tool comes with three new cursors: the vertical point type tool, the vertical area type, and the vertical path type. All these type effects can be copied and used in Photoshop.

2.19

2.20

2.21

> **TIP**
>
> When using type from Illustrator, remember type in Photoshop is transformed into pixels when you choose Paste as Pixels. This means the type cannot be edited after it is put into Photoshop. Extensis Corporation makes a third-party plug-in for Photoshop called *PhotoTools*. You can use PhotoTools to create multiple typefaces, colors, and sizes. Once you press the OK button in PhotoTools, the type changes to pixels and cannot be edited again. For more on Extensis' PhotoTools, see Chapter 5: "Photoshop and Illustrator with Third-Party Plug-Ins."

2.22

USING PATHS FROM ILLUSTRATOR

Paths or vectors you created in Illustrator can be used in Photoshop. You can create paths in Photoshop with the Pen tool, but it can be time-consuming. In Illustrator, you have the convenience of the other drawing implements like the Ellipse, Rectangle, Star, Polygon, Brush, and Pencil tools. You can use these tools to create complex paths, and then either copy and paste these paths as pixels or drag-and-drop the paths into Photoshop. The Path option in Photoshop enables you to save a path for a selection without the hassles of channels. You can easily make a selection from a path by choosing the Make Selection option from the pop-up menu of the Path palette and vice versa.

After the path is copied into Photoshop, you can save the path or paths. You can also use outlined vertical type as a path in Photoshop into which you can paste an image (2.23). Beyond type, you can create amazing spirograph-looking paths in Illustrator with as few as two commands.

Here's how to create a spirograph shape in Illustrator:

STEP 1 Drag out a star shape with the Star tool. Keep holding down the mouse key and add more points by using the up arrow on your keyboard. Release your mouse button when you have about 12 points on your star (2.24).

STEP 2 With the star shape selected, choose the Zig Zag filter from the Filter ➢ Distort menus. You need to choose the Illustrator Distort filters you see. In Illustrator, filters are grouped as Illustrator filters first, third-party Illustrator filters next, and Photoshop filters last.

STEP 3 Check the preview box so you can see what happens when you change the settings. I set the Points option to Smooth. I adjusted the Amount slider to around 35, and I set the Ridges slider to 4 to achieve this effect (2.25).

2.23

2.24

Paths are much easier to create in Illustrator so it's natural you'll want to use this ability to the fullest extent. You can create a kaleidoscope effect using Illustrator's paths and Photoshop's textures. By first creating the shapes in Illustrator, you can access the paths in Photoshop and apply different colors and textures to create your kaleidoscope. In Figure 2.27, I created five different paths in Illustrator and pasted them into Photoshop. In the Paths palette you can

see the different names and paths created (2.26). I then selected one path at a time and created a selection I filled with a texture. I filled each different design with a different texture to create this kaleidoscope effect (2.27).

APPLYING EFFECTS IN PHOTOSHOP

Photoshop has many cool filter effects you can apply to any image or piece of an image. Power users of Illustrator and Photoshop usually start an image in Illustrator and finish it off in Photoshop with filters, noise, and lighting effects. While Illustrator is a

---

TIP

When you use the Star or Polygon tool in Illustrator, a keyboard shortcut exists to make your life much easier. While dragging out a star or polygon, press the up arrow to add more points or sides. (You must keep the mouse button pressed.) If you press the down arrow, it will delete points or sides. You can also press the ⌘/Ctrl key for the Star tool to adjust the "pointiness" of the star. When you get the star as pointy as you like, release the ⌘/Ctrl key first, and then your mouse button.

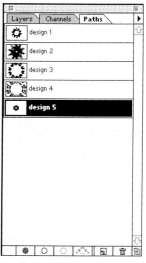

2.26

2.25

2.27

powerful program, it is limited in its effects where Photoshop's effects may seem endless.

All the images in the next section were started in Illustrator. Native Photoshop filters have expanded since Version 3 to add some artistic, sketchy, and texture effects. Third-party plug-in vendors expand Photoshop's ability to add amazing effects to a whole image or to only a selection of it.

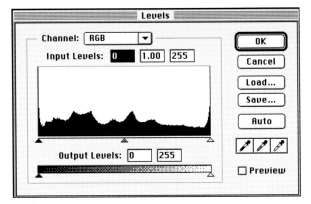

2.28

ADJUSTING YOUR IMAGE

Adjusting your image is the main reason you use Photoshop. You can use Levels or Curves to bring out sections of your image. The colors of your image can be fine-tuned with Hue/Saturation, Color Balance, or Variations. The final areas of adjusting can be done with the Transformations submenu of the Layer menu.

Levels and curves

The Levels menu adjusts the highlights, midtones, and shadows of the image. It also brings out the brightness and contrast of the image. You can adjust the dark, midtone, and light ranges of the whole image or just a selection of the image from the Levels dialog box (2.28). The Output Levels slider at the bottom of the Levels dialog box adjusts the whole tonal areas by sliding the black or white slider. The eyedroppers enable you to choose the darkest, midrange, and lightest tones right from your image. When I use Levels, I tend to change only the black and white sliders and leave the midrange alone. The midrange adjustment can cause some major color change, as you can see in Clarke Tate's *Surf's Up* (2.29).

2.29

Clarke created the surfer in Illustrator and used Fractal Design Expression to create the rest of the artwork. He then rasterized the image into Photoshop to apply smudging and texture with the Pointilize filter. The figure on the left is the original. The figure on the right has had the Levels adjusted. I chose the blue wave curl for the midtone range, which adjusted the colors of this image as well.

Precision tonal adjusting is done by using the Curves menu. The Curves dialog box has the same eyedropper concept as the Levels dialog box. The Levels adjusting only allows three tonal adjusting to take place. Curves,

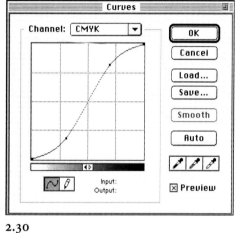

2.30

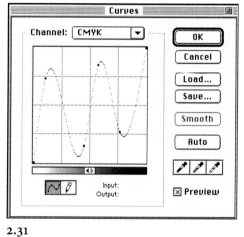

2.31

2.32

on the other hand, enables you to adjust 16 tonal ranges per color in the image. If your image is RGB, then you can adjust up to 48 tonal ranges with 256 values of that tone. If your image is CMYK, you can adjust up to 64 tonal ranges with 256 values of that tone. This concept may sound great, but curves can be difficult to work with and to understand.

I tend to go with the S curve when trying to achieve a balanced tonal adjustment (2.30). This setting is a good starting off base and usually gives me the adjustment I am looking for with a few minor tweakings. If I am looking for a totally different effect, I can use the pencil in the Curves dialog box or create my own wavy curve. For example, Figure 2.31 shows the Curves dialog box settings for Clarke Tate's *Surf's Up.* In Figure 2.32, the image on the left is the original artwork, and the image on the right has had a severe curve adjustment (2.31, 2.32). The major curve adjustment on this figure, which was originally done in Illustrator, created a texture-like effect on the background.

Many Illustrator images can benefit from the texture and lighting effects Photoshop's filters provide.

While filters are the first thing you might think of when you try to create an effect, don't rule out the standards of Levels and Curves. Both of these adjustments can create quite artistic and unparalleled effects.

Hue/Saturation and color balance

Color adjustment to an image is usually done with either the Hue/Saturation or Color Balance dialog boxes. With Hue/Saturation your options are many. You can colorize the whole image so it is one color tone or you can adjust all colors. By moving the Hue slider you can rotate the colors in your image. The Hue rotation may change the reds to blue, depending on where you move the slider.

The Precision logo by Joe Jones of Artworks Studio is comprised of four images. The original concept and design was started in Illustrator and then taken into Photoshop for texture and lighting effects. The top left is the original. I'll apply different aspects of Hue/Saturation to the other three. In the upper-right section of the logo, I made a selection and moved the slider so the reds would change to a blue hue. The setting ended up being −130 to get the blue hue (2.33). The lower-left logo had the saturation slider increased to +71, which flooded more color into the logo (2.34). The lower-right logo had the Colorize button checked and the Hue changed to an aqua-green color. The Saturation was set to 100 and the lightness increased to +27 to create a monotone logo (2.35). The complete figure shows all four logos, which gives this client the opportunity to compare the different versions (2.36).

The other color area you can work with is the Color Balance dialog box. The Color Balance adjusts the

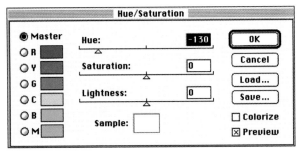

2.33

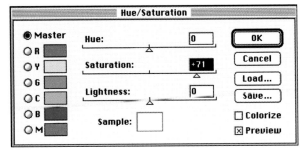

2.34

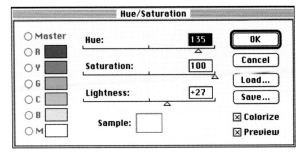

2.35

Color levels of your image or selection. You have sliders that produce opposite color effects. With a CMYK image, Cyan is the opposite of Red, so you can increase the Red or decrease the Cyan. Magenta and Green are opposites and Yellow and Blue are opposites. Traditional artists will recognize this as the opposite on the Color Wheel or complementary colors. With a RGB image, you have to decrease the amount of red and blue to decrease the magenta color of an image. The other options you'll find in this dialog box are to affect the Shadows, Midtones, or Highlights of the image. The Preserve Luminosity when checked will keep the original image's brightness, regardless of your color changes.

The Stone Cliff Vineyard & Winery logo by Joe Jones is subjected to various different adjustments in the Color Balance dialog box in Figure 2.37. This image was first started in Illustrator and taken into Photoshop to apply additional effects (2.37).

The top-left logo is the original logo, untouched. The top-right logo has the color balance adjusted more toward the red (+62), less green (−58), and more yellow (−65). Only the Shadows are affected by selecting the Shadows radial button. I unchecked the Preserve Luminosity to change the brightness of the logo. The bottom left logo is affecting the Midtone

ranges only. The red areas are increased (−37), the green areas are increased (+69), and the blue areas are increased (+27). This time I checked the Preserve Luminosity. The last image on the bottom right is affecting only the Highlights. Cyan is increased (−25), green is increased (+68), and yellow is increased (−62). The Preserve Luminosity is unchecked to create a new brightness.

Variations

In playing with the Variations option in the Adjust submenu of the Image menu, I used Glen Riegel's image called *Northern Clipper*. Glen created a rough sketch of the image in Illustrator. He then used Photoshop to create the terrain and textures.

In the Variations dialog box you'll find many options from which to choose (2.38). Similar to the

> **TIP**
>
> One thought to remember is you may want to try these effects on a copy of the original. Unlike some commands, once you have changed the Levels, Curves, Hue/Saturation, and Color Balance, the actions cannot be reversed. If you choose the numbers opposite of the original effect, this will not take your image back to the original color and tonal increments. A good idea is always to practice on a copy so your original won't be altered.

2.36

2.37

Color Balance dialog box, you can choose between affecting the Shadows, Midtones, and Highlights. The Saturation button changes the Variations dialog box to address the saturation or desaturation of your selection (2.39). The odd bright colors you see in the More Saturated area are an indication the area is already at its fullest saturation.

In the basic Variations dialog box, you can add colors to enhance your original art (2.40). Remember, the color opposite of another will cancel the original color. This means, if you add More Yellow and then add More Blue, nothing actually happens. Those two colors on the color wheel cancel out each other. I like the Coarse setting to get a rough idea of how the

image will look. Once I decide on the colors and lightness I want, I change the setting back to Fine and slowly adjust the colors. At any time, you can view the

TIP

If you don't create a selection (marching ants) around a section of your image, then any effect will be applied to the whole image. The same rule goes for Layers. If you are on a certain layer and don't create a selection, then the effect will affect your whole layer.

2.38

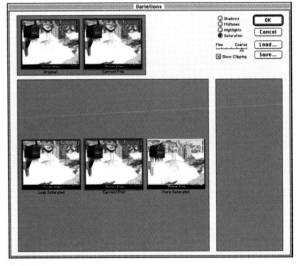

2.39

2.40

original compared to your changes. You can reset the settings to the original by pressing the Option key and hitting the Reset button below the OK button. You can also reset the settings by double-clicking the Original in the upper left.

Using the Variations dialog box is a wonderful way to adjust the colors in your image. The settings are more diverse and you can see the result in the upper area of the dialog box. Many users prefer to use Variations as opposed to Hue/Saturation or Color Balance because of its variety and ease of use.

Transformations

In Illustrator you can apply transformations like Rotate, Reflect, Shear, and Scale to your image. You can apply transformations in Photoshop, as well. Photoshop's transform menu is a little more expanded than Illustrator's. You can Scale, Rotate, Skew, Distort, Perspective, Numeric, Rotate 180°, Rotate 90° CW (clockwise), Rotate 90° CCW (counter-clockwise), Flip Horizontal, or Flip Vertical. All these transformations can be applied to the whole, or to just a selection of, your image.

Figure 2.41 shows a great use of the Transformation submenu. Eliot Bergman's *The Computer* (2.41) was initially done in Illustrator. The Illustrator image was then rasterized in Photoshop. In Photoshop, light and shadow effects were applied. To achieve the reflection, the computer box was copied to another layer and then transformed. The copied box was reflected and the opacity was altered to give it a more transparent look.

To create a reflection in a Photoshop image, follow these steps:

STEP 1 Open the image to which you want to create a reflection. I created a can in Adobe Dimensions and exported the image to Photoshop to add a basic background (2.42).

2.42

2.41

STEP 2 Drag the can layer to the little piece of paper at the bottom of the Layers palette. This will create a copy of the can layer (2.43).

STEP 3 Move the Layer copy below the original can layer.

STEP 4 Choose Flip Vertical in the Transform submenu of the Layer menu. Move the flipped can below the original with the Move tool.

STEP 5 Use the Transform submenu to add some perspective to the can copy. Use the Skew option and the Scale option to give the can copy a reflected look. Change the opacity of the can copy layer to 45 percent so the copy is transparent (2.44).

STEP 6 Add some light and shadow to finish the illustration (2.45). I used the Glass filter that comes with Alien Skin's Eye Candy.

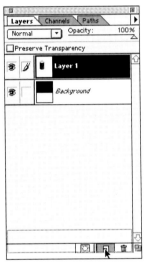

2.43

2.44

2.45

APPLYING PHOTOSHOP FILTERS

Photoshop's native filters include a wide variety of effects. Of these filters, there are two basic groups: the editing group and the effects group.

The editing group includes the Blur, Noise, Sharpen, and Fade filters. These effects can be used in editing, as well as in creating special effects. In Lance Jackson's *Workbook Ad* (2.46), he used the Blur filters to create some cool effects. The shoe in the foreground top is done in Illustrator and was kept out of the blurred effect to make it stand out a little more. In addition, the different effects of Blur, Noise, and Sharpen on a single image are shown in Figure 2.47 (2.47).

The effects group of filters are much more fun. Sjoerd Smit created *Hmmm...* in Illustrator and brought it into Photoshop to add texture, create a sky, soften edges, and create shadows (2.48).

Applying Photoshop filters to all or parts of an image can result in some quite artistic effects. You can use Photoshop to combine vector and pixel based images, and then apply one or multiple filter effects to finish your image. The following set of thumbnail images (2.49 through 2.56) shows just what the Photoshop filter effects will do to an image.

As you can see from the filter charts, not all filters produce the effect for which you may be looking. The Artistic filters show quite an array of different effects from Colored Pencil to Watercolor. The Brush Strokes filters produce different brush effects on your image or selection. The Distort filters can be fun to wreak havoc on family members or certain employees. The distortions that are fun are Displace, Pinch, and Spherize. The Pixelate filters produce pixel-like effects. The Render filters render Clouds, Lens, and Lighting Effects. The Sketch filters are the most drastic. Most of the Sketch filters change your original to a grayscale version. All except for the Water Paper effect change the color of your image to grayscale. Stylize filters create many outlining effects. Finally, the Texture filters create a texture to your selection.

2.46

Blur, Noise, and Sharpen

Original	Gaussian Blur	Motion Blur	Radial Blur
Add Noise	Despeckle	Dust & Scratches	Median
Sharpen	Sharpen More	Unsharp Mask	

2.47

2.48

Artistic Filters

1 Original

2 Colored Pencil

3 Cutout

4 Dry Brush

5 Film Grain

6 Fresco

7 Neon Glow

8 Paint Daubs

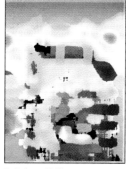

9 Palette Knife

10 Plastic Wrap

11 Poster Edges

12 Rough Pastels

13 Smudge Stick

14 Sponge

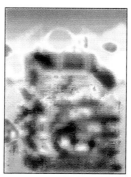

15 Underpainting

16 Watercolor

Brush Strokes

1 Original

2 Accented Edges

3 Angled Strokes

4 Crosshatch

5 Dark Strokes

6 Ink Outlines

7 Spatter

8 Sprayed Strokes

9 Sumi-e

2.50

Distort Filters

1 Original

2 Diffuse Glow

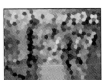

3 Displace

4 Glass

5 Ocean Ripple

6 Pinch

7 Polar Coordinates

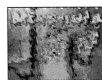

8 Ripple

9 Shear

10 Spherize

11 Twirl

12 Wave

13 Zig Zag

2.51

Pixelate

1 Original

2 Color Halftone

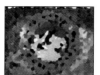

3 Crystallize

4 Facet

5 Fragment

6 Mezzotint

7 Mosaic

8 Pointillize

2.52

Render

1 Original

2 Clouds

3 Difference Clouds

4 Lens Flare

5 Lighting Effects

6 Texture Fill

2.53

Sketch

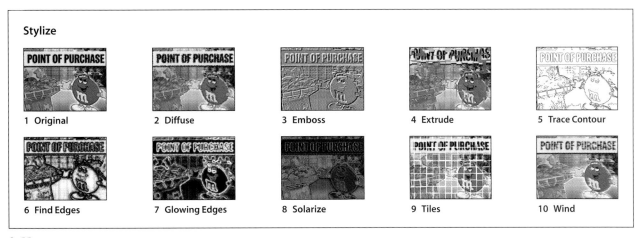

1 Original	2 Bas Relief	3 Chalk & Charcoal	4 Charcoal	5 Chrome
6 Conte Crayon	7 Graphic Pen	8 Halftone Pattern	9 Note Paper	10 Photocopy
11 Plaster	12 Reticulations	13 Stamp	14 Torn Edges	15 Water Paper

2.54

Stylize

1 Original	2 Diffuse	3 Emboss	4 Extrude	5 Trace Contour
6 Find Edges	7 Glowing Edges	8 Solarize	9 Tiles	10 Wind

2.55

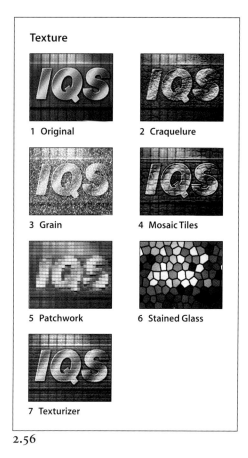

Texture

1 Original

2 Craquelure

3 Grain

4 Mosaic Tiles

5 Patchwork

6 Stained Glass

7 Texturizer

2.56

2.57

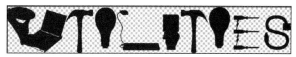

2.58

2.59

ADDING SHADOWS

Shadows are a major reason artists use Photoshop to enhance their Illustrator images. Yes, Illustrator can create shadows, but the effect can seem a little forced. A shadow created in Photoshop tends to have a smooth, natural quality. Without third-party plug-ins, creating a shadow can still be done, but not with the same ease.

If you copy and paste your Illustrator object into Photoshop, it automatically goes on its own layer. This makes your life easier when you create a shadow. Anytime you choose the Paste option in Photoshop, the object is pasted on a new layer.

To create a shadow, follow these steps:

STEP 1 Rasterize your Illustrator image into Photoshop (2.57).

STEP 2 Copy all the elements you want to shadow on their own layer. Make a duplicate of that layer by dragging the original layer to the Create New Layer icon (piece of paper). Turn off the Duplicate layer by clicking the eye icon.

STEP 3 Go back to your original layer and select the elements in that layer. Fill the selection with your shadow color by choosing Edit ➤ Fill (2.58).

STEP 4 Deselect the images and apply a Gaussian blur. I did a blur of ten pixels (2.59).

STEP 5 Show the other layers. Select your shadow layer and, using the Move tool, move the shadow to offset it (2.60).

Adding a shadow to any image is fairly easy. With third-party plug-ins for Photoshop, like Extensis' PhotoTools filter called PhotoShadow, you can achieve one-step shadows. Adding shadow to text is as quick as adding a shadow to an object. To add a shadow on your text, you can follow the same steps as you did in adding a shadow to your image. Not only can you add shadows, but you can add texture as well with one of the Photoshop filters.

TOP-TEN PHOTOSHOP FILTERS TO APPLY TO AN IMAGE

The following ten Photoshop filters are my personal favorite filter effects. While the other filters produce wonderful effects, I have found these ten in particular create a quick and amazing effect with little effort. Instead of applying the effect to your whole image, select only a certain portion for a more dramatic look.

1. CLOUDS FILTER

The Clouds filter found in the Render submenu creates great cloud-like effects from your foreground and background colors. I love using this filter to fix any skies I created in Illustrator that don't look quite right (2.61). If you keep applying the Clouds filter you get different cloud formations. You can keep applying the effect until you get the formation you want.

2. SPATTER FILTER

The Spatter filter is found in the Brush Strokes submenu. This filter creates a paint-like spatter of pixels. The effect is similar to a roughen effect. You can use this to add some texture (2.62).

TIP

I prefer to copy and paste text from Illustrator to Photoshop. This way, the text will automatically go on its own layer. When text is on its own layer, it is much easier to select to add shadows or texture to it. I also like to make my shadow on its own layer, so if I change my mind later, I can change the shadow.

2.60

3. CRYSTALLIZE FILTER

The Crystallize filter is found in the Pixelate submenu. The Crystallize effect is as if your images have been frozen into crystals. This is also useful in texturizing a blend/gradient background or even a background that is too plain.

4. MEZZOTINT FILTER

The Mezzotint filter is also found in the Pixelate submenu. This filter creates a pixelized dotted effect with noise added to it. It gives your Illustrator image a fine art look to your selected areas.

2.61

2.62

5. POINTILLIZE FILTER

The Pointillize filter found in the Pixelate submenu creates a pointilistic effect. The effect is as if your Illustrator image has been drawn with only dots. I think of it almost as an Impressionistic effect (2.63).

6. WATER PAPER FILTER

The Water Paper filter is probably one of my favorites. This filter found in the Sketch submenu creates a watercolor effect. The effect can be astounding on a whole Illustrator image giving it a purely artistic feeling (2.64).

7. GLOWING EDGES FILTER

I like the Glowing Edges filter found in the Stylize submenu for creating those neon effects. This filter takes the selection and makes the edges glow like neon. This effect works great on text from your Illustrator art (2.65).

8. TILES FILTER

The Tiles filter is found in the Stylize submenu. This filter creates little squares with white spaces between them. You determine the number of tiles and the offset. This feature is different from Illustrator's Object Mosaic, which creates squares with no offset. The Tiles has a random paper look, as if someone took scissors and cut up your Illustrator image.

9. WIND FILTER

The Wind filter creates a blown wind-like effect. This effect is unlike the motion blur, which tends to blur your image with motion. You choose the type of Wind you want. Either wind, blast, or stagger will create an effect from the right or left side. The Wind filter is found in the Stylize submenu. The Wind feature will give a motion-like feeling to your Illustrator selection or background.

2.63

2.64

2.65

10. TEXTURIZER FILTER

Texturizer is another favorite of mine. The Texturizer filter is found under the Texture submenu of the Filter menu. This filter can create a texture with Canvas, Burlap, Bricks, or Sandstone. You can increase the Scaling or Relief, as well as change the light direction. Sjoerd Smit used the Texturizer with the Bricks to create a background for his Illustrator image (2.66). There is no filter like this whatsoever in Illustrator, so to achieve this effect on your Illustrator image, you must rasterize in Photoshop.

2.66

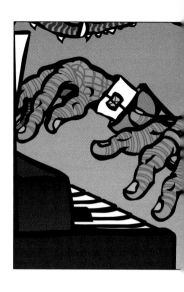

CHAPTER 3
PHOTOSHOP TO FREEHAND AND BACK AGAIN

Adobe Photoshop remains the most popular link between images created in multiple programs. The most popular debate is whether to use FreeHand or Illustrator for your vector-based art program. I firmly believe whichever program you start and continue with will be your favorite. I prefer Illustrator because I have used it since Illustrator 1.0. But FreeHand is also a powerful program that creates amazing vector images. When you combine FreeHand with Photoshop, there's no stopping you from creating great artwork. Further, third-party plug-in vendors, such as Extensis Corporation, KPT products, and Alien Skin have extended Photoshop's and FreeHand's editing ability.

In this chapter you'll learn the different file types you can work with in FreeHand and Photoshop. You'll also find out when to use Photoshop and when to use FreeHand. There are better files to work with when importing or opening files from Photoshop in FreeHand.

CHOOSING THE BEST FILE FORMAT

Importing a Photoshop image into FreeHand is done for a few reasons. One reason is to trace over and create vector-based art, which can be done to recreate a logo easily. Other artists sketch an idea, scan that sketch into Photoshop, and then trace over in FreeHand. Another great reason for taking a Photoshop image into FreeHand is to add type. While Photoshop has a type feature, it is limited because you can't edit the type.

Art is a collection of your subconscious, your dreams, your afterlife. It is a state to remain in.

BRIAN MCNULTY

The type in Photoshop also tends to look rough compared to type in FreeHand, which prints out smoothly.

FreeHand can open or import any TIFF, PICT, or EPS file. In FreeHand, you can choose File ➤ Open to open a file on its own page. If you want an image opened on an existing page, choose File ➤ Import. Importing a file will bring up a corner place cursor (3.1). You can click one time to place the image at its original size, or you can click and drag out the image to the size you want (3.2). Don't panic if the image looks horrible and rough; this is only the rough display in FreeHand. The image will print nicely.

FILE TYPES

A TIFF file can be embedded or linked into the FreeHand file. An EPS file would have to be sent along with the FreeHand file to the printer. The EPS file also can be embedded or linked, but the advantage of an EPS file is the DCS saving format that saves the four-color plates, as well as a fifth file for preview only. Saving a file with the DCS format is the preferred method when using high-resolution files from Photoshop. The drawback is the file size is larger than the TIFF.

To embed the EPS or TIFF into the FreeHand file, choose File ➤ Open (rather than File ➤ Import). An embedded file is part of the FreeHand file. This way you don't have to send the actual EPS or TIFF to the printer with your file. The catch is the FreeHand file size will be much larger.

RESOLUTION

Resolution is important when you start opening or importing Photoshop images. If you import a low-resolution Photoshop file into FreeHand to add labels, you'll print out a choppy, pixelized image with great labels (3.3).

A FreeHand file will print to the resolution of your printer. Photoshop files must have the resolution determined and set with the file before you print. When using a Photoshop image in FreeHand, you need to make sure the resolution of the Photoshop file will print at the quality you desire. You must find out what line screen values your printer can handle first. Then you can set the value of the line screen; the higher the line screen, the better the image will print. I like to double the line screen value to get the number I need to set in dots per inch. This way, I can have the right resolution from the beginning before putting the image into FreeHand.

A 1270 dpi printer, for example, has a line screen of 105 lpi. A 2540 dpi printer has a line screen of 133 lpi. Thus, a 1270 dpi printer would need a resolution of 210 dpi for an image to stay at 100 percent. A 2540 dpi printer would need a resolution of 266 dpi for an image to stay at 100 percent. If your image is going to be smaller or larger, you need to adjust the resolution accordingly. A common mistake is to have your image at a high resolution regardless of how the file will be printed. This results in a darker, more densely colored image because too many pixels are being used unnecessarily.

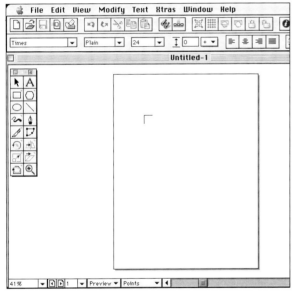

3.1

3.2

3.3

GETTING YOUR IMAGES INTO FREEHAND

Many ways exist to get a file from Photoshop into FreeHand. The most common way is to open or import the file. A typical way power users of Photoshop and FreeHand get a file into FreeHand is to copy and paste. Now, with FreeHand 7.0 and Photoshop 4, you are able to drag-and-drop files between the programs.

DRAG-AND-DROP

Drag-and-drop is now the fastest way to copy a file from page to page and from program to program. Drag-and-drop not only works between the Adobe programs like Photoshop, Illustrator, and PageMaker, but it also works with FreeHand. To drag-and-drop an image or vector, select the part(s) you want to drag, choose the Move tool, and then hold the mouse button down on the image and drag to your FreeHand document. The difference between this and copy and paste is, when you copy an image, it must go to the clipboard. This function takes more time to perform because a copy remains on the clipboard until you copy something else. The definite problem with drag-and-drop is when you drag a Photoshop image and drop it into FreeHand, the resolution changes to screen or 72 dpi (3.4).

COPY AND PASTE

Copy and paste is the most common way to get an image from one page or program into another. Copy and paste works with most software programs. Consider it the universal way to copy your images to another area. To copy a piece of an image from

> **NOTE**
>
> To drag a selection in Photoshop 4, you need to use the Move tool to drag-and-drop between documents or programs. If you don't use the move tool, nothing will drag-and-drop. If you are using Photoshop 3.0.4, you only need to drag with the Marquee tool.

Photoshop to FreeHand, select the piece(s) you want to copy, and then choose Edit ➢ Copy. In FreeHand, choose Edit ➢ Paste. This will paste the object you just copied into your FreeHand document. Unlike drag-and-drop, copying a pixel-based image from Photoshop retains that image's original resolution.

FREEHAND TO PHOTOSHOP TECHNIQUES

FreeHand provides the base for your image and Photoshop finishes the image by softening the edges and adding light, shadow, and textures. FreeHand can create the sketch of an image; Photoshop can give the image realistic touches.

Art done in FreeHand can benefit from Photoshop by adding textures and by softening the edges of the computer-looking lines. Photoshop can also add texture and depth FreeHand lacks. Text, illustrations, and logos can also be taken to the next level in Photoshop. With Photoshop's native filters, you can add depth, embossing, texture, and much more.

FreeHand is used to getting text with different typefaces and sizes into Photoshop (3.5). While Photoshop can do many things, text is not its strong point. You can create text in Photoshop, but you are limited to one size and one typeface per text entry. This leaves the artist to use other programs, such as Illustrator, to create text effects and Photoshop to add the depth, shadow, and texture.

3.4

OPENING YOUR FREEHAND FILES IN PHOTOSHOP

FreeHand files take less effort to bring into Photoshop than vice versa. In FreeHand, you can save your images as a FreeHand Document, a FreeHand Template, or an Editable EPS. Because FreeHand is vector-based, the resolution depends on the original Photoshop file in to which you are copying the file. You can drag-and-drop, copy and paste, or just open the file in Photoshop.

FILE TYPES

Opening a FreeHand file in Photoshop is as easy as choosing File ➤ Open. Before opening a FreeHand file in Photoshop, however, you must be sure it is saved as a Editable EPS in FreeHand. You must save this way because Photoshop can't open a FreeHand file in any other saved format. When you open the file in Photoshop you have a few options. You can choose the resolution, the color mode, the size of the file, and the background. Then, once in Photoshop, you can apply any filters or effects you wish.

TIP

When working with type from FreeHand, be sure to check the spelling of all type you take into Photoshop. Once the type is in Photoshop, it can't be edited to correct any typographical errors.

3.5

Test Tubes, by Sandee Cohen, shows a great use of a FreeHand file taken into Photoshop for finishing (3.6). Sandee used FreeHand's multiple blending option to create the bubbles along an arc. (For more information about Sandee's *Test Tubes*, see Chapter 9.)

USING PARTS OF PHOTOSHOP AND PARTS OF FREEHAND

When creating your art, you can work between two or more programs. You can also take parts of each program, like using clipping paths from Photoshop in FreeHand. You can take a path drawn in FreeHand and use it in Photoshop, and so on.

CLIPPING PATHS

A *clipping path* is a line drawn in Photoshop that creates a boundary around the image with a path. What this means is the image will only be seen within the path's boundaries. A clipping path is a way of masking out the pieces you don't want to view and only viewing the pieces you do want. Most people think of using a clipping path for QuarkXPress or PageMaker, but few know you can use a clipping path saved as an

3.6

EPS file in Illustrator. In this figure, I imported an image with and without a clipping path applied. (3.7).

USING COLOR FROM THE PHOTOSHOP IMAGE

You can select color from your pixel-based image in Photoshop and use it in FreeHand. The Eyedropper tool in the Xtra Tools window in FreeHand can "suck" up the color attributes of any pixel-based image. This is a great feature for the artist to match a color in the rasterized image.

USING PATHS AND SELECTIONS FROM PHOTOSHOP

Any path drawn in Photoshop can be used in FreeHand simply by copying and pasting the path into FreeHand. The drag-and-drop feature doesn't work with a path, so you *have* to copy and paste. What's nice about using a path is you can get an exact outline of an image you want to draw in FreeHand. If you are trying to trace a logo, you can select the path in Photoshop and copy and paste into FreeHand. In a sense, this is quicker than scanning and tracing over a photo. You already have the outline, now just fill in the vector art with color (3.8).

Selections can easily be copied and pasted into FreeHand. Rather than use the whole image, you can select only the section you want, and then drag-and-

drop the image into FreeHand. By dragging-and-dropping, you get only the selection, not the box with the whole image. When you use a clipping path, you get the whole image, but only the one section is masked. The file size will be larger when you save with a clipping path because it saves the whole image rather than just the section you want to see.

PASTE INSIDE

The Paste Inside option in FreeHand will create a cutout around your Photoshop image in FreeHand. A cutout is easy to create and a great way to cut out the parts of your vector art or raster art you don't want to view. The following steps outline how to use Paste Inside to create a cutout around your Photoshop image:

STEP 1 Import your pixel image (3.9).

STEP 2 Create the "mask" you want to be the cutout (3.10).

STEP 3 Arrange the created cutout over the pixel image where you want the image to show through.

STEP 4 Select the pixel image and choose Edit ➢ Cut. This will remove the image and place it on the Clipboard.

STEP 5 Select your created mask and choose Edit ➢ Paste Inside. This will place the image only within the created cutout (3.11).

3.7

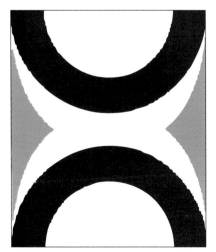

3.8

If you want to create multiple masks on one image in FreeHand, you can also do it with Paste Inside. Multiple masks can be done, but with one additional step. After creating your initial shape or importing your pixel image, create the mask shapes on top of the initial shape. You need to select all the mask shapes and choose Modify ➢ Join. Then you can cut your imported shape and choose Edit ➢ Paste Inside (3.12).

WORKING WITH TYPE IN FREEHAND

Some of the most fun you can have with Photoshop is creating cool effects with type. While Photoshop 4

improved the Type tool slightly, the tool still has a way to go. In Photoshop you are limited with using only one typeface and one type size per type entry. Many users turn to FreeHand for bringing type into Photoshop. Importing type from FreeHand is done by copying and pasting, dragging-and-dropping, or, if the whole document is used, by opening the file in Photoshop.

3.9

3.11

3.10

3.12

In FreeHand, you can also assign a different color for each letter of type. You can have each letter be a different typeface and size. Once you are creating your type, you can copy and paste or drag-and-drop it into Photoshop to add the jazzy touches. In this example, I applied various typefaces, sizes, and colors to the word *text* in FreeHand and then brought the image into Photoshop to add texture and shadow (3.13).

USING PATHS FROM FREEHAND IN PHOTOSHOP

Paths or vectors you have created in FreeHand can be used in Photoshop. Paths can be created in Photoshop with the Pen tool, but it can be time-consuming. In FreeHand, you have the convenience of the other drawing tools, like the Oval, Rectangle, Polygon, Freehand, and Variable Stroke. You can use these tools to create complex paths and then either copy and paste these paths as pixels or drag-and-drop the paths into Photoshop (3.14).

The Path palette in Photoshop enables you to save without the hassle of channels. You can easily make a selection from a path by choosing the Make Selection

> **TIP**
>
> When you use type from FreeHand, remember type in Photoshop is transformed into pixels. This means the type cannot be edited after it is put into Photoshop.

option from the Path palette's pop-up menu. You'll also want to save the path found in the same pop-up menu of the Path palette.

USING PHOTOSHOP AND FREEHAND FILTERS AND TRANSFORMATIONS

Photoshop has many cool filter effects you can apply to any image or piece of an image. Power users of FreeHand and Photoshop usually begin an image in FreeHand and finish it in Photoshop by adding filters, noise, and lighting effects. Since Photoshop 3, Photoshop has expanded its collection of native filters to add some artistic, sketchy, and texture effects. Third-party plug-in vendors have also expanded Photoshop's capability to add amazing effects to a whole image or to only a selection of it.

ACCESSING PHOTOSHOP FILTERS IN FREEHAND

FreeHand 7 enables you to access Photoshop filters right from within FreeHand. Copy or make an alias of the filters and put them in your FreeHand Xtras folder. You'll have to quit and relaunch FreeHand to activate these filters. The filters that will be available will show up under the Xtras menu with the label TIFF in front. Figure 3.15 shows a zoom radial blur applied to a TIFF image (3.15).

CHANGING AN IMPORTED IMAGE

FreeHand enables you to make your imported image transparent, to change the lightness/contrast, and to colorize your grayscale TIFF or EPS image. To create a transparent image, import your image and open the Object Inspector. In the Object Inspector, you can

3.13

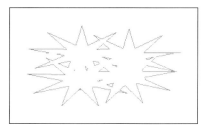

3.14

check a box called *transparent.* Figure 3.16 shows an imported image before and after checking the transparent box (3.16). To adjust an object's lightness and/or contrast, import an image and open the Object Inspector. Click the Edit button at the bottom of the Object Inspector panel. You can adjust the lightness and contrast, and then click the Apply button to see the effects (3.17). To colorize your grayscale

image, import your image first. Create your color in the Color Mixer panel. Add that new color to the Color List. Drag the new color on top of the grayscale image (3.18).

APPLYING FREEHAND TRANSFORMATIONS TO A PHOTOSHOP IMAGE

In FreeHand, you can apply transformations like Rotate, Reflect, Shear, and Scale to your image (3.19, 3.20). You can also apply transformations in Photoshop. You can Scale, Rotate, Skew, Distort, Perspective, Numeric, Rotate 180°, Rotate 90° CW, Rotate 90° CCW, Flip Horizontal, or Flip Vertical. All these transformations can be applied to the whole image or to only a selection of it.

APPLYING PHOTOSHOP FILTERS TO A FREEHAND IMAGE

Photoshop's native filters include a wide variety of effects. You can use one or more effects on your image. With Photoshop's selection abilities you can

3.15

3.16

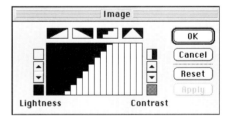

3.17

3.18

select the whole or just a portion of your image on which to create an effect. Two basic groups of filters exist: the editing group and the effects group.

The editing group includes: Blur, Noise, Sharpen, and Fade. These effects can be used in editing, as well as in creating special effects. The effects group of filters are much more fun. The effects main filters are: Artistic, Brush Strokes, Distort, Pixelate, Render, Sketch, Stylize, and Texture. Filter charts can be found in Chapter 2. The same effects you see in Chapter 2 will create the same effects with FreeHand.

TOP-TEN FREEHAND OR PHOTOSHOP EFFECTS TO APPLY TO AN IMAGE

I've always used Photoshop to add or enhance the background of my FreeHand images. The following effects are my personal favorites.

3.19

1. PASTE INSIDE

FreeHand's Paste Inside function enables you to put an object or image inside another shape (3.21).

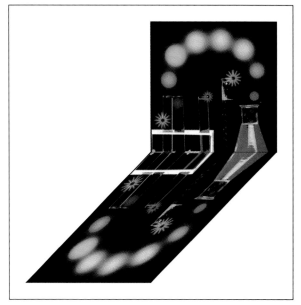

3.20

3.21

3.22

3.23

3.24

2. COLORIZING A GRAYSCALE IMAGE

FreeHand has the capability to colorize a grayscale TIFF or EPS totally. You simply drag the new color on top of the imported image and you have color (3.22).

3. CHANGING THE LIGHTNESS/CONTRAST

Changing the Lightness and Contrast of an imported image was usually done in Photoshop. You can change the lightness and contrast right from FreeHand. After importing your image, open the Object Inspector panel. If you click the Edit button at the bottom, you can adjust the lightness and contrast of your grayscale TIFF or EPS image (3.23).

4. MAKING AN IMAGE TRANSPARENT

Open the Object Inspector panel to view the options for your imported image. To make your selected grayscale TIFF or EPS transparent, check the transparent box in the Object Inspector panel (3.24).

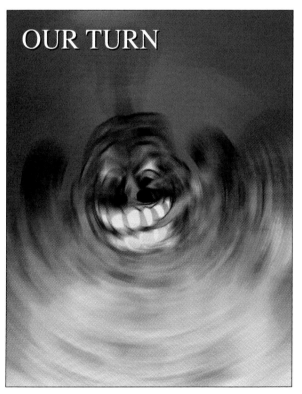

3.25

5. BLURRING AN IMAGE

Using Photoshop's Blur filter in FreeHand saves you from having to go back and forth between programs. If you take an image done in FreeHand, touched up in Photoshop, and brought back into FreeHand to add text, you can add the Blur filter to the TIFF image. Brian McNulty created *Our Turn* in FreeHand and Photoshop (3.25). He scanned in the sketch and cleaned it up in Photoshop. In FreeHand, Brian traced over the sketch and finished the image. I added the blur to the image.

6. MULTIPLE CUTOUTS

You can create some cool effects with multiple cutouts when you use type converted into paths. Remember, you can use Paste Inside when you work with text: Text is more than one shape you need to paste inside, but be sure to join all the paths you use as your cutout (3.26).

7. TRANSFORMING AN IMPORTED IMAGE

Any image imported into FreeHand can be scaled, rotated, reflected, or skewed. Here I used an image by Brian McNulty to illustrate the different views possible of a transformed TIFF image (3.27).

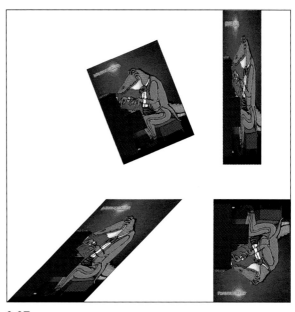

3.27

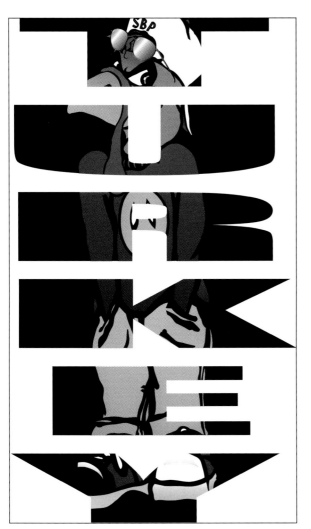

3.26

3.28

8. APPLYING A SHADOW WITH PHOTOSHOP

You can apply shadows within FreeHand, but something about Photoshop's soft realistic shadows seems better than vector-based shadows (3.28).

9. CREATING A TEXTURED
BACKGROUND ON YOUR FREEHAND IMAGE

With Photoshop's native and third-party filters, the backgrounds you can create are endless. This is a great way to jazz up your FreeHand file. *The Wrestler,* by Brian McNulty, shows a FreeHand image taken into Photoshop for the lightning texture to be added in the background (3.29).

10. ADJUSTING A FREEHAND
IMAGE'S LEVELS AND COLORS

With Photoshop's Adjust submenu, you can virtually change any vector art to a poster-like quality. Here I used the Adjust submenu to alter an image by Brian McNulty called *Crock* (3.30). I adjusted the image with the Hue/Saturation option. By rotating the Hues, you get a totally different look to the image.

3.29

3.30

CHAPTER 4
PIXELS TO VECTORS
AND BACK AGAIN

What is all this talk about pixels versus vectors? Well, Photoshop is a pixel-based program that displays your images by creating a bunch of little dots — or *pixels*. When you Blur, Sharpen, change color, or add any other effect, you are essentially changing the color of the pixels. If a selection is made and then deleted, the pixels are changed to your background color that, in Photoshop, is white. While it may look like you deleted a portion of your image, you actually changed the pixels to white. The image size will stay the same.

Illustrator, on the other hand, is a vector-based program. What this means is the illustrations you create in Illustrator are PostScript-based. *PostScript* creates a mathematical rendition of your lines and curves, and prints the image at the resolution of the output device. A definite difference exists between a pixel-based image and a vector-based image (4.1). This makes editing lines in Illustrator much easier than in Photoshop. When you edit a line in Photoshop, you essentially must erase the original line and redraw the new line in pixels. To edit a line in Illustrator, you simply drag the endpoint of the line to a new location and the line is changed. So, why should you ever use Photoshop? For one, you'll never get photograph-quality art from Illustrator like you can in Photoshop. To become a truly well-rounded designer, you need at least both Photoshop and Illustrator.

No matter what you believe in, believe in yourself first!

SJOERD SMIT

CHANGING PIXELS TO VECTORS AND VECTORS TO PIXELS

As you can see, relying on one program to do all your artistry is no longer enough. Typically, artists go back and forth between pixel- and vector-based programs. Often it is necessary to use Photoshop to scan in an image, and then to use Illustrator or FreeHand to open that file to trace over the image. After creating a nice line art image, the image can be taken back into Photoshop to add color, depth, and texture. When the image is complete, it may be brought back into Illustrator for text labeling or into a page layout program, such as QuarkXPress or PageMaker.

STARTING IN ILLUSTRATOR, ENDING IN PHOTOSHOP

Artist Sjoerd Smit has created some amazing illustrations using both Illustrator and Photoshop. Using an Illustrator file of a face and a skyline for a background, Sjoerd first copied, cropped, scaled, and placed the eye below the image (4.2). The eyeball was then taken into Photoshop to add light and realism (4.3) and brought back into Illustrator. In the original Illustrator image, the eyeball was masked into the

HMMM ...
Sjoerd Smit

61

Pixel-Based

Vector-Based

4.1

eye socket shape (4.4). This way, the eyeball has the touch of realism, as if it is looking at you. The background was filled in with Illustrator (4.5).

The Illustrator file was then taken back into Photoshop. Sjoerd used Photoshop's Neon filter to create a great blurred skyline. To create the clouds, Sjoerd selected the cloud color in the foreground and background colors. To create the actual clouds, he chose Filter ➢ Render ➢ Clouds. You can repeat this filter by pressing ⌘/Ctrl F. This repeats the last filter. When you repeat the cloud filter, different cloud formations are created.

Next, the image was selected, inverted, and then saved. KPT Vortex Tiling was used on the saved selection to curl the bits around the illustration.

4.2

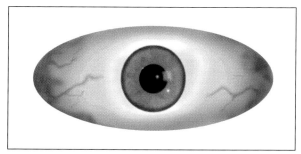

4.3

Photoshop's cloning and paint tools cleaned the background. To create the brick-look background, Sjoerd chose Filter ➤ Texture ➤ Texturizer and chose the brick texture. The final image truly showcases an excellent job of going from pixels to vectors and back (4.6).

SCANNING INTO PHOTOSHOP, TRACING IN FREEHAND

In planning an image or illustration, an idea usually starts with a sketch. Sometimes a rough hand-drawn sketch is all you need to get the creative juices flowing. A gesture sketch is a quick sketch that shows the action of an object and is a great way to start off an image.

Brian McNulty of Shark Byte Productions mastered the ability to turn a sketch into an amazing illustration (4.7, 4.8). After the sketch is fleshed out, it is scanned into Photoshop for any cleaning. The saved sketch is then opened in Illustrator or FreeHand to begin the tracing process.

4.5

4.4

4.6

In FreeHand, a variety of tools exist with which to draw. I favor the Variable Stroke tool. Using this tool, you can achieve an extremely accurate tracing of your original sketch (4.9). To give depth to uneven sketchier lines, you can set the variable stroke and use a pressure-sensitive tablet. The pressure-sensitive tablet is a godsend to all illustrators. The tablet enables you to record the pressure of your own hand as you draw. In FreeHand you need to access the Freehand tool by double-clicking it and choosing the Variable Stroke option. In Illustrator, you access the Brush tool in Pencil tool's pop-up menu and then double-click the Brush tool to set the variable brush options.

The sketch is traced over (inch by inch) in FreeHand to get the maximum amount of detail. In Photoshop, the color, depth, and textures are added in to complete the illustration, *Wrecking Ball* (4.10).

STARTING IN PHOTOSHOP, ENDING IN ILLUSTRATOR

Many artists start an illustration in Illustrator, take it into Photoshop, and then take it back into Illustrator to add text. A good example of this is *Bullseye* by Patricia Cheal. This illustration was created in Illustrator, and then taken into Photoshop to add the wood background. After softening in Photoshop, the image was taken back into Illustrator to add text (4.11).

As powerful as Photoshop is, it is not meant for altering text. Text isn't one of Photoshop's powerful features because the program lacks editing capability once text is created. In the type dialog box, you can change your mind as much as you want, but once you hit the OK button, the text becomes pixels (dots on your screen). Once the text is converted to pixels, it is no longer editable. This means you can't highlight the letters and retype any corrections. In Illustrator, and in other layout programs, you can easily highlight the text and retype any changes.

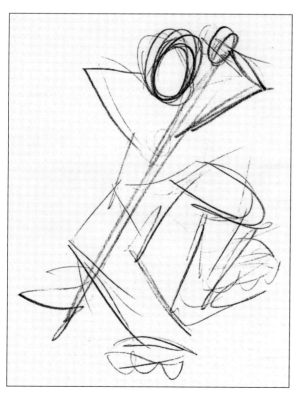

4·7

4.8

Because Photoshop isn't the best program with which to add type, in comes Illustrator. I often use Illustrator to add type to photos. When creating an illustration, I like to start in Illustrator to get the lines down and to fill in the basic colors. With Photoshop, I can soften the edges, as well as add depth, lighting effects, and texture. To complete the image, I open the file in Illustrator to add text, callouts, or a frame for the image (4.12).

4.11

4.12

4.9

4.10

4.13

4.14

LEARNING TRICKS OF THE TRADE

Joe Jones, of Art Works Studio, creates many images using ingenious tricks with Illustrator and Photoshop. In the logo he created for Precision Image Printing (4.13), Joe started the image in Illustrator as line art. Instead of rasterizing the file into Photoshop, Joe copied the paths and then pasted them into Photoshop as pixels. In doing this, he created a path in the Layers palette. Now Joe can save the path as a selection to access the path in the Channels palette easily. The logo can be raised and recessed easily accessing the different channels. In the channels, Joe can build lighting and texture maps to give the depth to his images.

Brian Warchesik, of Art Works Studio, created an amazing image called *Icarus* (4.14). He started with a series of pencil sketches, which he scanned into Photoshop, and then painted the art in Photoshop with a pressure-sensitive tablet. Brian created the wings in Illustrator to take full advantage of the vector's capabilities and he used Illustrator's layering capabilities to keep each detailed section separate. He then copied and pasted the paths into Photoshop in their own channels. When you access a channel, you can apply any of the filter effects to that channel to create different effects. Once Brian applies a filter effect, such as Add Noise, he can make the selection in the image from the changed channel and pull out texture or color. Finally, Brian manipulated the feathers in each channel to get the texture and subtlety of the colors.

CREATING PIXEL-BASED DROP SHADOWS IN ILLUSTRATOR

Illustrator can create soft or harsh shadows by using the Blend tool. Photoshop creates a soft, natural shadow using the Blur filter in a channel. You can then take these soft shadows into Illustrator to create an even softer, more natural shadow.

The following steps illustrate how to create a shadow for an Illustrator file in Photoshop:

STEP 1 Copy the path from Illustrator and choose Paste. Then you choose Paste as Pixels.

STEP 2 Save the selection as a channel.

STEP 3 Click the new channel you created to go to that channel.

STEP 4 Make sure there is no active selection by choosing Select ➤ None.

STEP 5 To create a soft shadow, choose Filter ➤ Blur ➤ Gaussian Blur.

STEP 6 Drag the slider high to create a soft shadow (4.15).

STEP 7 Click the CMYK channel to view the color channels.

STEP 8 Choose Select ➤ Load ➤ Selection. Choose the new channel.

STEP 9 Press Option Delete to fill in the selection with the foreground color (black).

STEP 10 If you are using only a grayscale shadow, change the mode to Grayscale before you save.

STEP 11 Save the file and in Illustrator choose File ➤ Place.

STEP 12 Send the Photoshop file to the back by choosing Object ➤ Arrange ➤ Send to Back. Move the file to look like a shadow on your object (4.16).

STREAMLINING YOUR PIXELS INTO VECTORS

One of Adobe's least-talked about, but vastly used, programs is Adobe Streamline 4.0. Streamline takes a pixel-based image and converts it into a vector-based

image. In the Color/B&W setup dialog box you have the choice of Limited Colors, Unlimited Colors, Use Custom Colors, and Black and White Only. Edge Smoothing, Custom Color Options, and Color Conversion are more options to clean up the image (4.17). Note, the more complex and accurate you want your conversion to be, the longer it will take to convert.

4.16

4.15

4.17

Here's how to convert a pixel-based image with Adobe Streamline 4.0:

STEP 1   Open the Photoshop image in Streamline (4.18).

STEP 2   In the Color/B&W Setup dialog box, choose your conversion settings. I chose Unlimited colors, Maximum edge smoothing, and more paths so my image would retain more detail.

STEP 3   Choose File ➢ Convert or ⌘/Ctrl+R. (If the image is large or complex, this may take some time.)

STEP 4   Instead of saving the file as an art file to take into Illustrator, it is quicker and easier to select all (⌘/Ctrl+A), Copy (⌘/Ctrl+C) and then in Illustrator, choose Paste (⌘/Ctrl+P).

STEP 5   In Illustrator you can save the file and mangle it to your heart's content (4.19).

You can make many adjustments to this converted image in Illustrator. Using some of the color adjusting features offered in Illustrator, you can change the colors without selecting each individual piece and recolorizing. Using Extensis' plug-in for Illustrator or

4.18

4.20

4.19

4.21

FreeHand called *VectorTools*, you can randomize the colors of the background in one fell swoop (4.20). If you don't have VectorTools, you can still create frames around your art — it will just take you longer. I added four frames with the Rectangle tool and on the last frame, I used a path pattern to give the streamlined image a finished look ready for printing (4.21). This type of imaging is what I call the *New Age Portraits*. It gives a different view of portraiting for pets or people. Not only does this work well for creating a different type of portrait, it can also be useful in creating textures and patterns.

WORKING WITH DIMENSIONS AND PHOTOSHOP

Adobe Dimensions is another great vector-based 3D program, which is actually easy to understand. While many 3D programs become too complex and difficult to use, Dimensions is easy to figure out without a manual (but, if needed, the manual is also easy to understand). With Dimensions, you can create new 3D shapes with a few mouse clicks. You can also copy and paste Illustrator paths to extrude or revolve around an axis.

Dimensions makes it easy to create basic shapes and to apply colors and properties. In Photoshop, you can add the background and texture to the shapes you create (4.22). In Illustrator (or even Dimensions), you can create a 2D image. In Figure 4.23, I created the letter *S* in Illustrator. I then copied the letter and pasted it into Dimensions, where I revolved and extruded it for two totally different results (4.23). The revolved *S* is only revolved 180 degrees so you can see the insides of the letter. The extruded *S* is filled in to create a chunky feeling to the letter. I then took these shapes into Illustrator to add a gradient to the face of the letters and change color.

TOP TEN SECRETS OF WORKING BETWEEN PIXELS AND VECTORS

The ten secrets you'll read about are my personal favorites for working between Photoshop and Illustrator. I find they increase my productivity immensely. They may also save you from hours of frustration.

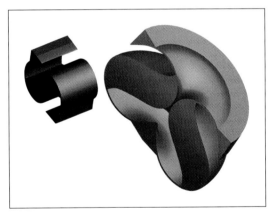

4.23

4.22

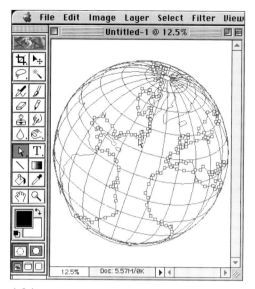

4.24

1. COPY PATHS FROM ILLUSTRATOR AND PASTE INTO PHOTOSHOP

Using Illustrator's amazing Bézier line creation capabilities you can create smooth, precise paths. You can then choose Paste as Paths into Photoshop into their own channels to be manipulated with ease (4.24).

2. ADD TEXT WITH ILLUSTRATOR

After creating an amazing image in Photoshop, open the file in Illustrator to add text, callouts, or a frame for your art (4.25).

4.25

4.26

3. SCAN YOUR SKETCH INTO PHOTOSHOP

Traditional artists still rely on the hand-drawn sketch as a starting point. Scan in your sketch in Photoshop, clean up the sketch, and paint in your color. You can add paths from Illustrator for fine-tuning specific areas. Another use of a scanned sketch is to take the cleaned up sketch from Photoshop into Illustrator to trace over and add color (4.26).

4. COPY TEXT FROM
ILLUSTRATOR INTO PHOTOSHOP

Unless you have Extensis' PhotoTools, your text choices are limited in Photoshop. Create text in Illustrator and change the text to outlines before copying the paths into Photoshop. This enables you to manipulate the text shape in the channels palette to create cool eVects (4.27).

4.27

4.28

5. USE PIECES OF PHOTOSHOP IN ILLUSTRATOR

Any selection you create and copy into Illustrator will display only the selection — rather than the whole image. This feature saves you from having to create a mask. The only catch is, when you copy and paste from Photoshop to Illustrator, you are limited to 72 dpi (4.28).

6. USE STREAMLINE TO CONVERT
PIXEL IMAGES TO VECTOR IMAGES

Adobe has a plethora of powerful programs. Adobe Streamline is fantastic to convert a pixel image into a vector one. With a vector image in Illustrator or FreeHand, you can adjust the lines, shapes, and colors as you wish (4.29).

4.29

4.30

4.31

7. DON'T FORGET THE "OTHER" VECTOR PROGRAM . . . DIMENSIONS

Adobe Dimensions is another great vector-based program that renders 3D images quickly and easily. After creating your 3D image, copy and paste or import it into Photoshop to soften the edges and create the background (4.30).

8. USE DIMENSIONS WITH ILLUSTRATOR AND PHOTOSHOP

Using Adobe Dimensions, create a 3D image. Copy and paste the Dimension image into Illustrator to complete the layout. Finish off the image in Photoshop (4.31).

9. CREATE SHAPES IN ILLUSTRATOR TO "MASK" IN PHOTOSHOP

Illustrator's vector capabilities enable you to create some amazing kaleidoscope effects in Photoshop (4.32). You can create many paths in Illustrator with ease and use those paths in Photoshop as channels. The channels can be activated as a selection and you can paste in textures or create your own textures in the selections.

10. USE PHOTOSHOP TO SOFTEN ILLUSTRATOR'S HARSH LINES

Photoshop comes with an amazing array of filters that enable you to soften the harsh edges of an Illustrator image (4.33).

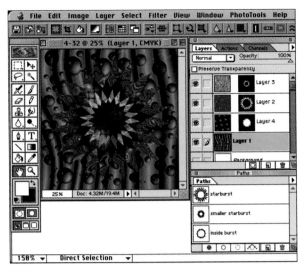

4.32

4.33

CHAPTER 5
PHOTOSHOP AND ILLUSTRATOR WITH THIRD-PARTY PLUG-INS

The third-party plug-in market has boomed! A complete designer probably has not only Photoshop and Illustrator, but also every third-party plug-in known to man. Many third-party plug-ins are on the market for Photoshop and Illustrator, but I'll highlight just some of the best of them here. While Photoshop and Illustrator are fantastic programs, they become even more marketable when plug-ins are added. From 3D effects to textures, the plug-in market has it all.

EXTENSIS CORPORATION

Extensis Corporation is the front leader in creating productive third-party plug-ins. Extensis has developed plug-ins for Photoshop, Illustrator, FreeHand, QuarkXPress, and PageMaker. The plug-ins for Photoshop include PhotoTools, Intellihance, and MaskPro. Extensis' Illustrator plug-in is VectorTools. Combine all the effects of the Photoshop plug-ins with the Illustrator plug-ins and you get some stunning results.

PHOTOTOOLS

Extensis' PhotoTools is a collection of eight plug-ins for Photoshop. Extensis has continued the special effects it created for QXTools with shadow, glow, bevel, and emboss. You'll also find a plethora of information in the PhotoTips. In the PhotoTools dialog boxes, you'll find the ability to zoom in or out, as well as to move your viewing area around.

All my work from 3D to Photoshop consists of some element created with Illustrator. There is rarely a day of the year when I'm not using Illustrator by itself or in concert with other programs.

CLARKE TATE

Intellihance Lite

Intellihance Lite is a *lite* version of Extensis' Intellihance plug-in. What makes this plug-in lite is it only works on RGB images and it doesn't have the fine-tuning controls of the full version. With Intellihance Lite, you can let the plug-in adjust your image to enhance and correct an over- or underdeveloped or too blurry photo. Using Intellihance or Intellihance Lite, you can change the light and dark levels to fix a too dark or light photo. If the image is blurred, you can also fix the blurred section using Intellihance or Intellihance Lite. By choosing the Preferences button, you can adjust contrast, brightness, saturation, sharpness, and despeckle your image. In each of these options, you have between three and six settings from which to choose. In Figure 5.1, the top half of the image was selected and had Intellihance Lite applied to it (5.1). If you apply Intellihance Lite, you can click the button *Enhance Image* to let the plug-in correct any imbalances on its own. This is similar to using Auto Levels from the Adjust submenu to fix an image. Auto Levels adjusts the light and dark without you controlling it. With Intellihance Lite's *Enhance Image* button, the plug-in corrects the contrast, brightness, saturation, sharpness, and despeckle, so you get five areas of correction being applied at once.

PhotoBars

PhotoBars will increase your productivity levels simply by giving you the ease of pressing a button, as opposed to searching through the pull-down menus (5.2). You can set up custom buttons, create your own toolbars, or edit toolbars to your specifications. You have the choice to Edit and Customize the toolbars. The SmartBar feature records the action as buttons in the pull-down menu in Photoshop, so you can create toolbars with the click of a button (5.3). In Photoshop, you

have to pull down to Adjust. Then go over to the secondary pull down menu and drag down to Variations each time you want to access the Variations option. With PhotoBars, you can make a button that enables you to access the Variations option with one click.

PhotoText

PhotoText is probably the most sought after feature of PhotoTools. PhotoText brings you the controls of text you have in Illustrator, FreeHand, QuarkXPress, or PageMaker. With PhotoText, you can make each letter of your text a different typeface, size, horizontal scale, and color. You can also adjust the tracking, kerning, leading, and more (5.4). PhotoText also enables you to have multiple strings of text. With the layering capability of Photoshop 4, all text automatically goes into its own layer. While all these features will no doubt excite you and make you want to do more tweaking to your text, once you press the check button, the text is still pixels and uneditable once it's accepted (5.5).

PhotoTips

PhotoTips is a compilation of insightful tips on using Photoshop 3 and 4, written by Deke McClelland (author of the *Macworld Photoshop Bible* series for IDG Books Worldwide). These tips can be viewed one at a time, or you can search for a particular area.

5.1

5.2

5.3

PhotoTips is better than Help options because more than basic help areas are covered in these tips. Tips you won't find anywhere are also in Photoshop's basic help functions. These tips are compiled from Deke's extensive knowledge of Photoshop, which goes beyond the basic areas you find in Photoshop's help area. The tips will make your Photoshop work more productive and show you an easier way to do things (5.6).

PhotoBevel

PhotoBevel enables you to create a variety of bevel effects to your selection. When you choose PhotoBevel, a dialog box appears that gives you many options for your bevel (5.7). You can choose your bevel type (inner or outer) and the shape of your bevel (flat, round, slope, or double bevel). The Edge Tolerance option sets the maximum, middle, or minimum edge to your bevel. Not only can you adjust the width of the bevel, you can adjust the softness, balance of highlight and shadow, and the intensity of the highlight and shadow. The angle of the shadow can

be changed by dragging a slider or typing in the angle you choose. The highlight and shadow color are defaulted to white and black, but you can choose any color for the highlight and shadow, as you wish (5.8). With the PhotoTools plug-ins, you always have the option to save or delete your settings.

5·5

5·4

PhotoEmboss

The PhotoEmboss plug-in has four types of embossing features: cutout, raise, edge, and blur. All four
show totally different embossing effects (5.9). The
embossing options are the amount in pixels, contrast,
softness, highlight intensity, and shadow intensity
(5.10). As with the other plug-ins, you can change the
highlight and shadow color and save or delete your
settings. The great feature of saving a setting is you
can drag to that saved name, instead of launching the
dialog box, and the effect will be applied.

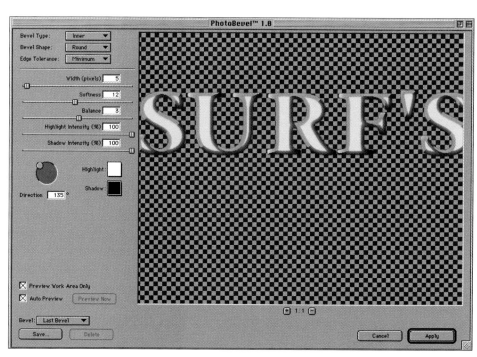

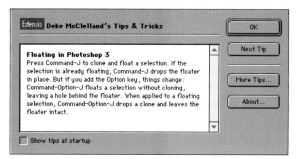

5.6

5.8

5.7

PhotoGlow

PhotoGlow applies a glow around the edge of your selection. Your two glow choices are edges and solid. What this means is, if you have a letter such as an *o* and solid is your choice, then the center of the *o* will be filled with the glow color. If edges is your choice, then the inside and outside edge of the *o* will have a glow effect applied (5.11 A and B). The PhotoGlow options include stroke width, radiance, and opacity. The stroke width is measured in pixels and determines the size of the glow. The radiance sets the softness or glow of the edge. The opacity is how intense the color of the glow will be. You can set the opacity to 100 percent and see the full color, or set it lower to 50 percent and get less color showing in through the glow. Figure 5.12 shows the opacity set to 100 percent for the maximum glow applied (5.12). The glow color can be any color you choose from Photoshop's color picker. You can save or delete any PhotoGlow setting.

5.9

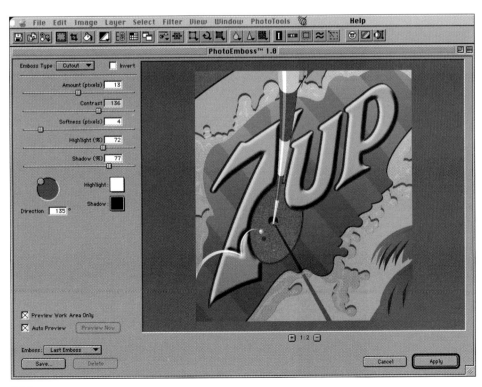

5.10

5.11A

5.11B

PhotoShadow

PhotoShadow creates a one-step shadow with such ease, you'll never use channels to create the soft selection again. As with PhotoGlow, you can choose to set a shadow on the edges of your selection or a solid shadow. You can also offset your shadow by dragging the X and Y Offset sliders to get a numerical offset. For the numerically challenged, you can hold down the Option/Alt key and drag your shadow to the location you want (5.13). The Blur slider will create a nice blurred edged shadow or none at all. The opacity setting determines how "see through" your shadow will be. You can choose any shadow color you want, as well as save or delete your shadow settings. One of the greatest thing about PhotoShadow is you needn't know much of anything about Photoshop to create a nice shadow (5.14). All you must know is how to create a selection for your shadow.

TIP

If you create your shadow on its own layer, you can change or delete the shadow later. Create your selection, and then click the new layer button. This will create the shadow on its own layer.

5.12

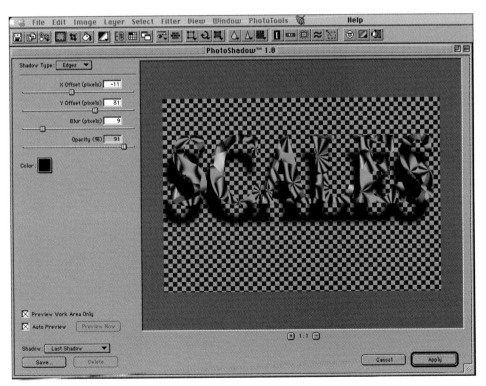

5.13

MASKPRO

MaskPro is a relatively new plug-in from Extensis that alleviates the hassle of masking out images (especially images with diverse backgrounds and

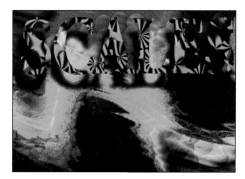

5.14

wispy foregrounds). Created for use with Photoshop, MaskPro saves time and frustration in selecting an image from the background.

The gist of MaskPro is you choose the colors you want to keep and the colors you want to drop from your image. Using the brush controls, you can soften the edge of your image from your background. Not only can you make minute adjustments to the brush, you can also adjust the threshold. The threshold will keep more or less of the image, depending on which way you drag the slider. Once you have brushed away the edge of the image you want to keep, you can use the Magic fill to erase the rest of the background (5.15). Now that the whole background is gone, you can create a path by choosing the Save/Apply option under the File menu. Probably the most exciting

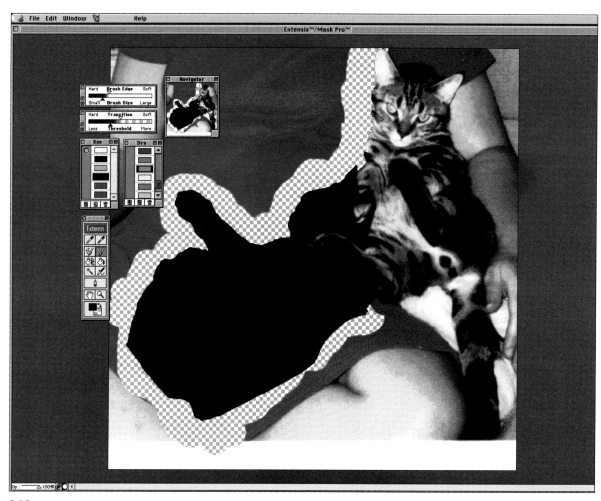

5.15

thing about MaskPro is you can have multiple undos in the dialog box! Everyone knows that in Photoshop you can only undo one time, but in MaskPro, you can undo multiple times.

Clark Tate used MaskPro to create *Surf's Up* (5.16). After opening the file in Photoshop, he used MaskPro for separating out the sun and art from the background. This way, Clark could create transparency effects of hidden layers.

INTELLIHANCE

Intellihance is a great landmark plug-in for Photoshop. Intellihance takes the hassle of image adjusting by putting the controls in one easily accessible area for Photoshop users (5.17). You can use the Quick Enhance option, open the Preferences, and choose your settings from the pop-up menu, or press the Fine Tune button for even more options.

5.16

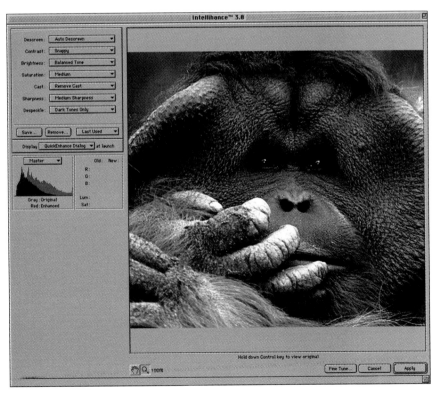

5.17

The Quick Enhance dialog box has three options: Enhance Image, Preferences, and Cancel (5.18). If you choose Enhance Image, the preference settings will be applied to your selection. What is truly great about the Quick Enhance is the settings will change from image to image. That is what makes Intellihance intelligent. It can look at each image differently and apply the necessary settings.

The Preferences option takes you into the Intellihance interface. You have seven options from which to choose: Descreen, Contrast, Brightness, Saturation, Cast, Sharpness, and Despeckle (5.19). You can save or remove any settings. Within these seven options you have from three to five pop-up presets from which to choose. As you choose any pop-up, you can see the preview in the preview window. To see the original image, press the control key.

The Fine Tune option takes you deeper into the Intellihance interface. In the Fine Tune dialog box, you have sliders for six options instead of standard presets (5.20). You can adjust the Cast, Tone, Descreen, Saturation, Sharpness, and Despeckle.

Each of these areas have sliders and/or eyedroppers you can manipulate.

- **Cast** removes the color cast some photographs may have. You can adjust the red, green, or blue and the cyan, magenta, yellow, and black, depending on the type of image. The eyedroppers can also remove cast by clicking the shadow, midtone, and highlights of your image.
- **Tone** is the same as brightness and contrast found in Photoshop. You use the eyedroppers or sliders to adjust the black point, midtone range, and white point of an image.
- **Descreen** removes the effects of a line screen that sometimes appear when you scan in an image from a book or magazine. Descreen blends an image that is blurred with the original. This option works much better than just blurring, because it retains detail.
- **Saturation** adjusts the amount of color in an image. Dragging the slider to the right saturates the image with more color. Dragging the

5.18

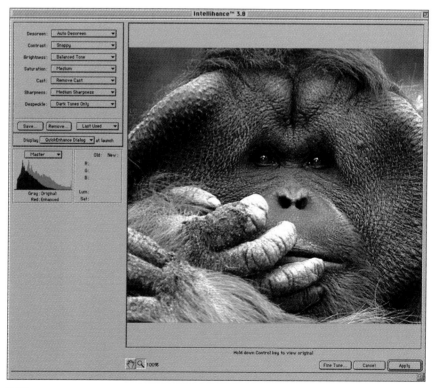

5.19

slider to the left desaturates the image or takes out a certain amount of color.

■ **Sharpness** adjusts the detail crispness of an image. The amount slider adjusts the sharpness. Definition controls whether you adjust the shadow, midtone, or highlights. The Threshold slider adjusts how pixels that are side-by-side will be sharpened. Smoothness will remove specks and flecks in the smooth areas.

■ **Despeckle** removes those nasty, tiny, different-colored pixels that ruin a large colored area. Amount refers to how much a blurred image will affect the original. The Threshold slider differentiates between the edge of pixels and noise. Limits adjusts whether dark or light pixels will be adjusted.

PORTFOLIO

Extensis' Portfolio 3.0 is a wonderful cataloging program that organizes your files into easily viewable, thumbnail-sized images (5.21). These files are cross platform and can be accessed at the same time by a Macintosh or Windows system. You can also access multiple Portfolio-saved documents at the same time. You can save graphic files, whole presentations, movies, sounds, text files, and more in your Portfolio file. I love using Portfolio to catalog all the artists' small JPEG files I receive. I can assign keywords to find a certain type of file or style of art easily. Not only is being able to catalog your art amazing, but the Portfolio document is also small and easily transferable for sending across the Internet for others to view.

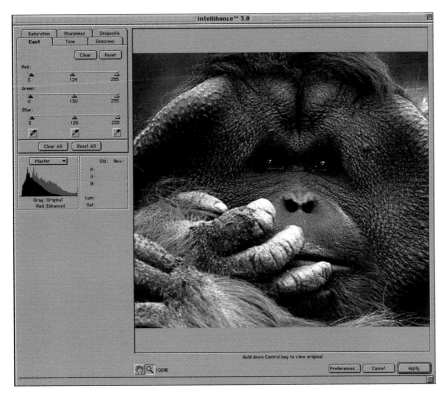

5.20

VECTORTOOLS

VectorTools has far outdone itself as a plug-in for Illustrator and FreeHand. This invaluable product has productivity features and options that have not been seen in a vector-based program. In the following list, I describe the Vector Tools features that will have you working in your vector program like never before — with amazing efficiency and productive results.

VectorBars

VectorBars come with 21 standard bars to view at will (5.22). VectorBars can be viewed as a floating palette or embedded as a toolbar. A floating palette can be resized and easily moved around your page. A *toolbar* is an imbedded bar — either vertically or horizontally — depending on your preference.

VectorBars are buttons that make accessing them as easy as pressing a button. Instead of dragging down through pull-down menus, you press a button. These buttons will quickly improve your efficiency in Illustrator.

SmartBar

SmartBar automatically creates a button and toolbar by recording the items you choose from the menu (5.23). You have the option to have SmartBar turned on or off. The little hammer icon will build a new bar with the buttons listed below in the SmartBar palette. The third button will reset the SmartBar back to an empty palette. With each little button, you can Command drag the button to any existing toolbar or you can build your own new toolbar.

5.21

VectorColor

VectorColor has brought the capability to change colors (as you do in Photoshop) to vectors and has added some new ways to change colors. VectorColor has five areas to access: Brightness/Contrast, Grayscale, Randomize, Multitone, and Edit Curves. In Illustrator, if you need a brighter color with more contrast, you'd have to create a whole new color and apply it to your path. With VectorColor, you can adjust the colors in real time on your selected path. The Grayscale option automatically changes all selected areas of color to different percentages of grayscale. The Randomize option will randomly replace a color with another color. This can have an amazing effect, especially on an expanded blend. Multitone will create a duo, tri, or quadtone. Edit Curves works similar to how it works in Photoshop. You can edit CMYK, RGB, or different combinations, such as only the Cyan and the Yellow colors. In Illustrator, VectorColor will affect gradient fills as well as solid colors. The following figure shows the original image above and the color-enriched image, which was altered using VectorColor (5.24).

VectorLibrary

VectorLibrary is an invaluable way to store and retrieve Illustrator or FreeHand images, paths, or text (5.25). Libraries are easily created by dragging-and-dropping your images, paths, or text into the VectorLibrary palette. New libraries can be saved and retrieved later, or you can continue to add images to the original library. You have the choice of viewing your objects in list (name) view or a thumbnail preview. All images, paths, or text you add to a library come in as an untitled name. You can give the new object any name you wish. These wonderful libraries can be exported and sent to your coworkers or friends.

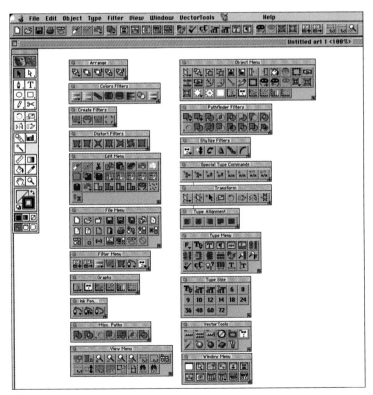

5.22

5.23

VectorNavigator

VectorNavigator enables you to view your Illustrator artwork easily from a resizeable floating palette (5.26). Photoshop 4 already has a Navigator plug-in; now Illustrator also has one. Navigation time is cut by this great feature that saves you from zooming in and out constantly to see where you are in your image. When you are zoomed in, you'll see a red box around the area you are viewing. You can resize the palette, change the preview, and easily move around your image by dragging the red box.

VectorObjectStyles

VectorObjectStyles creates style attributes for Illustrator objects (5.27). A style is defined by the Fill and Stroke attributes. Only path-based objects can have a style assigned. Once a style is created, you can easily apply this style to other objects. Another great feature is, if you need to change a style, you can do this easily in the VectorObjectStyles palette, rather than selecting all the individual pieces in your Illustrator image.

VectorShape

VectorShape is a distortion filter that projects your selection onto different shapes (5.28). You can project your selected path(s) onto a sphere, cylinder, or cone. You can also create a wavy, watery diamond, or a free projection. With any of these distortions, you can save your settings and remove unwanted settings. To access your settings, a pop-up menu is in the VectorShape palette. The other options in the VectorShape palette are to create a copy, use a ratio, maintain the layers, and add points. In the VectorShape palette, you can view in solid or artwork mode. If viewing complex images, you'll find a quicker preview in artwork mode. There is also a checkbox to show Unselected objects that are around your selected paths. VectorShape can create many cool distortions, especially when you apply more than one distortion on top of another. Type can also be distorted when it has been created into outlines.

5.24

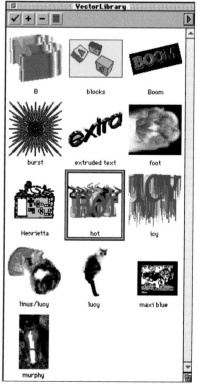

5.25

VectorTips

VectorTips contains a plethora of tips, tricks, and techniques that are amazing time savers (5.29). Ted Alspach provides the tips for Illustrator and Olav Kvern provides the tips for FreeHand. The tips Ted and Olav provide are better than using the Help functions because many of the tips are undocumented and advanced. They have given us their extensive knowledge in easy-to-access tips. The tips are not only helpful and insightful, but searchable as well.

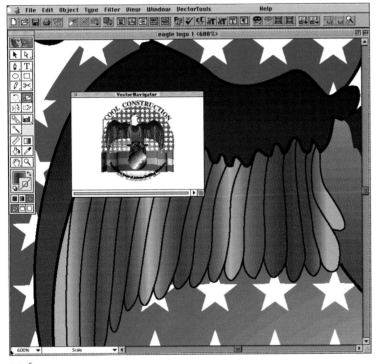

5.26

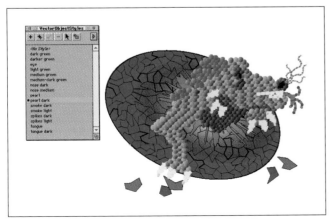

5.27

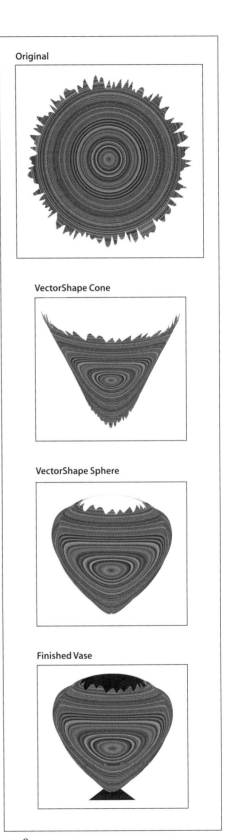

5.28

You can have these tips show at startup or access them from the VectorTools pull-down menu.

VectorMagicWand

VectorMagicWand finally gives users of Illustrator the convenience of Photoshop's Magic Wand, only better (5.30). The VectorMagicWand shows up in the VectorMagicWand palette and in the toolbar of Illustrator 7. The VectorTools pull-down menu has a pull-down access to the VectorMagicWand palette. The VectorMagicWand palette is where you'll find

multiple choices for using your VectorMagicWand. You can adjust the following tolerances: Fill Color, Stroke Color, Minimum Stroke Weight, Maximum Stroke Weight, Minimum Area, and Maximum Area. With the sliders available, you can have multiple areas to access at one time. The higher the tolerance setting, the more paths will be selected. The lower the tolerance setting, the fewer paths will be selected.

VectorFrame

VectorFrame creates an automatic frame on your selection, according to the size of offset you choose (5.31). With VectorFrame, you can apply one frame to all objects selected, to each object individually, or to each group. In the VectorFrame palette you have a pop-up triangle that enables you to save settings and to use presets.

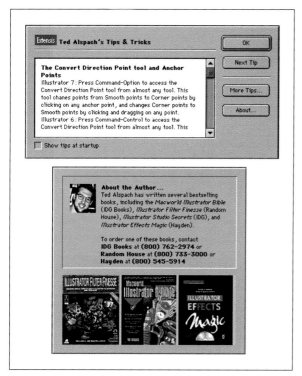

5.29

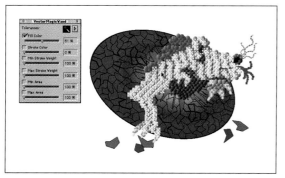

5.30

5.31

HotKeys

HotKeys are keyboard commands that quickly access VectorTools plug-ins. To see what the Hot Keys are, choose Hot Keys from the VectorTools pull-down menu. You can leave the default Hot Keys or change them to your liking. For a full listing of the default Hot Keys, see the following figure (5.32).

VectorTypeStyles

VectorTypeStyles is available only in FreeHand. VectorTypeStyles enables you to create a certain type style and assign it with a style name. Now you can easily change any type to have that style attribute. You can quickly change your selected type to be a certain font, style, size, leading, and color in one easy click.

VectorCaps

VectorCaps is available only in FreeHand. VectorCaps will quickly set the case for your selected type. Your case choices are lowercase, all caps, sentence caps, title caps, and random caps.

METACREATIONS CORPORATION

MetaCreations Corporation is the newly merged companies of MetaTools and Fractal Design. MetaCreations has created numerous plug-ins and stand-alone applications. Kai Krause is well-known in the graphics field as a leader of plug-ins with *Kai's Power Tools 3 for Photoshop* and *KPT Vector Effects for Illustrator*. (See Chapter 6 for more of MetaCreations stand-alone products.)

KAI'S POWER TOOLS 3

Kai's Power Tools 3 (KPT 3) contains 18 filters that enable you to create real-time effects. KPT 3 has tons of presets for you to use. These filters are incredible time savers when creating any special effects to part of or to your whole Photoshop image. You can also rasterize any Illustrator file into Photoshop to apply these affects.

KPT Gradient Designer

KPT Gradient Designer is one of the most used filters of the KPT 3 set. This filter enables you to design gradients from presets or totally create your own new gradient (5.33). You have six areas or options to choose from in the KPT Gradient Designer interface. The Mode is what type of gradient you want to create; you have 12 choices for mode. Loop is how you want the gradient to repeat or distort. Repeat is how many times you want to repeat the gradient; the maximum is ten repeats. Next, you can choose the Opacity. By dragging across the Opacity button, you can create a see-through gradient or a totally opaque one. Glue applies a certain style of gradient, from normal to procedural. Direction is the final option. If you have a linear gradient, you can choose the direction or angle of the gradient. You also must choose the color(s) you want to use in your gradient.

KPT Interform

KPT Interform is the combination of two textures (5.34). You can combine these two textures quickly and change their look and position. Not only can you create amazing textural backgrounds, but you can also save those background changes as a filmstrip for use in movies.

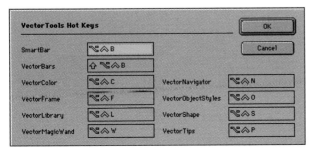

5.32

5.33

KPT Spheroid Designer

KPT Spheroid Designer is the only way to create unique spheres (5.35). You can create one or multiple spheres. You can choose from numerous styles of spheres, as well as the option to alter these presets to create your own type of spheres. As with KPT Interform, you can also create movies with KPT Spheroid Designer.

KPT Texture Explorer

KPT Texture Explorer goes that step beyond creating gradients. With KPT Texture Explorer, you can create textures beyond your wildest dreams (5.36). Not only can you create amazing textures, but you can choose the colors you want to use in your texture. To view the whole texture before accepting it, press the Kai logo in the upper-left corner.

KPT 3D Stereo Noise

KPT Stereo Noise is seen in almost every mall. This TV static-like noise is actually a 3D picture (5.37). You need to stare at the image for it to pop out at you. Few people can see the image immediately. If you're like I am, to see the 3D pop out at you, you need a piece of glass in front of the image on which to concentrate.

KPT Glass Lens

KPT Glass Lens is one of many small interface filters. This small interface offers less options than some of the bigger filters, but it still creates some stunning effects. The KPT Glass Lens has three options: Mode, Glue, and Opacity. In Mode, you choose between a soft, normal, and a bright light on the lens. The filter creates a bulged-out glass lens effect to your selection (5.38).

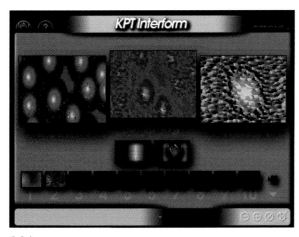

5.34

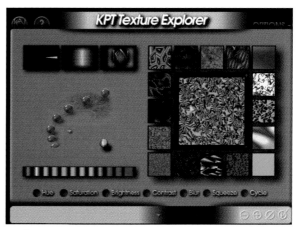

5.36

5.35

5.37

KPT Page Curl

KPT Page Curl creates a cool curled-page effect to your image. This looks as if the page is actually turning and you can see what is underneath that page (5.39). The options in KPT Page Curl enable you to control how much and how opaque the curl will be.

KPT Planar Tiling

KPT Planar Tiling can tile your image in parquet or perspective tiles (5.40). You choose which option you want and the filter will automatically repeat the selection and put it in a parquet tile or a perspective tile.

KPT Seamless Welder

KPT Seamless Welder makes tiles from rectangular selection (5.41). This creates a smooth, seamless edge between tiles. You can choose between the Seamless Welder, which creates tiles from outside the selections and the Reflective Welder, which creates tiles from within the selection.

KPT Twirl

KPT Twirl is another of the smaller interfaced filters that creates a twirled effect. You have to choose between a twirled effect and a kaleidoscope effect (5.42). To create the twirl or kaleidoscope, just drag in the small preview area to the desired effect. You can also adjust the Glue and Opacity in the KPT Twirl dialog box.

KPT Video Feedback

KPT Video Feedback creates a Video or Telescope swirling special effect (5.43). You can choose either Video or Telescope Feedback. The Video will create a rectangular perspective effect and the Telescope will create a circular perspective effect. As with the

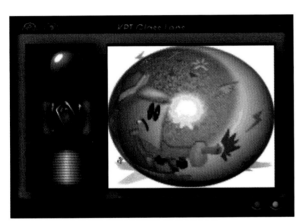

5.38

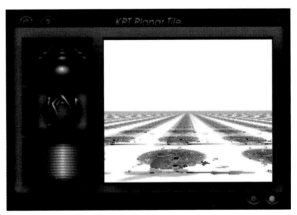

5.40

5.39

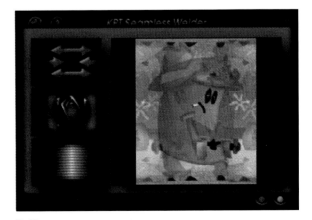

5.41

smaller filters, you can also adjust the Glue and the Opacity. To activate the effect, you need to drag in the small preview area to see the desired effect.

5.42

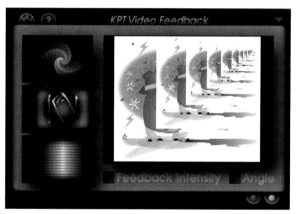

5.43

5.44

KPT Vortex Tiling

KPT Vortex Tiling creates a black hole effect into which your image gets sucked (5.44). You can choose between a normal or a pinched vortex. A normal vortex pulls your image into a center, which you specify. A pinched vortex will pinch in the center and enlarge the outside sections of the image. You can adjust the Vortex Radius to view more or less of your image being pulled on itself.

KPT Edge f/x

All the f/x filters come up as if you are viewing your image through a printer's loop. KPT Edge f/x pulls out the edges of your image and creates an outlined version of it (5.45). You can change the opacity and drag around your lens to see how this will affect your whole image. The three choices you have for edge are: normal, soft, and directional.

5.45

5.46

KPT Gaussian f/x

KPT Gaussian f/x applies a Gaussian Blur to your selection (5.46). You can drag the lens around to see the affect your settings have on the whole image. The intensity and opacity both can be adjusted to create a smooth blurred effect. You can have four types of Gaussian f/x: Blur, Weave, Blocks, and Diamonds.

KPT Intensity f/x

KPT Intensity f/x saturates your image's color if the intensity is set to 100, or can create a less saturated filmy look to your image (5.47).

KPT Noise f/x

KPT Noise f/x creates a pixelized noise to your selection. You have three options: Hue Protected, Grime Layer, and Special Color. The Hue Protected will retain the original hues from your image and only create noise in the color areas (5.48). Grime Layer will add a dirty darkened look to the noise. Special Color creates an overall noise effect to your image.

KPT Pixel f/x

KPT Pixel f/x creates a painted pixel look (5.49). You have three options from which to choose: Diffuse More, PixelWeather 1, and PixelWeather 2. All three options create a different painterly look. You can adjust the intensity and opacity of the effect on your image.

KPT Smudge f/x

KPT Smudge f/x creates a directional smear to your pixels (5.50). The smudge option affects all the colored areas with a blurred blend. The Drip option affects only the darker pixels.

KPT MetaToys f/x

KPT MetaToys f/x combines the Glass Lens and Twirl filters in a previewable lens. Although KPT MetaToys f/x doesn't seem practical, it does seem fun. You can view a twirl or spheroid effect through the lens, but it actually affects the whole image (5.51).

5.47

5.49

5.51

5.48

5.50

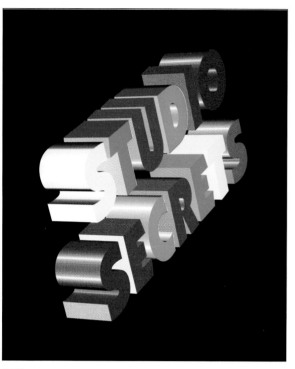

5.52

KPT VECTOR EFFECTS

KPT Vector Effects is a plug-in for Illustrator and FreeHand. These 13 plug-ins create some fantastic special effects. While some of the effects can be achieved without Vector Effects, it would take a long time to do it. Some of the effects you could not create without many hours of work and much difficulty.

KPT 3D Transform

KPT 3D Transform's name is a tad deceiving. While you can mimic 3D status with extrusion and an x, y, and z axis, actual 3D is still created using a 3D program like Adobe Dimensions. You can create some great extruded effects with KPT 3D Transform (5.52). With your selected path(s) you can rotate the x, y, and z axis, set the amount of extrusion, create a bevel with your extrusion, adjust the metallicity, create perspective, change the light source, and change the white and black point's color.

KPT ColorTweak

KPT ColorTweak gives you control over color in Illustrator or FreeHand. You can invert the color, change to grayscale, adjust the Brightness or Contrast,

Before KPT ColorTweak

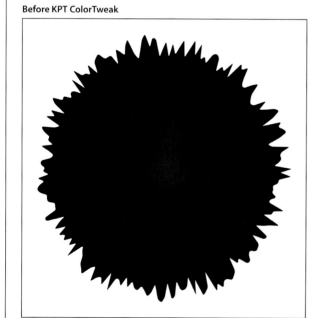

After KPT ColorTweak

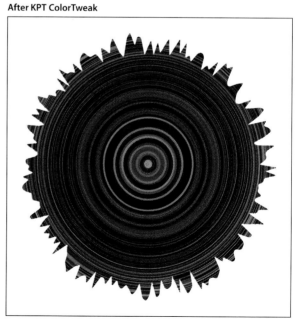

5.53

increase or decrease the Saturation, rotate the Hue values, and add or subtract a tint of cyan, magenta, yellow, or black. In the options menu you have a randomize option, which affects your selection when you rotate the hue (5.53).

KPT Emboss

KPT Emboss creates an emboss on your selected paths in one quick and easy step. You can create a hard or a soft emboss to your selection (5.54). You can adjust the contrast, angle, and the amount of emboss with sliders or you can Command-click the button and type in a numeric value.

KPT Flare

KPT Flare creates a starburst of light on your selected path (5.55). You can have multiple flares varying in sizes and shapes that can create a starry sky (5.56). KPT Flare will create an amazingly soft blend of light and shadow that would almost be impossible to create manually.

KPT Inset

KPT Inset will create an offset path with more finesse than Illustrator's Offset path. You can also see a preview of how far the path is being offset before you click the OK button. Inset path will create a second path on either the inside or the outside of the original with an exact spacing between the two paths (5.57).

KPT Neon

KPT Neon creates a neon light effect on your selected path or outlined text. KPT Neon creates neon tubes of which you determine the size and intensity (5.58). You start with any size line and choose KPT Neon. Here, you choose how thick you want the neon and how intense you want the highlight. If you Command-click the Intensity or Amount, you can type in a numeric value.

KPT Point Editor

KPT Point Editor enables you to move points and handles numerically with the *x* and *y* axis. You can also move the points in the preview box and the numeric values will correspond to your new positions.

5.56

5.54

5.55

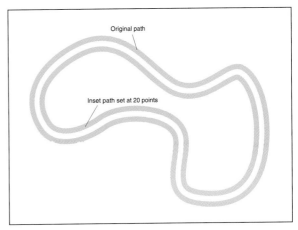

5.57

KPT Resize & Reposition

KPT Resize & Reposition enables you to change the size and position of a selected object. You can type in the new width and height values or enter a percentage to scale. By changing the *x* and *y* values, you can move the object a determined amount.

KPT ShadowLand

KPT ShadowLand creates three different types of shadow (5.59). A *Zoom shadow* is a shadow that goes back in a perspective and can rotate around, as well. A *Soft shadow* creates a softened shadow to your selected path. A *Halo shadow* creates a soft halo edge to your selected object. The General controls include: Scale, Steps, Distance, Angle, From what color, and To what color. You can scale the shadow to create a perspective shadow. If you see actual banded steps, you can increase the number in the Steps control to soften the blending of the shadow. Any setting you create can be saved for later use.

KPT ShatterBox

KPT ShatterBox breaks your selected fill into a determined amount of pieces. You have three choices for ShatterBox: Radial Shatter, Random Lines, and

5.58

5.59

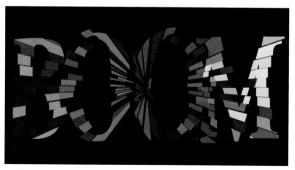

5.60

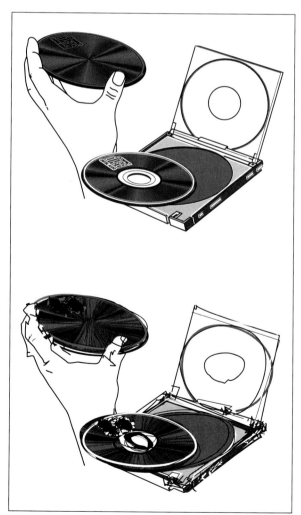

5.61

Random Curves (5.60). You can also set a fragment offset and radial disruption, which will move and distort the pieces out from their original. The Lighten and Darken options enable you to choose what percentage of the pieces will be lighter and darker. As with most of the Vector Effects, you can save and delete any setting you create.

KPT Sketch

KPT Sketch creates a sketchy quality to your selected objects. You can achieve a hand-drawn look to your images with the drag of a slider. You can have a Color Stroke, Pen Stroke, or a Width Stroke to create your sketchy look. The Stroke slider enables you to choose the stroke width, and the Amount slider enables you to choose just how sketchy you want your object (5.61).

KPT Vector Distort

KPT Vector Distort is actually seven additional plug-ins all wrapped up into one. You can Swirl, Spherize, Rotate, Magnify, Zig, Zap, or Zig Zag a path or outlined type (5.62). The last setting is Warp Frame, which takes you right to the next plug-in so you can apply an envelope setting to your path.

KPT Warp Frame

KPT Warp Frame pushes your selected object into an envelope frame. You can adjust the frame to any setting you like or you can use the many presets that come with KPT Warp Frame. When viewing the presets, you can press Command-Option-Spacebar and see your selection in each of the presets (5.63). This way, you get a minipreview before you choose a frame. You can always adjust the preset to create your own frame and save your new preset.

Original

KPT Vector Distort Spherize

5.62

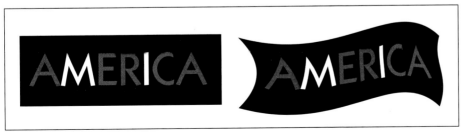

5.63

ALIEN SKIN SOFTWARE

Alien Skin has brought us plug-ins for Photoshop and Illustrator. The Photoshop plug-in is called Eye Candy 3.01, which is the upgrade of the original product called Black Box. The Illustrator plug-in, called Stylist, enables you to attach styles to your vectors. Both the Photoshop and Illustrator products increase your productivity, as well as create some really cool effects.

EYE CANDY 3.01

Alien Skin Software upgraded its Black Box line of Photoshop plug-ins to Eye Candy 3.01. These 21 plug-ins for Photoshop create amazing effects with

the click of a button. You have quite a variety of special effects to choose from and the dialog boxes are clean and easy to use.

Antimatter

Antimatter inverts your image's brightness, while keeping the hue and saturation values. There is no dialog box; it automatically applies the inversion to your selection (5.64).

Carve

Carve will create a carved or chiseled effect to your image. By using light and shadow with beveling, you create a 3D carved-in look (5.65). You can control the Bevel Width, Shadow Strength, Smoothness, and Bevel Shape. There are ten presets to choose from or you can create your own.

Chrome

Chrome creates a metallic effect on your selection. You can produce a chrome, gold, copper, and many other cool effects (5.66). The Controls you can play with are: Bands, Softness, Variation, and Contrast. There are 11 presets to use or from which to start. You can adjust the sliders to create your own effects and save those as new presets.

Cutout

Cutout creates a hole in your selection (5.67). It creates this illusion by filling in the center with white and adding shadow to the edges to create a 3D hole

5.64

5.65

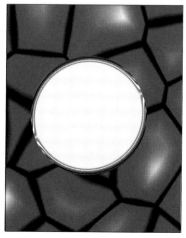

5.66

look. You can adjust the Direction, Distance, and Blur, as well as choose from ten presets.

Drop Shadow

Drop Shadow produces a shadow beneath your selected area (5.68). This quickly adds a 3D feeling to your image. You can choose the direction, shadow distance, and any color of shadow, and you can choose or launch from 13 presets.

Fire

Fire makes a flame (as if you are setting your selection on fire) around your selection (5.69). You need to create a selection first for this filter to work correctly. You can choose from ten presets and you can control the flame width, flame height, movement, and a random seed.

Fur

Fur does just what it sounds like. It creates a fur-like effect to your image (5.70). You can choose from 11 presets and you can create your own. The controls you adjust are: Wave Spacing, Waviness, and Hair Length. This one is a blast to try with a person's face, but be sure only to select the skin — not the hair — eyes or mouth to get a really hilarious effect (5.71).

Glass

Glass looks as if you put a glass top over your image (5.72). You choose the width of the bevel, the space between flaws, the thickness of the flaws, opacity, refraction, highlight brightness and sharpness, and the direction of light. You also choose the color of the glass. Choose from ten presets or you can create your own.

Glow

Glow creates a glowing edge around your selection (5.73). You control the width of the glow, the opacity, the opacity dropoff, and the color of the glow. You can save any settings as a preset, so you have it anytime you open Photoshop.

5.68

5.69

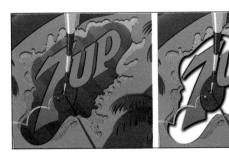

5.67

HSB Noise

HSB Noise produces noise in a selection using Hue, Saturation, and Brightness (5.74). The controls you set are Hue Variation, Saturation Variation, Brightness Variation, and Opacity. You have ten presets to choose from or create your own.

Inner Bevel

Inner Bevel produces an embossed look to your selection (5.75). The selection will look as if it is popping up from the rest of your image. You control the Bevel Width, Shadow Strength, Smoothness, and Lighting

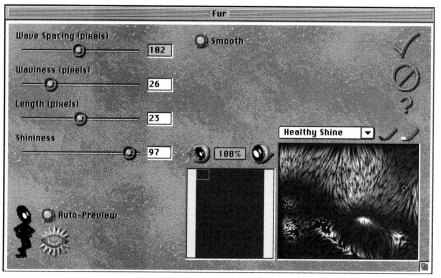

5.70

5.71

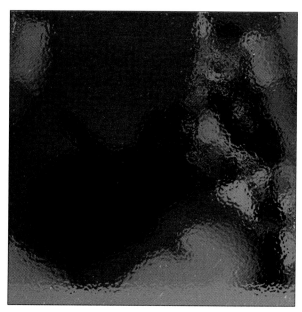

5.72

direction. You can choose from ten presets or create your own settings.

Jiggle

Jiggle creates a bubbling distortion to your selection (5.76). This jiggle effect looks bubbly, Jello-like, or shattered. You control the Bubble Size, Warp Amount, Twist, and Movement Type. You can choose from ten presets.

Motion Trail

Motion Trail smudges your selection outward in one direction (5.77). You determine the Length of the trail, the Opacity of the motion, and the Direction the trail will go.

Outer Bevel

Outer Bevel is similar to Inner Bevel except the raised look appears on the outside of your selection (5.78). You control the Bevel Width, Bevel Shape, Smoothness, Shadow Depth, Highlight Balance and Sharpness, and the Lighting direction.

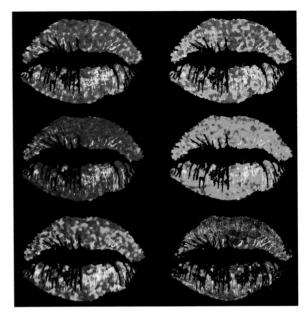

5.74

5.75

5.73

5.76

Perspective Shadow

Perspective Shadow makes a shadow behind your selected area and the shadow appears to go back in space (5.79). You determine the Vanishing Point Direction, Vanishing Point Distance, Length, Opacity, Blur, and Shadow color. Choose from ten presets or you can create your own.

Smoke

Smoke is similar to the fire filter once the fire has been extinguished. With the Smoke filter, you create various smoke effects behind your selection (5.80). You determine the Wisp Width, Wisp Height, Breakup Amount, Breakup Roughness, Inside Masking, Edge Softness, Random Seed, and Inside and Outside colors.

5.77

5.78

Squint

Squint creates a blur similar to what you'd see if you needed glasses (5.81). You determine how strong a prescription your eyes need. Unlike Gaussian Blur, which blurs evenly, Squint gives you that double vision, if it's dragged far enough.

5.79

5.80

Star

Star creates polygons with ease (5.82). You can quickly create any star pattern without having to use Illustrator or FreeHand. You set the Number of Sides, Indentation, Scale, *X* and *Y* shift, Opacity, Orientation, and Inner and Outer color. You can have a maximum of 50 sides to your star.

5.81

5.82

Swirl

Swirl will smudge your image by using whirlpools (5.83). You set how far apart the Whirlpools are, the length of the Smear, how much of a Twist, and the Streak afterward.

Water Drops

Water Drops sprinkles water across your selection (5.84). You set the Number of Drops, Edge Darkness, Opacity, Refraction, Drop Color, Random Seed, Highlight Brightness and Sharpness, and Lighting direction. You can choose from presets or create your own water drops.

Weave

Weave takes your selection and, from it, creates a woven pattern (5.85). You choose the Ribbon Width, Gap Width and color, Shadow Depth, Thread Detail, and Thread Length. This is another great filter to try on a person's skin to give them a creepy, woven look (5.86).

5.83

STYLIST

Stylist, by Alien Skin Software, is a plug-in for Illustrator. This plug-in uses style sheets to organize your complex images by organizing your art into groups. Stylist also can save special effects as styles so they can quickly and easily be applied to a selected path. Stylist has over 100 preset special effects from which to choose. Some of the presets include Millipede, Soft Shadow, Chain, and Railroad track (5.87).

5.84

5.85

5.86

TOP TEN THIRD-PARTY PLUG-IN EFFECTS FOR PHOTOSHOP AND ILLUSTRATOR

1. PHOTOTEXT

PhotoText by Extensis enables you to do things with text in Photoshop like never before (5.88).

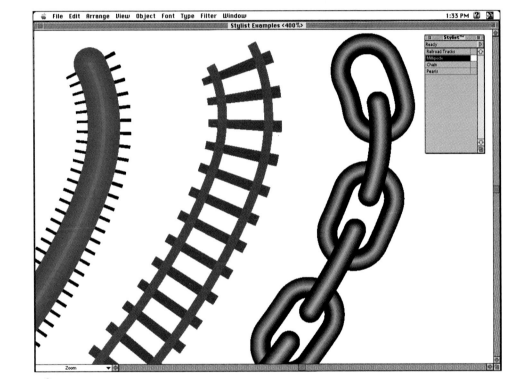

5.87

5.88

5.89

5.90

2. PHOTOSHADOW

PhotoShadow by Extensis creates shadows with such ease and comfort, you'll never use channels again (5.89).

3. PHOTOEMBOSS

PhotoEmboss takes the idea of emboss a step further and uses it to create depth by popping out images (5.90).

4. VECTORSHAPE

VectorShape by Extensis enables you to shove your selections into shapes and even to wrap text around an image (5.91).

5.91

5. VECTORCOLOR

VectorColor by Extensis gives Illustrator users the control over their color like they have in Photoshop (5.92).

6. KPT SPHEROID DESIGNER

KPT Spheroid Designer by MetaCreations enables you to create amazing spheres like never before (5.93).

7. KPT PIXEL F/X

KPT Pixel f/x by MetaCreations creates soft painterly effects on your pixel image (5.94).

5.93

5.92

5.94

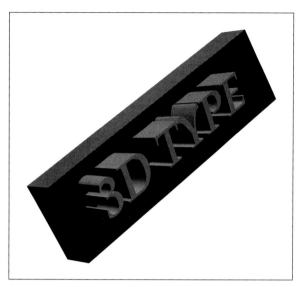

5.95

8. KPT 3D TRANSFORM

KPT 3D Transform by MetaCreations enables you to create amazing extruded effects, even with outlined text (5.95).

9. FUR

Fur, by Alien Skin Software, is one of the most fun filters to create a fur texture on a selection. Pick a friend or relative and turn him or her into a beast (5.96).

10. HSB NOISE

HSB Noise by Alien Skin Software adds some fun effects by adding noise with hue, saturation, and brightness to your selection (5.97).

5.96

5.97

CHAPTER 6
PHOTOSHOP AND ILLUSTRATOR WITH OTHER APPLICATIONS

In the graphics industry, knowing only one or two programs just isn't enough. Most artists and graphics people alike use Photoshop and Illustrator with other programs. Whether you use a 3D program or a page layout program, you need to know how your programs will interact together. From QuarkXPress, PageMaker, and programs from MetaCreations such as Kai's Power Goo, to 3D programs and Web pages, you'll find a plethora of information about working with Photoshop and Illustrator and other applications in this chapter.

WORKING WITH METACREATIONS PRODUCTS

As you may know, MetaTools and Fractal Design evolved into MetaCreations Corporation. Within MetaCreations, you'll find KPT products and Fractal products. These stand-alone applications add another dimension to creating amazing images with Photoshop and Illustrator. While Photoshop and Illustrator are fantastic programs, they can't do everything. Using other applications increases the potential of Photoshop and Illustrator. You can start an image in Illustrator, combine it with a Photoshop image, and then take a Bryce image to complete the background. The possibilities are endless.

The technological advances offered to the artist by the digital revolution oblige us to create revolutionary work.

BILL ELLSWORTH

KPT PHOTO SOAP

MetaCreation's newest product on the market is KPT Photo Soap. This stand-alone application enables you to clean up like never before. Because of the easy repair ability, Kai's Photo Soap is great for any level user.

Soap, like Goo, consists of rooms you enter to perform a variety of tasks. You can explore a total of eight rooms: Map Room, In Room, Out Room, Prep Room, Tone Room, Color Room, Detail Room, and Finish Room. The main use of Soap is to adjust the tone, color, and detail of an image; in the Finish Room, you can add text or backgrounds. The following steps outline how to fix a scratched image with Photo Soap:

STEP 1 Open the image in Soap by choosing the In Room and File (6.1).
STEP 2 Click the Details button to enter the Details Room.
STEP 3 Using the magnifying glass, zoom in on the scratched area.
STEP 4 Click the Paintbrush and start painting over the scratch (6.2).

6.1

STEP 5 When the scratch is fixed, exit by choosing the Out Room (6.3). In the Out Room, you can save or print the file.

Kai's Photo Soap not only can fix images, but you can also add backgrounds, textures, edges, and cartoon characters. Soap can open Photoshop, TIFF, JPEG, FlashPix, BMP, and PICT files. You can also create your own albums in which to store your files. One of the many fun things you can do with Soap is to add cartoon images to your photos. Soap has a library of cute cartoons for you to choose from. Here's how to add toons to your image:

6.2

6.3

PHOTOSHOP AND THE MOVIES, MUSINGS FROM MARK J. SMITH

THE FOLLOWING are some off-the-cuff musings from artist Mark J. Smith about production work and how Photoshop was an integral part of solving some difficult problems he faced working on various lower budget films. Mark discusses his experience working with Concorde/ New Horizons to produce the digital FX for two films in Showtime's film series. If you can, visit Mark's Web page (`http://home.earthlink. net/~digitaldrama`), which will help you understand some of the things Mark discusses.

"This was the second time we worked for Concorde/New Horizons. We may never have worked on films at all if it were not for the good graces of Roger Corman himself. For those unfamiliar with Roger Corman, he is considered one of the kings of the low-budget arena. We were ecstatic to get our first digital film and to work with Roger. We would soon learn the meaning of low budget.

"We were hired to do the digital FX for two films of the 13-film Showtime series. The first was called *Black Scorpion,* with Joan Severance. The second film was a remake — the second remake — of the

STEP 1 Open the image to which you want to add cartoons in the In Room (6.4).

STEP 2 Click the Finish button to enter the Finish Room.

STEP 3 Click the Objects bar to access the cartoon characters (6.5).

STEP 4 Click and drag a character to your image or double-click the character to place it in your image.

STEP 5 Add as many cartoon images as you want. You can move them by clicking and dragging them to a new location (6.6). When you finish, click the Out button to enter the Out Room where you can save or print the file.

BRYCE 2

Bryce 2 is a program that enables you to create 3D landscapes. Bryce 2 images can then be combined with any Photoshop image you create. With Bryce, you control the sky, clouds, type of cloud cover, weather, and more. Artist Bill Ellsworth, in my opinion, could be the foremost expert on using Bryce 2. Bill has used Bryce in many landscapes; he then takes them into Photoshop to finish off the image. In the next few paragraphs, Bill explains his use of Bryce and Photoshop to create his collection of images.

6.4

1957 classic, *Not of This Earth.* (In 1988, Roger himself remade the film with former porn actress Tracy Lords. This was a god-awful film. How do you account for another remake by the same guy eight years later?) The second remake was to be Concorde/New Horizons' first endeavor into digital FX.

"On *Not of This Earth (N.O.T.E.),* we did 63 digital FX for the film. We were very proud of what we did, considering the money we had. Because of the naiveté on their part, as well as ours, there were a myriad of things that made a difficult shot all the more time-consuming and complex. This also became the time I became a devout believer in the power of Photoshop.

"One scene in particular had to do with the jellyfish attacking and killing one of the actors in his office. The actor was Mason Adams, who is best known as the voice of Smuckers Jam. How appropriate that he should be whacked by an alien jellyfish.

"Allow me to set some points about digital FX mixed with live action. No matter what transpires, there should always be a clean background plate filmed in any scene that requires computer graphics. Why? Well, for starters it is the only record of events on a clean set, before actors are present.

"A second point that should be made is a clean background plate needs to be running footage. Film grain is an integral part of what makes film look different than video. The other is it is 24 frames per second, not 30 as in video. Film grain is something you don't really notice until it isn't there."

See Chapter 7 for more of Mark's musings into the digital FX work he did for *Not of This Earth.*

BIOTA Advertisement

"This image ran as an advertisement for the band, Biota, in *Mondo 2000* magazine. I created it in Photoshop — from several low-resolution Bryce and Photoshop images — by creating a new blank document at the correct size and resolution of the ad and pasting in the small source images, and then fading and blurring them together" (6.7).

Buried Dreams

"This one started out by collaging together a couple Bryce images. The resulting image was pretty boring, so I applied KPT3's Spheroid Designer and Vortex Tiling to the entire surface. The two Sphere-like things were created by floating an oval selection and applying KPT3's Gradient Designer in various apply modes" (6.8).

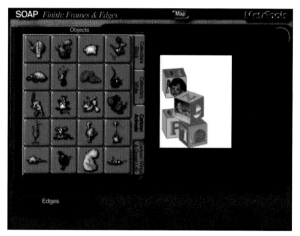

6.5

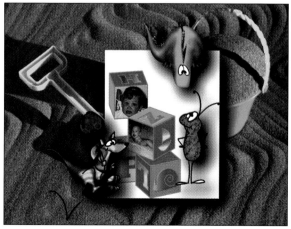

6.6

6.7

Contact

"This is, again, a collage of low-resolution Bryce images. The overall composition and 'feel' of the image comes direct from the low-resolution Bryce source image. To make it look good at a higher resolution, I applied Photoshop's Lighting Effects filter to a slightly blurred copy of the image and applied that to the scaled-up original, effectively removing the pixelation and creating a new, interesting texture. Several other Bryce images were added via various apply modes using the same process" (6.9).

Into the Labyrinth

"I made a tiled pattern from a small Bryce Image and seriously distorted the center of the resulting image with KPT3's Gradient Designer, Twirl, and Planar Tiling filters. The two green filigrees are KNOT generations that have been enhanced (stretched, twisted, and so on) in Photoshop" (6.10).

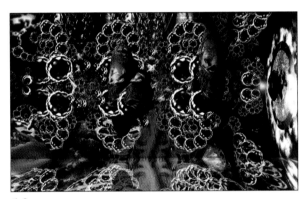

6.8

6.9

Spheroid Invader

"This image started as a Bryce background over which I applied KPT3's Spheroid Designer using various apply modes" (6.11).

KAI'S POWER GOO

Kai's Power Goo is probably one of the most fun software packages you'll ever work with. I have never had as many laughs and fun as I do when I use Goo. With Goo, you can smear, grow, shrink, and pretty much

6.10

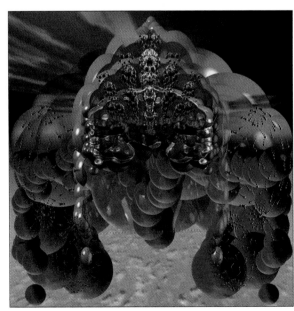

6.11

mangle any image. You can also fuse two images together. For instance, you can give a bald guy the curly locks from a gorgeous model. If that isn't enough fun for you, you can save steps in-between and make them into a "Goovie" to watch later.

STEP 1 Open the image you want to "Goo" by clicking the In Room and choosing the image from the File menu (6.12).

STEP 2 Click the top rainbow dots to access some Goo features.

STEP 3 Click the Smear button and drag the image to create a peanut shape (6.13).

STEP 4 Click the Out button to get to the Out Room so you can save the file (6.14).

Another fun use of Goo is to fuse together images. You can take the great features of one image and replace the not-so-great features on another image.

The following steps illustrate how to fuse together two images:

STEP 1 Click the Fusion Room (6.15).

STEP 2 Choose two images by clicking the In button and selecting your images.

STEP 3 Click the Paint button and move the crosshairs to the image you want to copy. Make sure the image you want to copy to is the middle image.

STEP 4 As you start to paint, you'll see the new features coming out (6.16).

STEP 5 You can use the Smooth button to even out skin tones and harsh edges (6.17).

STEP 6 If you want, you can change the image you are copying to and alter another feature (6.18).

After you have the image you want, you can save the image. To save any Goo image, click the Out button at the lower-right of the image. In the Out Room, you can save the image as a Goovie, a file, an animation, or send it right to the printer.

PAINTER

MetaCreations' Painter is a fabulous program that has the natural artist in mind. When you combine this amazing program with a pressure-sensitive tablet, there is no end to what you can do. Painter enables you to simulate actual painting on selected canvas with any artist's materials. Painter can start with a new document for you to create on the fly or you can bring in any photo or scan as a starting off point.

Painter works on both the Macintosh and the PC with the Drag-and-Drop feature. This means you can

6.12

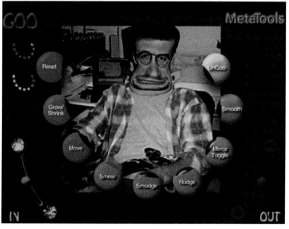

6.13

6.14

select any part or whole section of a Painter image and drag-and-drop it into another program, like Photoshop. Painter can save out as TIFF, PICT, EPS, Photoshop 2.0, Photoshop 3.0, PICT, Targa, PCX, BMP, GIF, JPEG, Pyramid, and Painter's standard RIFF file. Painter can also import and export to Illustrator.

The floating palettes are one of Painter's strengths (6.19). These palettes are customizable. From the palettes, you can access a wide range of drawing and painting tools, as well as special effect brushes. With the ability to make selections, like Photoshop, you can apply brushes to a section instead of the whole image (6.20). All in all, Painter is an amazing program and, in combination with Photoshop and Illustrator, you can create images like never before. You can start your ideas in Illustrator, then paint them in Painter, and finish them off with light, blurring, or additional textures in Photoshop.

Figure 6.20 shows an image created by Bill Ellsworth that incorporates using Photoshop with Poser and Painter (Poser is another great program by MetaCreations). Bill used Poser first to create the figure. The images from Poser can easily be taken into Painter or any other program. Poser figures can take on life with the click of a button. You can choose from many preset poses. In Painter, Bill added the texture and lighting to the body. You can also create any skin-like colors you wish. Painter enables you to design as if you were actually using a paintbrush, pencil, chalk, or many other tools found in an artist's workbox. In Photoshop, Bill created the starburst background. You can also create textures with KPT 3.0 or you can bring in a Bryce image to a selection in Photoshop to create a kaleidoscope effect.

6.15

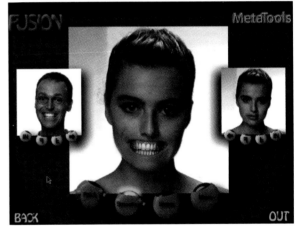

6.17

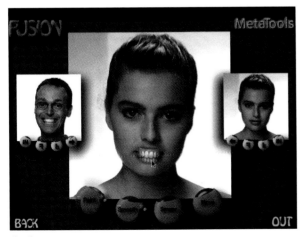

6.16

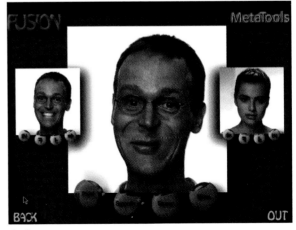

6.18

WORKING WITH
QUARKXPRESS AND PAGEMAKER

Page layout is the ultimate end of the artistic process. Usually after finishing your image in Photoshop and Illustrator, you place the image in a page layout program like QuarkXPress or PageMaker. After you add text with your images, the page layout program can do your final output.

QUARKXPRESS

QuarkXPress is one of the leading page layout programs among artists, designers, and publishers.

QuarkXPress enables you to combine text, images, and create layout for books, newsletters, and reports. As with the Illustrator versus FreeHand debate, QuarkXPress and PageMaker are in the same boat. I personally believe that whichever program you start with will be the one you love.

QuarkXPress can use any Illustrator EPS, Photoshop EPS, TIFF, PICT, or even JPEG files. Even though QuarkXPress will accept many different types of files, certain files will print better than others. Figure 6-21 shows a page laid out in QuarkXPress for the chapter opener of a book. The layout was done by Ted Alspach (6.21).

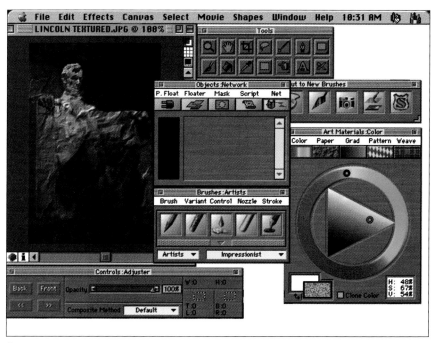

6.19

6.20

PAGEMAKER

PageMaker is another page layout program. PageMaker can place images that are saved as PICT, TIFF, EPS, GIF, WMF, and EMF (6.22). Figure 6.23 shows a page of Ted Alspach's *PageMaker for the Macintosh Visual Quick Start Guide* (6.23).

PageMaker has a set of tools you can use to do some basic drawing. This doesn't mean you can toss Illustrator, but it does mean, for some basic shapes, you can do it all in PageMaker. The Drawing tools include: Line, Constrained Line, Rectangle, Rectangle Frame, Ellipse, Ellipse Frame, Polygon, and Polygon Frame. You can add a stroke and frame to these shapes you create.

> **TIP**
>
> **Illustrator and Photoshop files can be dragged-and-dropped right into PageMaker. This makes placing images a breeze in page layout.**

> **TIP**
>
> **When using an EPS file, you can save the file in Photoshop with a lower-quality preview JPEG or TIFF (6.22). The file may not look as crisp in QuarkXPress, but it will print as the high-quality EPS. This way, when you have many images, it won't take as long to load the images.**

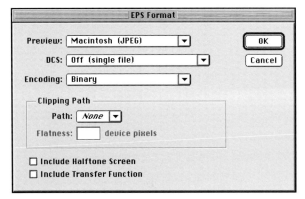

6.22

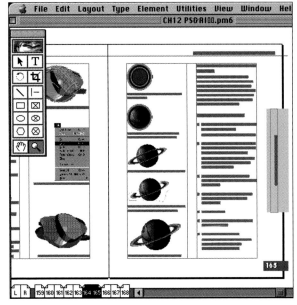

6.21

6.23

WORKING WITH 3D PROGRAMS

Another natural blend of programs with Photoshop and Illustrator is 3D programs. For example, many times you can use Illustrator's 2D paths as a guide to create a 3D image. And while 3D programs are quite powerful, you'll still want Photoshop to soften and combine a background image.

Artist Eliot Bergman is quite the master of the 3D world. His images (6.24, 6.25) illustrate his beautiful handling of 3D combined with Photoshop. Eliot uses Alias Sketch! and Alias RenderQ! as his 3D programs of choice. He uses Illustrator to start the basic sketch of the image, and then he takes the Illustrator image into Alias Sketch! or Alias RenderQ! to create the extrusions and render the initial background. In Photoshop, Eliot adds more contrasts, lights, and textures as needed.

Alliance, by Michael Tompert (6.26), illustrates a chess scene. To create the work, Michael started with a scan of actual chess pieces. He then used Strata Vision to create the 3D world. In Photoshop, Michael finished off the scene with highlights, shadows, and textures. The main tip he can offer is to use Photoshop to create depth. One of the differences of a 3D-created image and an actual photo is a 3D-created image has perfect focus from front to back. Using Photoshop to blur the background adds that touch of realism. (See Chapter 11 for more examples of Michael's work.)

6.24

6.25

6.26

EXTREME 3D

Macromedia's Extreme 3D is a stand-alone application that enables you to create 3D modeling, animation, and rendering (6.27). Extreme 3D also works hand in hand with FreeHand, Director, xRes, and Authorware, all Macromedia products. With Extreme 3D, you can take a 2D vector image from FreeHand or Illustrator and turn it into a 3D dream.

Artist Andrew Faw uses Photoshop to create texture maps that he applied to flat shapes in Extreme 3D. Andrew continually works back and forth between Photoshop and Extreme 3D to create his renderings. *Common Desktop Environment*, or *CDE* (6.28) illustrates Andrew's extensive use of Illustrator, Photoshop, and Extreme 3D. Andrew created the text letter *D* in Illustrator and used KPT Vector Effects to make the *D* look 3D. In Photoshop, Andrew creates all the textures he applies in Extreme 3D. (For more information about the creation of *CDE* and for more examples of Andrew's work, see Chapter 8.)

Extreme 3D enables you to render to certain file formats. You can render to a PICT, Targa 24 and 32 bit, and Quicktime movies on the Macintosh platform. If you are on a Windows platform, you can render to a BMP and 24- and 32-bit file formats.

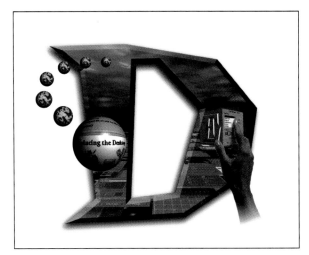

6.28

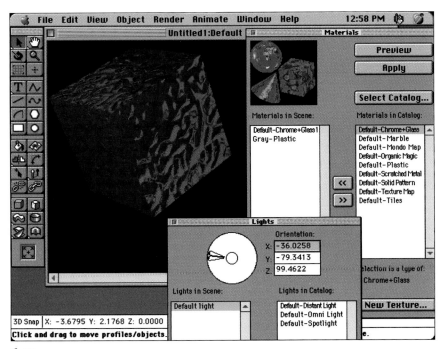

6.27

ADOBE DIMENSIONS

Adobe's 3D rendering program is Dimensions. While Dimensions is not as powerful as other packages, it still gets the job done with ease. Because of Adobe's drag-and-drop between programs feature, rendering images is made much easier. For example, you can create your 2D image in Illustrator, extrude the image in Dimensions, and then finish it off in Photoshop.

Dimensions doesn't enable you to address lighting, reflective surfaces, object shadows, skinning, or transparency, though. But don't let this stop you from using Dimensions! What Dimensions has over other 3D programs is that it prints out in PostScript. This means the art you create is resolution independent. You needn't worry about the size of the image or the resolution of the file. It's like Illustrator — you don't have to set resolution. Now, if you do happen to combine everything in a Photoshop file, then you must make sure the Photoshop file has the right resolution before adding your combined parts.

While Illustrator, with its gradients, can create a somewhat 3D-looking sphere, Dimensions adds the shadow and depth on the object Illustrator can't (6.29).

WORKING WITH THE WEB

Accessing the World Wide Web is of interest to most everyone. Not only do we want to get on the Web, we also want our own page on the Web. You can create images in Photoshop or Illustrator — or a combination of both — and place them on the Web. Now with Illustrator 7, you can export an image right from Illustrator and have it Web ready. Photoshop's Version 4 has made Web export even easier than it was before. You can easily export a file from Illustrator or Photoshop by following these steps:

STEP 1 Open the file you want to export to the Web.

STEP 2 Choose File ➢ Export. This brings up the Save dialog box. Click and drag to the GIF89a export option (6.30).

STEP 3 Give the file a name and click Save. This brings up the GIF89a Options dialog box (6.31). The palette I tend to choose is Adaptive. This way my system limitations aren't imposed on those viewing my images. If you check the Transparent check box, the white page background will become transparent in your Web page. This way, your object will be viewed on the background color you set up for your Web page.

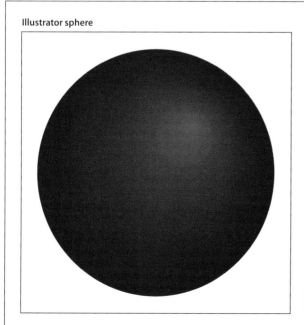
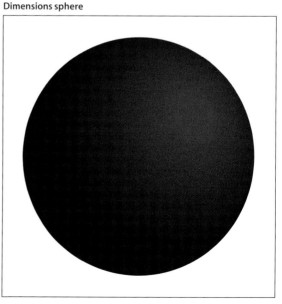

Illustrator sphere

Dimensions sphere

6.29

STEP 4 Click the OK button. That's it! Now you add the file in your Web page program and you're all set.

Now that you can export a file for the Web in Illustrator, you need to know how to do it in Photoshop. Note, you have a few more options to choose when exporting your file in Photoshop.

STEP 1 Open the file you want to export to the Web.

STEP 2 Choose Image ➢ Mode ➢ Indexed Color. You cannot export until you have done this first. This brings up the Indexed Color dialog box, which enables you to choose your Palette, Color Depth, Colors, and Dither options (6.32). Click OK.

STEP 3 Choose File ➢ Export ➢ GIF89a export. This brings up the GIF89a dialog box (6.33). Here you can set a color to become transparent if you want. Click OK.

STEP 4 Last, a Save dialog box will appear after you pick your transparent color (6.34). Enter the name of the file and link it to your Web page program. You link it to the Web program by typing in the same name you saved here in the Web page program.

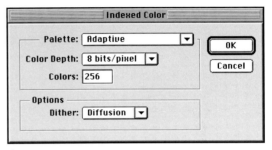

6.32

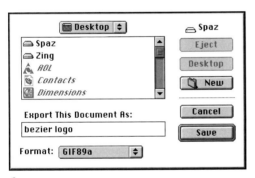

6.30

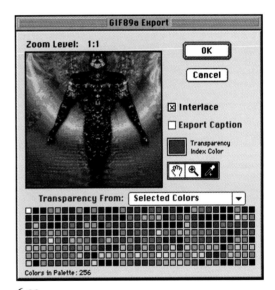

6.33

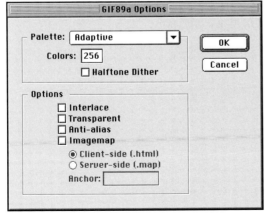

6.31

6.34

Remember, when you work with Photoshop and resolutions, to view images on the Web you only need a resolution of 72 ppi (pixels per inch). This is because our computer screens only display a resolution of 72 ppi. No need exists to go any higher. The other benefit to this lower resolution, is the images view more quickly. Nothing is more frustrating than trying to view a Web page with higher resolution files and having it take a long time.

Figure 6.35 shows a Web page created by artist Patricia Cheal. This Web page originally comes from a series of postcards for kids that incorporates Photoshop, Illustrator, and PageMaker (6.35). Patricia started the original concept in Illustrator as a sketch. In Photoshop, she smoothed out the colored areas and added some of the lighting effects in the sky. In PageMaker, Patricia combined the images with the text. She then turned them into easy to navigate Web pages.

6.35

CHAPTER 7
TRACING PHOTOS AND USING HAND-DRAWN SKETCHES

Many traditional and nontraditional artists alike can't jump right in and start drawing. Starting an image from a sketch or a photo is much easier. Photoshop not only enables you to scan in a photo or a sketch, but you can also clean up the image and dim it for tracing in Illustrator. Many artists I have worked with constantly use this method in their creation process. In this chapter, we will discuss how to use a photo or a sketch to create some great images with Photoshop and Illustrator. You can use a photo to trace in Illustrator. You can use a hand-drawn sketch to flesh out in Photoshop. You can also use an inked sketch and enhance it with Photoshop or Illustrator . . . the possibilities are endless.

TRACING IMAGES

To trace an image in the old days, you would get out your tracing paper and place it over the image you want to copy. After hours of painstaking inking—as well as a cramp in your hand—you would have a fairly good copy of the original image. With the wonders of computers and the fantastic graphics programs available, you can now create similar, but far more exciting, images from tracing. Many artists today trace from a sketch or photo they took. This trace is a jumping-off point of some amazing images.

The line between what is here now and what can only be imagined is a path for us to edit.

BRIAN WARCHESIK

THE FISH

Geno Coppotelli created this whimsical fish using an image he drew by hand first. This sketch was brought into Illustrator so Gene could trace the basic fish shapes. He brought the shapes into Photoshop to add depth, light, and texture. Geno describes his creation process:

"The basic shape of body, eye, eyelid, and fins were created in Illustrator. The shapes were filled in with different colors. The shapes were then copied and pasted into Photoshop. Each color was saved as a channel. Depth was added by loading the shape selection, feathering and inverting the selection, and intersecting the original selection and the feathered selection. I used Curves to lighten the center and darken the edges. The scales of the fish were created by applying a standard Photoshop pattern in render, texture fill to the red channel of the image. The ferns were embossed lightly and colored by using Hue/Saturation. The Lighting effects filter was added to increase depth. The edges were shaded in the same way as the fish.

ICARUS
Brian Warchesik

"The pond was drawn in Photoshop. I used blue as a fill. This pond was duplicated and the top layer put over the fish. Its opacity was set to 40 percent to give that underwater effect. A circular marquee tool was used to delete the area where the body of the fish should appear like it is entering the water" (7.1).

7.1

When you trace a photo, you may find it a bit hard to see the lines you are drawing. If you open or import a photo for tracing in Illustrator, the image will display in full color or intensity. In Illustrator, you can choose to dim an image, but this tends to make your redraw time long. I like to dim my photos in Photoshop so I can easily see the image and the lines I am drawing on top. The following steps outline how to dim a photo for tracing:

STEP 1 Scan in a sketch you want to trace into Photoshop (7.2).

STEP 2 Adjust the vels to clean up the scan.

STEP 3 Using Contrast in the Contrast/Brightness dialog box, increase the contrast to make your lines stand out more (7.3).

STEP 4 Dim the image by using the Output Levels slider and drag the black slider toward the white slider to lighten the image (7.4). Save the image as a TIFF or EPS.

STEP 5 Launch Illustrator and choose File ➢ Open. Double-click the sketch you saved as a TIFF or EPS.

STEP 6 Using the Pen and Brush tools with a Wacom or another type of pressure-sensitive tablet, begin to trace the image (7.5).

PHOTOSHOP AND THE MOVIES, MUSINGS FROM MARK J. SMITH

IN THIS SECTION, Mark explains how they blend the actor's shots with the jellyfish. The problem area to fix is the author is looking too high for the actual beast's height. In Photoshop, Mark explains how they fix this problem.

"Now back to the scene. The jellyfish was sent to kill Mason in his research lab. In the film, the jellyfish was quite large (seven feet in body length, not counting the flowing, glowing tentacles). In the studio, the set apparently had no ceiling to it. On film, it appears as a normal eight-foot ceiling. As the shot was acted out, Mason turned around to find this creature had invaded his personal space. Mason stood stunned, almost hypnotized, by the sight of the beast.

"On the profile shot of the beast facing Mason, the actor looks as though he is standing toe to tentacle with something much larger. Granted it is very difficult to act to something that wasn't there, but the original footage had Mason craning his neck like he was looking at the clouds, not something that was supposedly standing right in front of him. The animal floated, but had to be

7.2

7·3

confined to the room's space. The ceiling was only 8 feet high, not 40 feet. What were we to do? Photoshop to the rescue!

"Obviously we were going to remove the actor's head and then reposition it into the proper angle. This brings up the point I made earlier about shooting a clean background plate. We could have eliminated Mr. Adams' head and replaced the information that was missing from the scene. When we removed his head, there was no background plate! Therefore, we removed his head by drawing a very accurate selection around his head, up to, but not including, his collar. We kept his head in the copy buffer until it was needed.

"Now, as our intention was to rotate his head into the right orientation, this would have left areas exposed that had not been photographed. There is no tool I use more in Photoshop than the Rubber-stamp tool. With clever guesstimating, I was able to use the rubber stamp tool to borrow other exposed areas to 're-invent' what would have been there had it been photographed *sans* actor first (clean background plate).

"Thankfully, two things helped immensely: The area to replace was small and the area was not very busy; therefore, surrounding information was easily borrowed to create this new background."

See Chapter 11 for more of Mark's explanation of the digital FX work he did for *Not of This Earth*.

TRACING IMAGES FROM SKETCHES

Some of the more artistic graphic people out there will hand-draw their own sketch to start. Sometimes it's easier to jot down ideas or sketches on paper first.

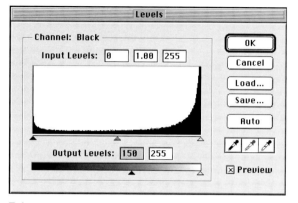

7.4

7.5

You'll find many of the "thoughts" you wrote down are good enough to trace.

ICARUS

Brian Warchesik is much more than an accomplished artist. He starts many of his images from pencil sketches. (One great benefit of drawing this way is you avoid any copyright problems!) In *Icarus* (7.6), Brian uses his sketches with Photoshop and Illustrator. He takes full advantage of Illustrator's Pen tool and with Photoshop, he enhances colors and softens the background.

"The process involved in this work began through a series of pencil drawings that were scanned into Photoshop. Much of the work was then painted using Photoshop's Adjustment layers and a Wacom tablet. None of the work here has been clipped from photos or brought in from other applications, such as Bryce. It all began with hand-rendered sketches.

"The wing is specifically where Illustrator's vector capabilities were taken full advantage of. I started by

7.6

tracing the basic shape of the wing from a scanned sketch. I began developing detail on separate layers in the Illustrator file. Each layer of the wing was then pasted as paths into Photoshop. The feathers themselves were manipulated in channels to give the subtle differences in the details."

USING INKED SKETCHES WITH PHOTOSHOP AND ILLUSTRATOR

So far you've seen how you can use rough sketches with Photoshop and Illustrator. Let's expand on the sketch idea. If you've spent time creating a beautiful sketch, you don't have to re-draw it to use the image in Photoshop or Illustrator. You can scan in any sketch and, in Photoshop, you can colorize it or just enhance the tones. These sketches can be placed or opened in Illustrator to be combined with other elements for your final rendering.

TV WORLD

Joe Jones of Art Works Studio created *TV World* using hand-inked sketches. These small elements were placed in Illustrator with the other elements of the image. Joe then took the Illustrator file and opened it in Photoshop to add the textures and finish off the illustration.

"*TV World* was a fun project, but with a tight deadline of three days. The file was built in Illustrator (7.7). The figures and planes were actually hand-inked images traced in Illustrator. All type was created from Illustrator type paths. I always wanted to do a design that repeats itself.

"I incorporate all kinds of textures in my stuff. In this case, I went to the local metal scrap yard and got a really good piece of rusty metal. I used that metal texture in the world-earth image, as well as the strange moon in the background. I used Photoshop to soften the blends and finish off the color" (7.8).

7·7

7.8

USING ILLUSTRATOR
TO FINISH YOUR IMAGE

Typically, Illustrator is used to add type to images. Because Photoshop's type capabilities are somewhat limited, it is natural for you to turn to Adobe's vector program to add type. Not only can you start an image in Illustrator to enhance in Photoshop, but many times you'll take this image back into Illustrator to add type and print separations. While Photoshop can print files and separations, it doesn't recognize spot colors. You can print spot color separations from Illustrator.

7.9

AFRICA SHIRT

Artist Patricia Cheal starts many images in Photoshop and uses Illustrator to add type. Here she describes the process she used to create this image for a T-shirt (7.9).

"The Africa shirt is a T-shirt design that was to be printed in two colors. I used Photoshop to assemble the montage of sketches. The file was placed in Illustrator to add text and to print the separations."

TRACING IN FREEHAND

Just as you trace an image in Illustrator, you'll do the same in FreeHand. *FreeHand* is the "other" illustrating program and many artists solely use one program or the other. The idea of tracing in either program is basically the same. You first open or import the image you want to trace. Next, you use the tracing tool of your choice. Many prefer using the Pen tool for accurate tracings. You can also use the Brush or FreeHand tool for a sketchier tracing.

WRECKING BALL, WRESTLER, LOUNGE LIZARD

Brian McNulty starts most of his images from sketching an idea on paper. His true artist nature comes through when he doodles. These doodles are turned into full-blown illustrations. Brian uses FreeHand to trace over these sketches. In the next paragraphs, Brian describes some of his techniques for tracing his sketches:

"*Wrecking Ball*, *Wrestler*, and *Lounge Lizard* were primarily created in Macromedia FreeHand 7.0. The backgrounds on all three were created in Photoshop 4.0 and imported into FreeHand as a Tiff.

"The original sketch was scanned in with a 300 DPI scanner because I didn't want the drawing to be too exact (7.10, 7.11, 7.12). The contrast was set higher to give an 'edgy' feeling so that when I traced, not auto-traced, the sketch in FreeHand, the scan would bring out little nuances I never imagined or originally drew."

"I zoom in to 200 percent and set the line weight to .5 in FreeHand. I then outline the artwork in red, exactly as the scan looks. I use red to see the lines over the sketch. This creates a line drawing with no fills.

7.11

7.10

7.12

"After finishing with the outlining, I delete the scan. I change all the lines to black with a black fill to see what might be filled with black. I needed to make new lines for those areas that aren't filled with color, an overlay, if you will. I filled those areas with the desired color. I then chose 'Send to Back'. I fixed any lines that didn't look correct and then the piece of artwork was finished and ready for display" (7.13, 7.14, 7.15).

USING ADOBE STREAMLINE

Adobe Streamline is a great program that converts pixel-based images into vector-based images. Using Streamline, you can convert any photo into an editable vector-based image to be altered in Illustrator. Streamline can trace images, but to get a truly accurate trace, you'll want to trace the image in Illustrator or FreeHand. Streamline can create a painterly look to your image.

The following steps take you through the process of using Streamline on a photo. Because Streamline has upgraded to 4.0, the program has become much easier to use. For example, Streamline will actually "read" the image and determine the best way to trace it. You can change the settings to be whatever you want. I prefer to let Streamline think for me.

STEP 1 Open the photo you want to convert in Streamline (7.16).

STEP 2 Adjust the Color/B&W Setup under the Options pull-down menu (7.17). Here is where you can specify Limited Colors, Unlimited Colors, Custom Colors, Black & White only, Edge Smoothing, and Complexity.

STEP 3 Choose File ➣ Convert (⌘/Ctrl+R). The more complex the image, the longer it takes to convert.

7.13

7.14

7.15

STEP 4 You can save the image as an Illustrator file, or copy and paste the file into an Illustrator document. I prefer to copy and paste.

STEP 5 In the Illustrator document, you can see the painterly look the converted image has (7.18).

STEP 6 You can use any Adobe or third-party filters to adjust the image further (7.19). I selected the sky and applied KPT Shatterbox of the MetaCreations KPT Vector Effects plug-ins.

7.18

7.16

7.19

7.17

7.20

ALTERING VECTOR IMAGES IN PHOTOSHOP

Any image you create, whether in Photoshop or Illustrator, can always be altered for better or worse. Photoshop can fix images as well as offer alternative renderings of your original. By using Levels, Curves, Brightness/Contrast, Hue/Saturation, Color Balance, as well as Photoshop filters, you can create some beautiful different variations of your image.

Ted Alspach created *Lucy Ann* (7.20) by scanning a photo into Photoshop. He adjusted the image in Photoshop before taking it into Streamline for conversion into a vector image. After Streamlining the image, Ted used Illustrator and various filters to create the painterly look to the image. He added text and the black border to finish the illustration.

"I imported *Lucy Ann* into Photoshop for further experimentation. I thought the image would make a great poster showing different effects. I used Levels on the original image to crisp up the edges. After playing around with altering the color and applying various filters, I adjusted the Curves on some of the images. The image now has variety for its poster printing" (7.21).

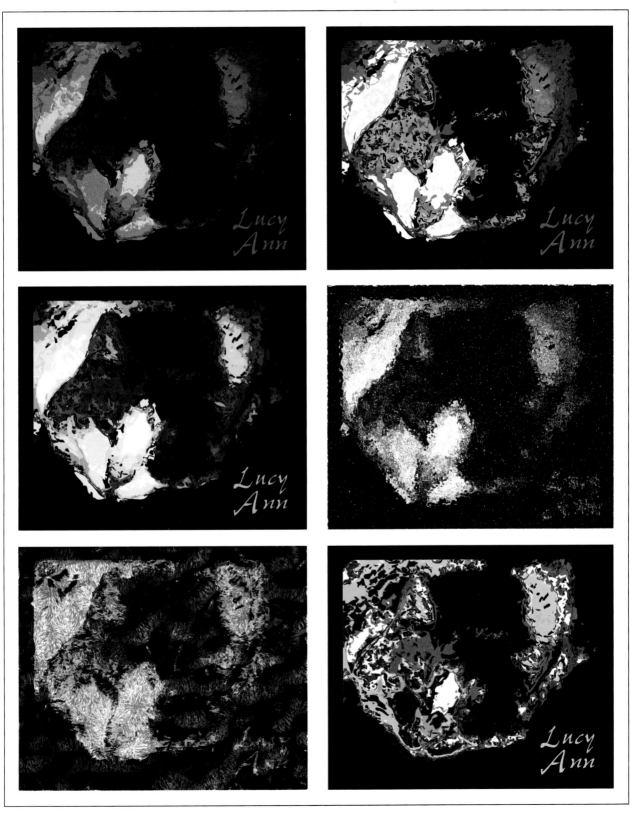

7.21

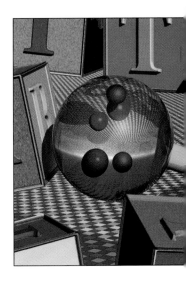

CHAPTER 8
LOGOS, TYPE, AND IMAGES

L ogos, type, and images are part of everyone's daily life. Anywhere you look, you'll
see some example of the powers of
Photoshop and Illustrator in creating
these images. Not only can you create
beautiful artwork with Photoshop and Illustrator,
you can also use these programs to finish off your
business identity. Eye-catching logos, started in
Illustrator or FreeHand, can have some startling
effects and textures applied by using Photoshop.

*When someone asks how 3D scenes or
worlds are created, my general response
is to say, 'Do you remember the papier-
mâché volcano you made as a kid? First
you started with some chicken wire and
put on your paper skin, which was then
painted to look real.' 3D modeling is
like that!*

GLENN RIEGEL

LOGOS

Logos are everywhere. Driving along a road, you'll
probably see a logo for a product being advertised on
a billboard. Logos are essential to any business identity. A *logo* is the image you remember when you
think of a certain product or company. The artists in
the following section have incorporated the use of
Photoshop and Illustrator in creating logos for their
clients. As with many great logos, Illustrator or
FreeHand is the starting point and Photoshop is the
finishing program.

MUELLER BEER

Gerard Chateauvieux used Photoshop and FreeHand
to create a logo for the Mueller Beer company. He
used FreeHand for pieces of the logo and Photoshop
for mapping. The finished image shows a beautifully
rendered logo on a bottle and a glass of beer.

"This model demonstrates the ability to use two
identical pieces of geometry to apply two texture

maps in Photoshop. I employed this technique on
both the glass and the bottle. I used existence of surface and environment mapping on the two separate,
but identical, shapes. By scaling one of the objects
slightly smaller than the other, the two surfaces do
not interfere with each other. I created the labels in
FreeHand, and then rasterized, masked, and cropped
them in Photoshop. The environment map is a
grayscale map with a greenish color added to the
specular and roughness settings in the Mondo Map
shader" (8.1).

BORG

Joe Jones created this logo focusing on the letter *B*.
He started the image in Illustrator to get the basic
shape and letter combined. In Photoshop, Joe used
scanned metallic textures to create the texture of the
logo. Joe explains his process in creating this logo.

"This piece was developed for my accountant, Joanne Borg. This was originally drawn in Adobe Illustrator. Then I imported those simple paths I created into the full-blown Photoshop version (8.2). This is key for great bevel work. I first laid in a good marble texture, and then I built a series of channels and texture maps for lighting effects. I also created special layers working with different modes to give the raised areas a cool chrome effect. One thing I do in my pieces is always to give the drop shadows a little color, usually a blue or purple cast. Shadows in real life are never just black" (8.3).

TYPE EFFECTS

The best way to create type is in a vector-based program like Illustrator, unless you have a third-party product, such as Extensis' PhotoTools. PhotoTools has a filter called *PhotoText,* which enables you to create type as you would in a vector program. After the type is created, you can import the text into Photoshop. In Photoshop, you can create any image and in Illustrator, you can finish off the image by adding type.

DIGI HONG KONG

Pamela Hobbs has created quite a style of her own. She feels it is better to create her own look and to make it as individual as possible. Pamela's images have an exotic feel to them. She incorporates her Photoshop images with a 3D program for a dramatic image.

The digital artists group based in Hong Kong, DIGI, held an exhibition of International Digital Artists. Pamela Hobbs was selected to represent the San Francisco Bay Area. The exhibition was based on an

8.1

8.2

8.3

open assignment, for which the only requirement was the image must have the word DIGI within it. Pamela said when she thinks of Hong Kong, she thinks of night life, hotels, cabarets, food, and restaurants (8.4).

To create *Digi Hong Kong* for the International Digital Artists exhibition, Pamela followed these steps:

STEP 1 I created the word DIGI in Specular Infini D. I wanted a very crisp and dimensional feel to the word, so I used a lot of refractions in the rendering features. I used spot lights and glass. I imported the rendered file to Photoshop.

STEP 2 I scanned packets of food, ramen noodles, bottles, cigarettes, and such by placing them directly onto my flat bed scanner.

STEP 3 Using Photoshop's Hue, Saturation, and Brightness controls, I was able to adjust these values.

STEP 4 I dropped the ramen into the background by using the opacity setting in the layers palette at 20 percent.

STEP 5 I retouched the color of the bottle using the pen tool to make a selection around the highlighted areas and then apply color levels to specific areas to bring out the sharp highlights.

STEP 6 The wings on the woman are stock images. Her dress is a customized noise filter mode from the pre-set Kai Power Tools menu.

STEP 7 Her stockings are made by using the custom-blend feature in Photoshop and by adding a highlight to the area where the leg would shine through the stocking.

STEP 8 The whole image was then flattened and I applied a drop shadow.

DECADE PIECE

Laurie Grace's images are found in many publications. For *Decade Piece*, she combined Photoshop, Illustrator, and Dimensions to create this eye-catching piece. With all the various small images, Laurie manages to blend them together with color.

"The decade pieces were made as graphics for an in-house corporate news show. They all begin with

Photoshop backgrounds and all were put together in Photoshop with layers, layer masks, shadows, and more. I created the type in Illustrator and brought it into Photoshop. Some of the artwork is in Illustrator and some is in Dimensions. The flame is coming from the Olympics image and the flag is in Dimensions" (8.5).

FAMILY PC, KIDSGUIDE, RESTAURANTS

Wayne Vincent's cartoonish images are fantastic advertisements. His whimsical style comes across in these three pieces. The original hand sketches were traced over in Illustrator and smoothed in Photoshop. Wayne completed the image by adding text in Illustrator. Wayne created *Family PC*, *Kidsguide*, and *Restaurants* (8.6) initially in Illustrator. He started the images as sketches and used them as a template in Illustrator. After rendering the template as paths and adding fills, Wayne opened the file in Photoshop. By copying the paths from Illustrator, he used the paths to create masks for the soft-edged drop shadows.

8.4

8.5

8.6

COMMON DESKTOP ENVIRONMENT

Andrew Faw explains how he created the image *Common Desktop Environment* in his own words. This image shows a great use of KPT Vector Effects (a plug-in for Illustrator). Andrew used Photoshop as a combining program, as well as for special effects.

"This piece was created for X Inside Inc. They needed an image for their licensed software version of *CDE* (*Common Desktop Environment*). The software is a set of building blocks for the Graphical User Interface (GUI) for PCs running the UNIX operating system. We decided we wanted the piece to have the feel of direct interaction with the software, as well as incorporating the letters *C, D,* and *E.* The *D* for *Desktop* was to be the most important element in the image" (8.7).

The hardware Andrew used to create *CDE* included: Powermac 9500 with 64MB RAM, 2GB hard drive; Sony 200 SF 17" monitor; Wacom 6 × 9 tablet; LaCie Silverscanner; APS DAT drive; and Epson Stylus ProXL color printer. Software used: Adobe Photoshop, Adobe Illustrator, Kai's Power Tools, KPT Vector Effects, and Macromedia Extreme 3D.

To create the image, Andrew followed these steps:

STEP 1 After discussing the project with my client, I had him mail as many screen captures as possible to me, showing examples of the interface. These were all screen resolution (72 dpi) GIF images. I converted them to 32-bit color PICT files in Photoshop, and then I applied them as texture

8.7

maps to several flat shapes in Extreme 3D. I adjusted the levels of the pieces to create the floating scene. I had to duplicate the shapes many times to get enough for the receding landscape.

STEP 2 I then created a large (roughly 7" × 7" × 300 dpi) Texture Explorer background in Photoshop. I applied this as a texture map to a large shape under the floating rectangles in Extreme 3D.

STEP 3 For the sky, I started with a clip art photo of clouds and adjusted the angle using the free transform tool in Photoshop. I played with the color using the Hue/Saturation tool, and then I applied a black to transparent gradient on the lower-half so it looks like it's receding into the background. I placed the final render of the floating screens on top of the cloud background. This completed the backdrop for the illustration (8.8).

STEP 4 At this point I had to consider how to create the beveled *D* look to the image. In Illustrator, I used a *D* I liked and gave it a beveled look using Vector Effects 3D Transform (8.9). I placed a copy of my backdrop image in Illustrator to help me get the proper placement. I created an empty box the same size as my placed Photoshop artwork so I could open the Illustrator files at the same size and resolution as my Photoshop file. I created the bevels using shades of gray, leaving the rest of the

letter transparent. I saved that as one file. I then created a *D* that ran along the very outer edge of the bevel and filled it with black and saved that as a second file. To apply the bevels and mask in Photoshop, I opened the solid *D* file in Photoshop as a grayscale at the same resolution as my backdrop image. I copied it to a new channel in my backdrop image. I used the solid *D* channel as a layer mask on my background image (8.10).

STEP 5 For the bevel, I opened the bevel file as grayscale and copied the image to a new layer above my background. I wanted to keep some of the white

8.9

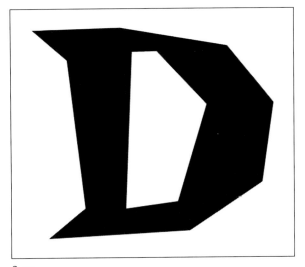

8.10

8.8

8.11

8.12

areas of the bevel, so I lowered the opacity of the bevel layer until it gave me the desired effect.

STEP 6 To create the *E* box, I built a cube in Extreme 3D with texture maps of screen captures, and then I used the 3D type tool to create a beveled *E*. I placed the *E* right against one face of the cube (8.11). I shot a photo of my sister's hand (with silver nail polish) and ran that over to a one-hour photo service (it was a tight deadline). I scanned the hand to Photoshop and used the dodge and burn tools, along with some cloning, to touch up the photo. I placed the photo on a layer above the rendered E cube. Between the cube and the hand layers, I inserted another layer and painted in some of the shadows. Once satisfied, I copied the cube to my back-drop file, placed it beneath the D bevels, and placed the hand above the bevels. This gave the look of the cube being inside the *D* and the hand reaching in from the outside (8.12).

STEP 7 For the little spheres in the letter *C,* I created a nice texture in Photoshop using Texture Explorer (I get a lot of mileage out of that plug-in). I saved the texture as a PICT and used it as a texture map in Extreme 3D. I placed the spheres and set the lighting roughly to match other elements in the piece. I rendered the shapes with an alpha channel to aid my placement in Photoshop (8.13). For the "Introducing the Desktop" sphere, I used one of the screen captures my client sent me and applied the KPT Glass Lens filter, no fancy 3D work there. This would also have worked with the smaller spheres, but I wanted a little "authentic" depth.

STEP 8 At this point, the image was near completion. I only needed something to set the E cube off the background. I inserted a layer between the backdrop and the cube, copying the D layer mask from the background. I airbrushed in a yellow glow and adjusted the layer transparency to set off the artwork properly.

STEP 9 Finally, I duplicated the original solid D channel I'd created earlier. I applied a Gaussian Blur filter, and then offset the channel to the lower-right. In a new layer behind everything, I loaded the blurred *D* as a selection and filled it with black. I adjusted the transparency of the layer until I had a drop shadow I liked.

STEP 10 I always render 3D objects with an alpha channel. This is a blessing for simplifying the compositing of several images in Photoshop.

BUSINESS CARDS

Why pay someone to create your business identity? You can create any business card you want using Photoshop with Illustrator and other programs. Illustrator can add the text and Photoshop can jazz up the background.

DIGITAL DRAMA

Mark Smith created his business card with help from Perry Harovas. He enlightens us here with his creative process and provides some insightful tips on getting the best buy for your cards.

"While I did most of the work on this card, it was based on an original rendering by my partner, Perry Harovas. He should also be credited for this.

"The business card started out as an advertisement, but was later scrapped for something else. It was later redesigned. Perry had rendered the original in Bryce 1.0. The entire ad was in a different aspect ratio than it is now. Perry rendered a clean blue area, which we would eventually have text applied to in Photoshop for the ad. I'd never used Quark in my life. He used Bryce to render the raised area that reads VISUAL FX. Bryce is a good raytracer and did a neat effect of water iciness. The ad never went anywhere. Sometimes things just don't strike you as interesting anymore. It was later cropped in Photoshop to the aspect ratio of a business card. The resolution was pretty good.

"Perry put our company information on it and that was that. I hated it. The VISUAL FX part was cool, but the card did not knock me out. The original card Perry designed had a great deal of wasted blue space. This was the area that now is occupied by the swirl. Let me digress. We use a Fuji Pictography printer, a $22,000 printer owned by a sister company. This printer is capable of producing photo quality output; it is virtually indistinguishable from a color photo. I tell you this because we never got any Digital Drama cards printed. We lost tons of money on cards we did not like. We always printed a sheet of ten, which was enough to get by. We often called our cards *Cards du jour*. It was cool to print cards for a specific purpose — 10 or 20 at a time — and instantly! If we went to a trade show or to SIGGRAPH, we could make cards specific to where we were going to pass them out. We eventually used to kid that when we were famous, these cards would be collectors items, like baseball cards. Sometimes, not too many got printed and circulated. Those would be the rare ones.

8.13

"All right, back to the design. As I said, the card was ugly and I never used mine. It was a bad design. Too much openness. The card was meant to be an ad and that area was to be filled with lots of really good stuff about Digital Drama. I liked the VISUAL FX part, though. It appealed to me. One day, while looking for material for our Web page, which I was building, I found that card I hated. A company that does what we do should not be placid — it should emote something representative of what you are all about.

"I'm a big fan of Tim Burton. In particular, the stop-motion classic film *The Nightmare Before Christmas*. The characters are really great. I have them adorning my personal *geekosphere* at the studio. There is a Compathat that creates fonts. They are called *t-26*. The fonts are very interesting looking. I wanted to use one of their fonts. It expresses a look. To make it generic enough so it could be easily altered to suit different people's names and titles, I added the black margin running along the bottom of the card. I did this in Photoshop by adding the blackness at the bottom with PS's Canvas size option. It enabled me to add this margin at the bottom quite easily. I experimented several times to get the right amount of black. The reason is, as I added the black to it, the card's aspect ratio was no longer that of a business card. Each time after adding black, I used PS's Image size function to alter the image into the proper aspect ratio. After some trial and error, I found the right amount of black I wanted. This altered the aspect ratio of the original picture slightly. While this seemingly lacks artistic integrity, I look at it more as the difference between italic and normal print. Honestly, it did not alter the picture noticeably.

"The big open blue space had to be dealt with now. In keeping with the Burtonesque type thing, I reached for several ideas that didn't pan out. Finally, I thought about a KPT plug-in called *video feedback*. It's the same tool Kai Krause used in his famous Absolute Vodka ad and I liked the effect. I grabbed the blue area with the lasso tool. I made sure this selection encompassed a portion of the raised area that said VISUAL FX. The tool is rather interactive and I was soon able to fill that blue void with something cool and substantial. If the region is too large, it looks very chunky. I wanted the curling infinity change to be as subtle as it could be. I found a nice balance.

"By incorporating the raised section of the original Bryce, rendering it really added to the 3D-ness of it all. Especially the pronounced white highlight — or in 3D parlance — the specular hot spots. I actually did this KPT Video Feedback maneuver before I added the text. This enabled me to grab the newly added bottom black margin at the bottom and to incorporate that into the KPT filter. This ever-so-slightly bent part of the blue up and away from the black, creating a more logical transition between the black and the blue. It was no longer just two diverse colors clashing, but rather a slightly warped transition that made a difference.

"Finally, I used the Magic Wand to select the black area inside the curled warp. Using the Magic Wand, I also selected a good portion of the black margin. I then used the square selection tool to deselect the text and the newly formed black margin area. My main focus was to fill that black area with something, even if it was slight. I used Alien Skin's Eyecandy filter Toolset (formerly Black Box) for this. The filter I used was Carve. This gave a new 3D meaning to the darkness. It made it look as though it was raised ever-so-slightly and gave it a really interesting organic look. Kind of like the tail of the Lochness Monster, or something that should have scales. I used the Filter to alter the brightness and sharpness of the highlights just enough to make it interesting. The text about our company was added directly in Photoshop. This completed the card.

"Finally I used the Canvas Size feature to add 100 percent more space to the side of the card and five times the amount of space on the bottom of the card. This essentially left me space to copy the original card and paste it down on the newly formed blackness to create a sheet of business cards 2×5 for a total of ten cards per sheet" (8.14).

MENU DESIGN

The creation of images using type is endless—from advertisements and business cards to menu designs. Restaurant opportunities especially abound. Once you create the menu, you can expand and create the signage, business cards, and letterhead.

BULLSEYE MENU COVER

Patricia Cheal gets the restaurant theme jump-started with her creation of a menu cover. Once the initial logo and theme gets approved, she can design the business identity for the whole restaurant chain.

The Bullseye image was created for a menu cover design, as well as for a table tent card. Patricia created the art in Illustrator. The image was copied and pasted onto a photo of wood in Photoshop. The art was feathered and filled with black to give that *burned-in* look. The file was saved and placed into Illustrator. In Illustrator, the original image was pasted on top of the burned-in look (8.15).

SIGNAGE

The following *Macworld Expo* image was created with Illustrator, Dimensions, and Photoshop. This image by Lance Jackson shows a natural flowing between programs. Lance started the image in Photoshop, and then used Illustrator for text and Dimensions for bending the text. Back in Photoshop, he blended the image together seamlessly.

8.14

MACWORLD EXPO

"The image *Macworld Expo* was commissioned for the 1996–97 Macworld Expositions in San Francisco and Boston. The base file is a montage of video and photographic scans saved as a Photoshop 2.5 document (8.16). The Illustrator files 'Macworld Expo text,' 'Expo.ill.wideangle,' and 'Expo.ill.telescope2,'

8.15

8.16

were exported from the Dimensions program. With the instructional help of a friend, Joe Shoulak, I used the Dimensions program to set the text 'Macworld Expo' on a cylindrical shape. The results were exported from the Dimensions program and saved as Illustrator files (8.17). I imported the Illustrator file into Photoshop 2.5 and saved it. I then imported this file into the base file. An intermediate working file was saved. In this file, the text is imported as 100 percent normal. At this point, the text is too strong and not integrated into the composition (8.18). I went back to the original base file and selected and copied parts. I copied parts in varying degrees of opacity of the central yellow light beam back onto the red text. By copying and pasting, I was able to tone down and integrate the text into the central yellow light beam. I used this technique of repetitive copying and pasting to create the final image" (8.19).

8.17

IMAGES

The next artists display some wonderful images they created by using Photoshop, Illustrator, and a 3D program. As you read their descriptions on how they created the art, you'll see how useful it is to work with multiple programs to create some eye-catching images.

COLUMN

Eliot Bergman used Photoshop, Illustrator, and Alias Sketch to render the image, *Column*. In reading his explanations, you see how easy it is to create an image that looks like it took hours to complete.

"Although this image looks complex, it was deceptively simple to generate. First, I drafted a circle in Illustrator. Smaller circles were rotated around the circumference, grouped, and cut, using the Object ➢ pathfinder ➢ Minus Front, to create a serrated edge. This shape served as the plan for the column. In a separate file, I set the type for the words 'public finance.'

8.18

"Next, I imported the type file into Photoshop and saved it as a grayscale PICT. In Alias Sketch!, I imported the Illustrator plan for the column, extruded it, and selected a PICT file of marble to apply as a cylindrical color map. The serrated edge of the Illustrator circle is what gives the column its fluted appearance. For the base of the column, I again used marble for color, but I imported the Photoshop PICT I created for use as the type bump map, relief set to 4 percent.

"An orthographic view was used to keep all of the elements in the scene square. The image was rendered in Alias RenderQ! Because there were no reflections or refractions, long rendering, rather than ray-tracing, was used. Render size was 8½" × 11", 300 ppi.

"Finally, an Illustrator file was merged with the render in Photoshop to create the characters that appear to float through the scene (8.20). The degree of opacity for these characters was set in the Layers palette."

FAST TRACK

With *Fast Track*, artist Lance Jackson shows us the ease in which he uses multiple programs to create an image. Like the image he created for the Macworld Expo (explained previously in this chapter), Lance used Illustrator to create the initial text and Dimensions to distort the words. He used Photoshop to put it all together with the base images with which he starts.

"*Fast Track* was originally commissioned by *Worth* magazine to illustrate the obsessive behavior some people exhibit when using a particular investment software program. The base file is a group of video and photography images merged together using Photoshop (8.21). The Illustrator files are two text files where the characters were placed on a curved path or several paths and manipulated using the scaling, rotating, and distortion tools (8.22).

"For the text, *The secret of my success*, I used the Dimensions program to rotate the text along an ellipse to a point that would comfortably fit the existing ellipse above the man's head in the base file (8.23). I saved the Dimensions file. While in the Dimensions

8.19

8.20

8.21

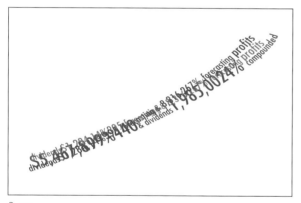

8.22

program, I saved and exported the file as an Illustrator file. I then imported the Illustrator file into several layers in Photoshop. On each layer I used the opacity features, such as hard light, multiple, lighten, and darken to add variation in the text files. Subsequently, I added other parts of the existing base file, such as the Saturn-like ellipse in the background on top of the text files, in varying positions to add a sense of speed and motion. In a sense it is digital painting, adding, removing, and adding still more layers to the file. It is painting without turpentine, brushes, and rags. Also, it is an attempt to graft a fourth-dimensional feel in a two-dimensional image. When the text and background were satisfactorily merged to a believable point, I flattened and saved the file" (8.24).

D[AI]SY

Artist Andrew Faw created *D[AI]sy* as an experimental piece for his portfolio. "Much of my work is more product-oriented, so I needed to come up with an imaginary 'dream job.' I had been reading a book with some great explorations on how artificial intelligence might manifest itself. There were shades of HAL 9000 from the film *2001*. I remember seeing *2001* with my dad when I was very young. I loved it, but I was scared to death by the astronaut flying end-over-end into space. I haven't decided whether I think the idea of artificial intelligence is appealing or ominous, but

8.23

8.24

there is definitely enough material in my head for an illustration or two. *D[AI]sy* was born (8.25).

"There are two distinct categories to this piece: the background and the objects. I started the background with a couple of pieces (8.26, 8.27, 8.28). One is a clip art photo of some cool textured cloth. I created a full page, 300 dpi KPT Texture Explorer piece in Photoshop. I combined them in Live Picture, so I could quickly mush around the bright texture with a big distortion brush. I then applied a luminance mask based on the values in a photo of a cloud. This enabled me to let only the bright background show through in a subtle way. It was too much just to drop it in.

"I love using Live Picture with Photoshop. I can create lots of huge files of textures and images and type in Photoshop, and then do much of my compositing in Live Picture without worrying about altering my original Photoshop files. It really frees me up to experiment more with both.

"In the foreground, I created a big eye by applying a photographic iris to a sphere in Fractal Design Detailer. I used Detailer to render the big eye because it was a simple object (8.29). The pipes were created in Ray dream designer with a subtle marble texture. I applied Texture Explorer to them in Photoshop using 'procedural—minus' glue setting to make it look

mapped on the pipes (8.30). Whenever I do 3D work for collages, I make sure to render with an alpha channel to aid in compositing later.

8.26

8.25

8.27

"The type for the song from *2001* was created in Adobe Illustrator and put into a perspective view using KPT Vector Effects 3D Transform filter (8.31). I imported the type into Photoshop and painted on it with the preserve transparency option checked in the layer palette. Once painted, I duplicated the layer,

8.28

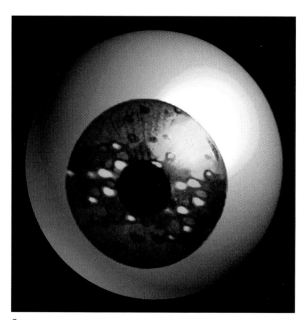

8.29

unchecked the preserve transparency option, and applied a motion blur to the lower layer. Once I had modified the type to my liking, I used the merge visible option in the layers menu. I saved the transparency of the layer to a new channel, flattened the image, and saved the file as a TIFF with alpha channel for converting and compositing in Live Picture (8.32). For the type shadow, I copied the mask from the type layer in Live Picture to a new monocolor layer and painted it black with transparency set to about 40 percent. I placed the shadow layer behind the 3D pipes.

"When I was ready to work on the rat, I actually set a circuit board on my scanner instead of shooting a photo and waiting for processing. I used the Hue/Saturation adjustment in Photoshop to pump up the color a little and then I applied KPT Texture

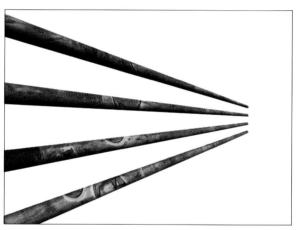

8.30

8.31

Explorer to get a little more texture going on. I played with the glue options in Texture Explorer until I got an effect I liked (8.33).

"I used the layer mask option in Photoshop to create the circuitry in the rat. I placed the circuit board on a layer above the rat. I created a layer mask on the circuit layer. Doing this enabled me just to airbrush the circuit board into the areas on the rat's body that I wanted (8.34). Because a layer mask leaves your full image in place on the layer, it also makes it easier to go back in later and repaint or to add more areas of the artwork. In Live Picture, I placed the rat on a layer above the pillar. I painted some shadows in on a monocular layer to make the rat look more like it was actually standing on the pillar.

"At this point, I had all my elements together that I had created in Photoshop, Illustrator, and Detailed. Live Picture was a good place to combine everything; however, all the compositing could have been done in a similar manner in Photoshop. I mainly chose Live Picture to take advantage of outputting the image at any resolution (dependent only on the quality of my lowest resolution objects). Live Picture is also a little less memory intensive for very large images. My final document can be output at about $15" \times 15" \times 300$ dpi with very good results.

"Photoshop is hands down my all-time favorite creative software package. Between native Photoshop features and third-party plug-in filters, the sky's the limit. Even when Photoshop isn't the starting point of my artwork, everything seems to pass through it at some point, even if it's just to touch up a 3D render or to combine some type and imagery and make it look just right."

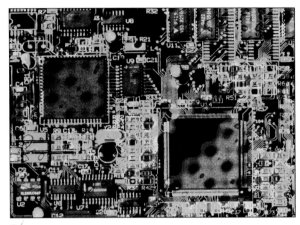

8.33

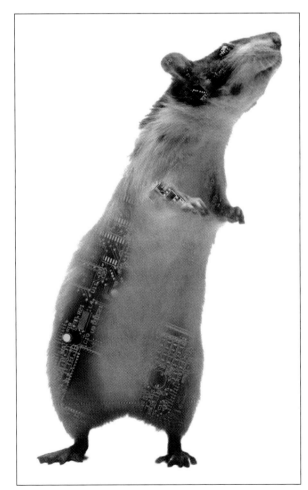

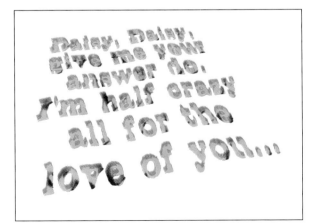

8.32

8.34

CHAPTER 9
REALISM AND FINE ARTS

Achieving a realistic image from man-made art is the goal of many artists. Creating an image solely from the mind and having it look like something from the real world is rewarding. On the other end of this spectrum is to create an artistic piece from an actual photograph. When you make this photograph look like a fine art painting, you cross from the tangible to the artistic. These techniques may be opposite, but both show the range of a truly great artist. In this chapter, you'll see how some artists approached creating realistic-looking buildings, people, and objects from an idea. You'll also see how to turn a scanned photograph into a work of art.

BUILDINGS AND LANDSCAPES

You may come across the need to create a series of buildings or to create a landscape for the background of your object. Photoshop and Illustrator work together beautifully to create a building in perspective. You can use Illustrator to create the line work and Photoshop to add color and the background. Bryce 2 by MetaCreations is a fantastic program to use for creating realistic and fantasy landscapes. By combining the Bryce image with an object in Photoshop, you have easily created a scene.

Although the computer has enabled us greater control and speed, the traditional disciplines and theories of both photography and illustration are just as relevant as they ever were.

DARREN SPROTT AND ROSS EASON

WHEELING

Wheeling, by Phil Free, was created using Photoshop, MetaCreations Poser, and Bryce 2. Bryce is wonderful for creating a background landscape. By using Poser to create the images, Phil captured the feeling of a human-type being. He created depth by placing a larger figure in the foreground of the image and smaller figures in the middle ground. This way, it seems as if the figures are going away from the viewer. Here Phil explains his process in creating this image.

"I created this image as a design concept for an annual report (9.1). The theme was *wheeling,* which is the term used when electrical companies trade electricity back and forth to each other.

"I started in MetaCreations Poser and created the guys who were going to push my wheels. I used Bryce to create the landscape and the wheels themselves. I put the guys, landscape, and wheels together in Photoshop. I added a little trail for them to push their wheels down in Photoshop, as well.

"I liked the image and I was getting excited about using Poser and Bryce, but the concept didn't fly with the brass and that was that. Maybe next time."

SHINY TURKEY 3

Mark J. Smith uses Bryce like many artists do to create a landscape. He uses Photoshop to create the basic shape of an object. In Bryce, Mark completes the object and puts in the landscape and atmosphere.

"The Shiny Turkey 3 image was a Bryce rendering based on a black-and-white picture I created in Photoshop. The object is a symmetrical latticed object created from a black-and-white rendering from Photoshop. I modeled the object from a Photoshop image and the rest was completed in Bryce" (9.2).

RANDOM VEG

Random Veg is another beautiful image. To create this image, as with his previous image, Mark used Photoshop to create the basic black-and-white shape of an object. In Bryce, he combined the maps he created in Photoshop to make the terrain. After the image was basically put together, he used Photoshop to finish the image.

"Many of my images are rendered in Bryce, but are originally created from various programs that get composited in Photoshop. Bryce has a tool, which takes a depth map in formation or grayscale height in formation, and uses those maps to create objects. Photoshop is always the program I use to create the maps. Many times I used Photoshop to paint the black-and-white maps that create terrain in Bryce. The object in *Random Veg* was created from a black-and-white map and latticed in Bryce. Bryce renders beautifully, but I still alter and tweak the final result in Photoshop" (9.3).

9.2

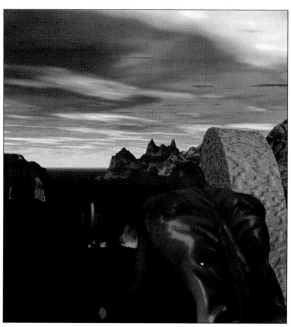

9.1

9.3

NOKIA

The purpose of *Nokia* is to show that Nokia Telecommunications' wireless system solution provides coverage for all environments. The art director wanted to show rural and city locations, as well as a train tunnel in the same illustration (9.4). Robert Forsbach followed the idea of the art director to create this stunning illustration.

9.4

9.5

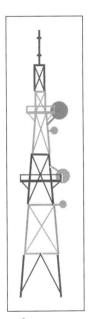

9.6

"I began by creating the landscape in Bryce. The buildings and train were originally created in FormZ and saved as DXF files. Unfortunately, there were problems importing the DXF's into Bryce (one or more sides of an object would be missing), so I ended up recreating almost everything in Bryce (9.5). The radio tower in the landscape was created in Illustrator (9.6).

"On the left is a close-up of the train's wire frame done in Bryce (9.7). On the right is a close-up of the same train done in FormZ. It's a shame that I could not import the DXFs, because, as you can see, it's much easier to align complex objects in FormZ (9.8).

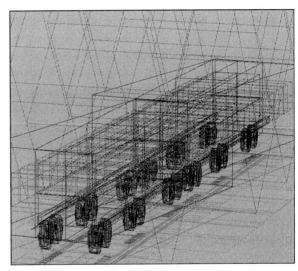

9.7

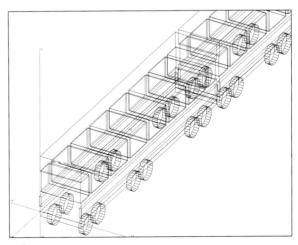

9.8

9.9

9.10

"I used Photoshop to clean up as many of the alignment problems as I could. For example, the roof of the building on the left (9.9) doesn't quite rest on the top, so I added to it in Photoshop. I cut out the land with the lasso tool and pasted it onto a foreground layer. I brought in some trees and pasted them into a middle ground layer. Then the trees could be scaled and moved around freely" (9.10).

BRIDGE

Robert Forsbach created *Bridge* for his client, Memorex Telex (Agency: Memorex Telex; Art Director: Steve Parker). The following steps outline those steps Robert took to create the image:

STEP 1 The first rough sketch was done in Illustrator (9.11).

STEP 2 In Illustrator, I changed the man's pose, got rid of the rails on top of the bridge, and started adding flat colors (9.12).

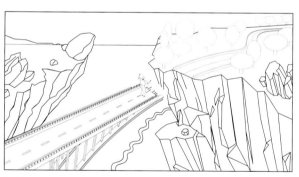

9.11

9.12

STEP 3 I brought the art into Photoshop and blended and added noise to the shapes. I brought one tree in and then squashed and stretched it to make all the other trees. The art director asked me to add more height to the illustration so we could see more sky.

STEP 4 When I was finished, I brought the Photoshop file into Painter to add an overall texture (9.13, 9.14), and the image was complete (9.15).

PEOPLE

People are probably the most interesting subjects you can work with in Photoshop and Illustrator. One typical use is using a photograph of people and combining a background in Photoshop. Sometimes you need to create an advertisement showing people and a product. Photoshop can easily combine the people with the product without ever having to set up a big shoot.

9.13

9.14

9.15

THE RIDE

The Ride, by Darren Sprott and Ross Eason, was created for UnderWater World, Sunshine Coast, in Australia. The amusement park had put in a new simulator ride and needed a "hero" shot of the simulator (9.16). No clean way existed to take the shot showing the models' faces, so Darren and Ross decided a shot with some retouching would be required. Darren is the art director for the UnderWater World account and Ross is the photographer.

The shoot

Darren first produced a "rough" of the proposed shot and Ross organized two models. The models where placed into the simulator before opening time early one morning and a large fan was employed to blow back the models' hair. The black walls of the simulator where draped in white, so Ross would have an easier job when it came time for deep etching. A wide range of photographs were taken with the models actually screaming, even though the simulator wasn't running.

The 3D model

The first simulator ride used at UnderWater World is a glacier roller coaster. Darren (after riding on the simulator more than enough times to do his research) began to make his model. First a large irregular shape was created with a jagged front. Then this was extruded with a slight bevel to soften the top edges. This formed the base for the ice cliffs and ground. Next, another irregular shape was created

that fitted inside the ice cliffs. Again this was extruded. This was simplified and many points where added to it. Darren then selected points and groups of points, changing their *Y* axis values to create the snow-covered hills. Points that dropped below the zero mark exposed the ice extrude. These snow hills extended much higher up into the shot than is shown here because many of them were going to be retouched out (as described later).

Light poles with spot lights in them where placed around the model in different locations. The Ice Station was created by lathing a circle to create a *torus* (donut shape). A bump map texture was created in Photoshop and applied to the torus. This created the ridged and plated effect on its surface. The exit tunnel was created by extruding two circles and applying a striped material to it with a bump. The ice track was built by sweeping two profiles along a path. One profile used the ice material from the base, while the other profile had the snow material applied that was used for the hills. A carriage on the roller coaster was created and placed on the ice track. This was going to be blurred, so not much detail went into it.

One of the most important aspects of creating the background was to make sure the lighting and colors were muted enough to allow the simulator and models to dominate the final composition. It is tempting to make each component as vibrant and sharp as possible, but this leads to a final picture without a focus.

Photoshop retouching

Ross deep-etched the models and simulator from the background, and then placed the background 3D model in on a separate layer. Storm clouds that had been shot earlier were placed over the background and rubber stamped downward to create a soft, yet realistic, horizon. The background was Gaussian Blurred, and then Ross applied a slight radial blur to bring movement to the picture. The focus of this radial blur was the opening of the exit tunnel.

On a separate layer, Ross generated a movement blur from the models and simulator, and then he softened the effect and placed it over the top of the composition, but offset from where it had originally been. This effect creates movement and also interest. An UnderWater World logo was manipulated and positioned on the front of the simulator.

9.16

SHOJI

Artist Eliot Bergman created this beautiful image called *Shoji*. Eliot used an image he scanned into Photoshop. By combining elements from Illustrator and Alias Sketch! in Photoshop, he made this image a work of art.

"The image of the figure was scanned and retouched in Photoshop. Because it was a grayscale scan, I converted the file to RGB and adjusted Hue and Saturation to simulate a color scan. I deleted the original background, applied a gradient, and saved the file as a PICT for later use. I also created the color and bump maps for the lantern in Photoshop.

"In one Illustrator file, I drafted grids for the wood frames of the shoji screen and rectangles that would later be used for the rice paper. I converted the grids to outlines, saved the file, and imported it into Alias Sketch! In Sketch!, I extruded the grids, or frames, but left the rectangles as planes. Another plane was drafted directly in Sketch! and positioned behind the model of the screen, to serve as the model for the map of the figure. In a second Illustrator file, I drafted a profile for the lantern. I imported the profile of the lantern and revolved it 360 degrees.

"In Sketch!'s Materials dialog, I created four materials: wood, rice paper, lantern, and figure. The color map of the wood was a PICT file from the Sketch! catalog. I tiled the map and specified a cubic projection. I chose white for the color of the rice paper and assigned an index of refraction for its transparency. The bump map for the paper was a PICT file of a fractal pattern, again from the catalog. I tiled the map and specified a planar projection for the material. For the lantern, I imported the files I had created in Photoshop and assigned a spherical projection. The last map was the image of the figure I had retouched in Photoshop.

"I composed the scene, selected an orthographic display to keep the elements square, assigned the materials, saved the file, and rendered the image using Alias RenderQ! Because the rice paper had a degree of transparency, ray-tracing was essential" (9.17).

BALANCE

In *Balance*, Eliot used Poser and Alias Sketch! in conjunction with Photoshop. As many of us do, he used Photoshop to touch up the final combined image. Photoshop not only touches up images, it can also enable you to add lighting and shadow effects.

"The first step was to create a model for the figure in Poser. I posed the figure, exported it as a DXF file, and imported the model into AliasSketch. In Sketch! I created the board, ball, and ground plane — using primitives from the toolbox — and composed the scene. The pattern for the ground plane was an image that was drafted in Illustrator, saved as a PICT in Photoshop, imported into Sketch!, and tiled.

"Next, the image was rendered in Alias RenderQ! using ray-tracing. Render size was $8^1/_2$" × 11", 300 ppi.

"Last, I opened the render in Photoshop and retouched any flaws in the figure. I then applied a Lighting Effects filter, flattened the image, and converted the file from RGB PICT to CMYK TIFF" (9.18).

9.17

9.18

OBJECTS

DURACELL

Duracell is another image by Eliot Bergman. Eliot continues to astound us with his use of Alias Sketch! with Photoshop. This image was used in Duracell's annual report. The movement upward is a great visual demonstrating the company's projections.

"The first step was to draft a profile for one battery in Illustrator. I imported the profile into Alias Sketch!, revolved it 360 degrees, duplicated it four times, and positioned the duplicates.

"Next, I imported five files I had created in Illustrator, one for each color map. These files were saved as PICTs in Photoshop and applied as cylindrical color maps in Sketch. I selected a background from the Sketch catalog and rendered the image using ray-tracing in RenderQ! Render size was 4" × 5" × 300 dpi.

"I opened the render in Photoshop, created several layers, and airbrushed lines to indicate motion. I flattened the file and converted it from RGB PICT to CMYK TIFF. The image was used to illustrate Duracell's annual report" (9.19).

BAG

Tom Neal and Brad Neal are the lifeblood of Thomas Bradley Design. Their efforts in using Illustrator and Photoshop show techniques never seen before in realism. The use of blends is extraordinary. *Bag* was done for United Display Craft (9.20). The client sent a bag to be used as a reference. Tom and Brad took a photograph of the bag to use as a tracing template in Illustrator.

They did all the line work in Illustrator. The blends were created in Illustrator following the curves of the bag. The key to blending successfully is choosing a color and making tints and shadows from that color. More important than the colors is creating many small blends to create the realistic-looking shadows and highlights. You also have to see the whole picture. If you focus on just one blend, it may look a little strange, but in combination with the whole image, it is beautiful.

Once the complex line work was finished, Tom and Brad rasterized the image in Photoshop. Photoshop was then used to airbrush the edges of the blends to soften the look of the bag.

9.19

9.20

CAR INTERIOR

Car Interior looks like a photograph (9.21). Tom Neal and Brad Neal strike again with their astounding illustrator started images. The interior looks real to the touch. They created the *Car Interior* for their client, Lincoln-Mercury. Like their work to create *Bag*, Tom and Brad created the detailed line work in Illustrator concentrating on the blends. Once the blends were complete, they used Photoshop to soften the edges of the vector art.

TEST TUBES

Test Tubes was created by Sandee Cohen, who teaches at the New School for Social Research Computer Instruction Center in New York City. Her detailed explanations and extraordinary thought processes in using Photoshop and FreeHand show why Sandee is truly outstanding in the graphics field. She created this image moving efficiently between Photoshop and FreeHand.

STEP 1 "The original file consisted solely of the stock photo of the test tubes on a black background. I needed to make some sort of artwork that would show the actions of the chemicals or the activity of the science. I decided I would like some sort of artwork that indicated one test tube's contents were moving up and mixing with another test tube's contents.

STEP 2 "To accomplish this look, I decided I wanted 'bubbles' that would grow out of one test tube, move along an arc, and then shrink back into the other test tube, changing color, size, and sharpness along the way.

STEP 3 "I started in Photoshop with the Pen tool and created an open path that moved from the blue test tube over to the red beaker. I then copied that path and pasted it into a FreeHand document.

STEP 4 "In FreeHand, I created four circles: small, large, large, and small (order is important to show the movement). I then turned the four objects into a blend. FreeHand is better to use than Illustrator for creating multiple blends with ease.

STEP 5 "I then selected the blend, as well as the pasted arc, and chose the FreeHand command 'Join Blend to Path.' I then adjusted the number of steps in the blend until I had the proper number of circles along the path (9.22).

STEP 6 "I copied the objects from FreeHand and pasted them into Photoshop as pixels. This created a new layer with the circles, which I positioned using the arc path as a guide.

STEP 7 "I needed to blur the circles. I wanted the blur to move along the path, however. This would mean the objects at the bottom of the path would have less blur than the objects at the top of the

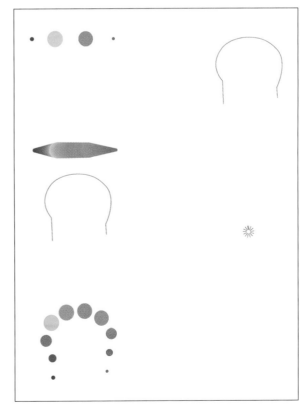

9.21

9.22

path. The blur would reduce as you moved to the bottom of the path.

STEP 8 "After much trial and error, I created the following technique. First, I needed to cut the path in half at the top. Because Photoshop doesn't have a knife tool, I pasted the path into FreeHand and used the knife tool to cut it.

STEP 9 "I also needed to change the direction of the path. Because I had drawn the path myself, I knew both paths moved in a clockwise direction. But I needed the left side of the arc to start at the top and move counter-clockwise. I did this by choosing the command 'Reverse Direction.' After having split the path and changed the direction of one, I copied and pasted the paths back from FreeHand to Photoshop. This time, I pasted them in as paths rather than pixels.

STEP 10 "I now could use the half arc to create an Alpha Channel to control the blur. I went to the channels palette and added a channel. I made the foreground color white and the background color black. I then chose a huge brush size for the paintbrush, and set the brush options to fade a certain number of steps from foreground to background colors.

STEP 11 "Still in the new channel, I took the half arc path and dragged it onto the Stroke Path icon at the bottom of the Paths palette. Because both paths started at the top and ended at the bottom, this had the effect of creating an arc that was thicker at the top and thinner and less white at the bottom. This would become the mask for my blur.

STEP 12 "Back on the circle layer, I loaded the channel I had just created. The mask meant any filter would be applied in an arc path, increasing from the bottom to the top.

STEP 13 "Finally, I decided I needed a little more pizzazz to add to the effect. In FreeHand I created a little 'twinkle' object that consisted of a line rotated around the copies. All the lines started in the center and moved outward.

STEP 14 "I pasted the twinkle object onto its own path layer in Photoshop. I positioned it over one of the circles. I then set the brush size to be really thin with a certain number for the fade and a complimentary color for the foreground color. I dragged the twinkle path onto the Stroke Path icon in the Paths palette. Because all the lines started in the center and moved outward, the stroke was heavier in the center and lighter at the edge. I moved the twinkle path around to another circle and repeated the process.

STEP 15 "I find this much more convenient than defining brushes because paths are resolution-independent. While a brush for one resolution could not be used with another file, a path can. I also made other twinkles that finished off the image" (9.23).

GALLERY ART

Sometimes I like to create an image purely for an artistic reason. I have images I have had printed and framed as art in my home. After creating for advertisements, book covers, and reports, it's nice to make an image that pleases your eye. Some of the images in this section not only please the eye, but are also functional in your work life.

BJORKLAND

In *Bjorkland*, Mark J. Smith continues with the symbolism of the bird, as in some of his other pieces. He works between Bryce and Photoshop to generate this

9.23

haunting image. Mark creates a beautiful balance of light and shadow in this image.

"The weird stone bird overlooking the cliff was originally done as a black-and-white height map in Photoshop. This was the first object I created in this way, which I generated in Photoshop. The symbol of the stone bird appears in several other pieces I have done by drawing a black-and-white picture. The white symbol on a black background can be used in Bryce to create a symmetrical latticed object. Any grayscale value other than black will be used to create a part of the geometry of a lattice object in Bryce. What's cool is I can use some interesting Photoshop tools to enhance the model in Bryce. If I want to distort the model with a twist, I can't do it in Bryce. The current version of Bryce is limited in the object modeling department. But by bringing the black and white picture of the bird back into Photoshop, I can create a slight twirl of about 30 degrees. Now when I import it back into Bryce, the object it creates is twirled, as well" (9.24).

CANNON

Matt Hoffman created *Cannon* by combining a 3D program with Photoshop. He takes advantage of the textures from a CD collection. I use CDs with stock photographs, textures, and landscapes to combine with my images in Photoshop. You can also start with a stock image and totally revamp it as an original creation of your own.

"The barrel of the cannon was just a simple lathe created in a 3D program with a mondo map texture molded on it in Photoshop. I added a slight bump map of granite, specular map of stucco, and an environment map of clouds (all from the Wraptures CD-ROM). The supports on the side, the platform on the bottom, and the cannon-balls are all organic magic applied to simple objects. The texture on the wooden floor I got from the Wraptures CD-ROM and enhanced it with Photoshop (I just accented the colors a little more). The clouds in the back were done in Photoshop" (9.25).

LUMINA

Lumina, by Phil Free shows a beautiful blend of a photograph turned into a gallery-worthy piece of art. The image shows a religious theme. Phil created a soft glow to give that heavenly feeling.

"Every now and then, I have to take a vacation from my normal corporate images to keep my brain from imploding. This was one of those exercises.

"In this image, Erica, a theatrical costume designer, is posing with one of her crinoline creations. Erica is in front of an old plaster wall on top of a table I covered with cheese cloth to give it an ethereal effect (9.26). Her feet were positioned over the edge of the table like a floating religious icon, so I decided she needed an aural glow.

"I scanned the black-and-white print, which was toned a medium brown, and brought it into Photoshop. I then selected the table and the slip and copied the selection to a new layer. I inverted the selection, darkened it with Levels, and gave the layer a darken only attribute. Finally, I selected the wall area

9.24

9.25

and the bottom of her slip and gave the edges a glow with the dodge tool" (9.27).

CURTAIN OF CONFUSION

Phil Free created *Curtain of Confusion* for an annual report. This is a perfect example of an artistic image used in the real world: his use of imagery to show the curtain revealing a clearer view. Phil uses Ray Dream Designer and Photoshop. In Photoshop, he loves using KPT 3.0 by MetaCreations.

"I created this image for the cover of our corporate annual report. We were trying to clear up some confusing terms and situations. I came up with this curtain that makes things look fuzzy and hard to discern and the little hand that pulls the curtain back, so the metaphorical images could be more easily seen (9.28).

"I created and rendered the dollar chart with Ray Dream Designer (9.29). I photographed the models and the curtain in the studio with tungsten light accentuated with a hand held flashlight that I painted over the models during long exposures (9.30, 9.31).

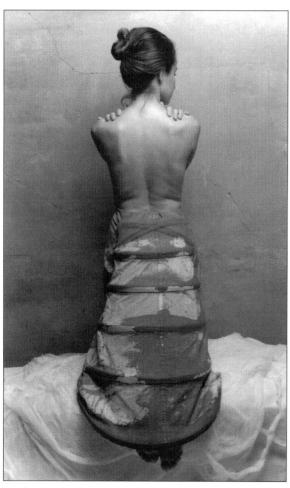

9.26

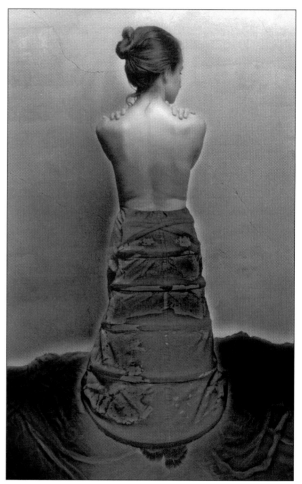

9.27

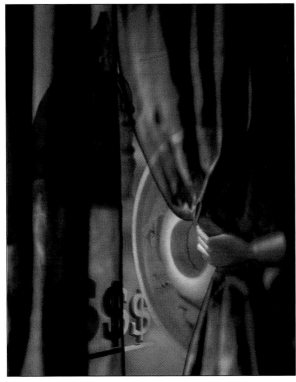

9.28

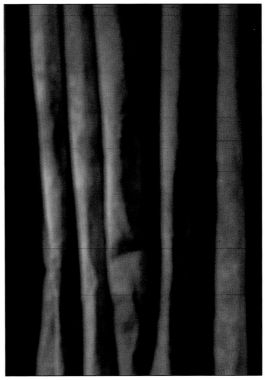

9.30

9.29

9.31

9.32

9.33

9.34

The newspaper article was simply typed into a layer in Photoshop, and then twisted and rotated to look like a page.

"All the elements were placed in layers over a background I created in KPT's Texture Explorer. The purplish, confused-looking effect was achieved by using the difference mode in the layers, with a bit of creative masking."

ALT PICK

To create *ALT Pick*, Lance Jackson used Illustrator in conjunction with Photoshop. He used the same basic image multiple times, layered on itself. After layering the images, Lance used Photoshop's opacity and lighting features to finish this cool illustration.

The image is composed of three horizontal strips. The top strip is a combined video and photography montage. The middle strip is a traditional image scan of a sepia diazod print. The bottom strip is a combination of multiple Illustrator and Photoshop files.

9.35

9.36

"For the bottom strip, I copied and pasted the two Illustrator files (9.32, 9.33) along a horizontal line in Photoshop, using varying degrees of opacity. I next placed two more Illustrator files (9.34, 9.35), in different positions along the horizontal line. To define the color fields in the image, I imported the Photoshop file several times on top of the group of images (9.36). I used the opacity features — such as hard light, multiple, lighten, and darken — to add variation in the color files. The combined strip was then added on the top two strips to complete the composition (9.37). The file was then flattened and saved (9.38).

JAVA HAPPY

Lance Jackson's use of Illustrator with Photoshop is amazing. With *Java Happy*, Lance successfully uses Illustrator to create the basic object and Photoshop to combine the object with a photo he tweaked.

"To create the background, I began with a video cam generated. This image was manipulated and the color enhanced in Photoshop a year earlier (9.39). I drew the coffee cup and head image in Illustrator, using a pencil sketch as a template (9.40). I then imported the Illustrator file into a layer in Photoshop. Using the feather tool with varying degrees of pixel selection, I removed parts of the coffee cup and head. Subsequently, I added other parts of the coffee cup and head in varying positions for a sense of speed and motion. Areas of the face and coffee cup were also copied onto layers where the color was adjusted and saturated. The file was flattened and saved (9.41).

CAMEL MAGIC

To create *Camel Magic,* Victor Claudio used KPT 3.0 textured background, Photoshop's ripple distort, and cool animals. Victor created a whimsical image combining the funky background with some great animal images.

"To create the Photoshop illustration, I started with a KPT texture (Super Turtle) as my background. I then took a scan of the camel, silhouetted with the path tool, and added a drop shadow using Alien Skin. The flamingo and rhinoceros were treated the same way (after many attempts with a variety of images that did not work). The finishing touch was to add some blue — in this case, a butterfly — in three places

9.37

9.38

around the composition, to which I used the Zig-Zag filter under distort. All of the preceding was done using Photoshop's layers to optimize the positioning of all objects" (9.42).

9.39

9.40

VOLCANIC DALI

Volcanic Dali is a nonserious take on a Salvador Dali theme. All elements were drawn with Photoshop tools and filled in with KPT filters. Victor describes how he used these tools to create this Dali spoof.

"I had just received KPT tools, and while experimenting with some of the texture settings, this illustration came to be. The mountain landscape was 'drawn' with the lasso tool and using the KPT texture explorer; Luminous Tourmaline (Minerals) was used for the fill. Some adjustment using the Mutation tree was done. The lava was also drawn with the lasso tool, with the KPT texture Fire Information (Fire) as the fill. The smoke was done by selecting the area with the lasso tool (feathered) and using the gradient tool to add different warm grays. The smudge tool and Gaussian Blur gave this combination its smoky texture. The melted clocks began with a circle, filled with KPT Texture explorer 'Golden Sweeps' (Metallic), the button on top had the same fill and was drawn with the circle tool as an oval. Details were added with the pencil tool. The face of the clock was a smaller white

9.41

circle with a light blue radial fill and numbers added with the type tool. The face was then pasted on top of the original metallic circle (which now became the clock's case). The melted drops were drawn with the lasso tool with a Golden Sweeps' fill. The clock and drop were then slightly distorted with the Wave (distort) filter, and cloned to different sizes to add perspective. After positioning the clocks and fine tuning the smoke, all layers were flattened" (9.43).

HERA'S SUPRISE

Hera's Suprise is a humble tribute to the master, Salvador Dali. Artist Victor Caludio says Dali was Bryce before Bryce! He creates this fabulous image by keeping in the theme of Dali-like art. I would love to use this soft image in any room because it gives me a calm, relaxed state of mind when I look at it.

"The object of this piece was to use Bryce, without it overpowering the finished product, the mythological theme occurred as the piece progressed. Starting with a Bryce sky and water as my background, I opened the Bryce document in Photoshop. Here I added the female, flying heron, and goat taken from various scans, which I again silhouetted with the path tool. The dolphins were copied from their original back-ground, using the lasso tool set at a 24-pixel feathering (for a soft edge around their water), and then faded back to 30 percent onto a new layer. The water splash at the base of the jumping goat was selected from a waterfall scan with the lasso tool (reshaped using the clone tool), manipulated with a little motion blur, after which I added the Zig-Zag effect at the base to simulate water ripples. After positioning all objects on their respective layers, the finishing touch was the moon behind Hera, rendered in Bryce, and placed in the layer behind the female figure. It was selected and given the Glow effect, using Alien Skin. All layers were then flattened for the final piece" (9.44).

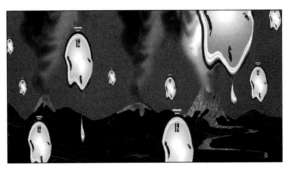

9.43

9.42

9.44

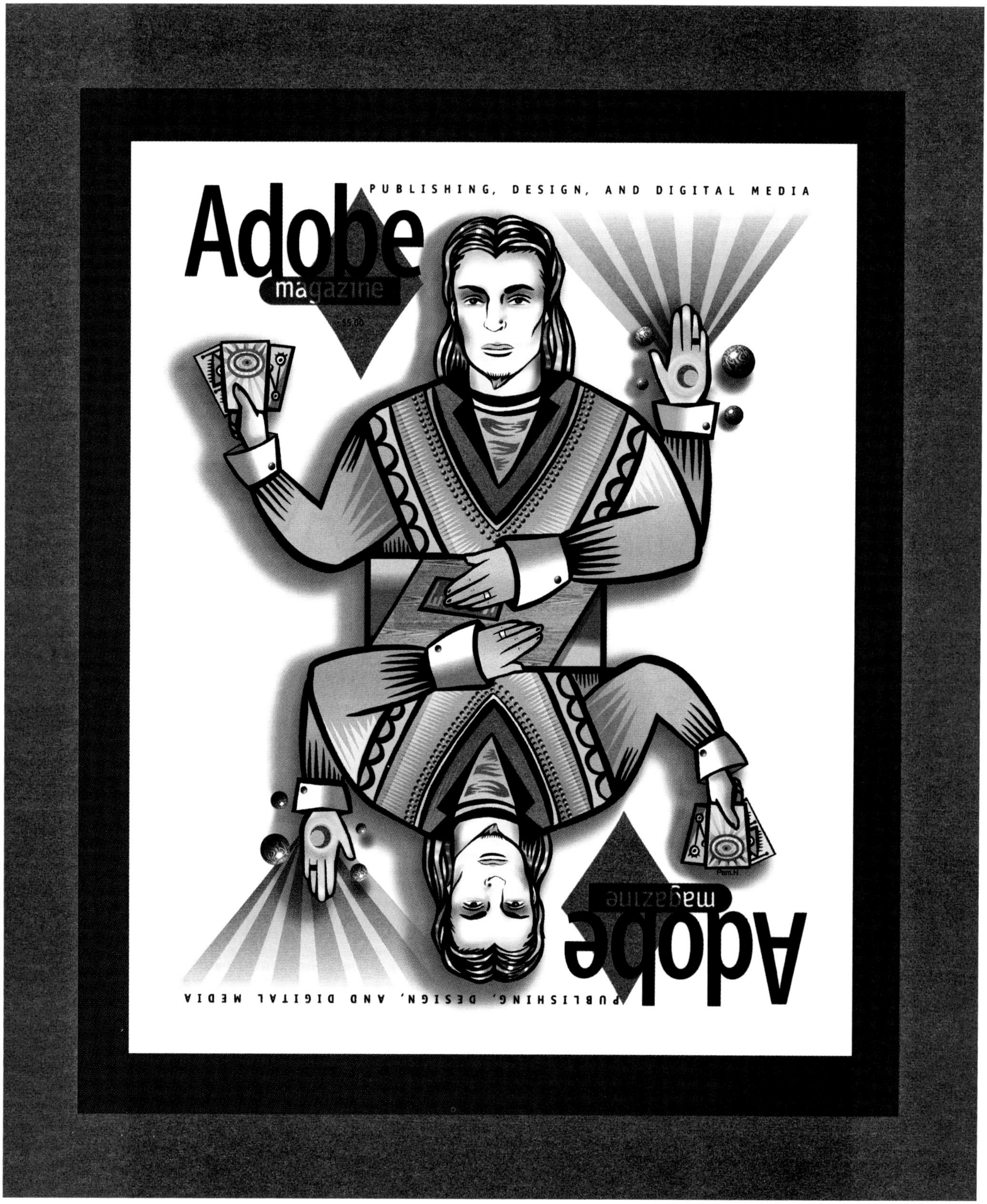
PUBLISHING, DESIGN, AND DIGITAL MEDIA
Adobe
magazine
$5.00

CHAPTER 10
PHOTOSHOP AND ILLUSTRATOR IN LAYOUT

The combination of Photoshop and Illustrator naturally falls in with creating page layout designs. You can use Illustrator to start the vector image, Photoshop to soften and add depth, and then go back to Illustrator for type and layout designs. You can explore many different aspects of type and layout — from magazine covers, book covers, and advertisements to cards, box designs, and movies.

MAGAZINE COVERS

One of the more popular ways of using layout is in designing magazine or book covers. To finish a cover, even with the most amazing photograph, you need to add type and lines in Illustrator. Many of the artists in this chapter go back and forth between Photoshop and Illustrator to create their finished covers. Then Illustrator is often used at the end for final output and printing ease.

CREATIVE BLACK BOOK

Pamela Hobbs created cover art for the *Creative Black Book*, which would be seen by advertising companies all over the U.S. Pamela uses Photoshop and Bryce with scanned 3D images, as well as stock photos.

"The project I had been given was on a tight deadline and I had a lot of research to do before hand. The *Creative Black Book* in New York City had commissioned me to do their cover art, which would be sent out to the head advertising and creative companies in

I try to combine my traditional work with the computer so it has more of a human touch to it. I used to think I would do everything on the computer, but why do something with technology if you can do it more efficiently by hand?

PAMELA HOBBS

the United States. I knew this had to be a dynamic piece, as it was going to be seen by everyone with whom I would like to be working. The subject given to me was anything that I felt inspired me as an artist in the form of a mask. The mask could be anything abstract, literal or any other format."

The following steps illustrate how Pamela created the cover art for the *Creative Black Book*:

STEP 1 "I drew an original drawing by hand, using brush and ink. I do this traditionally and not in the computer. I then scan in the drawings using Adobe Photoshop 4.0 (10.1, 10.2).

STEP 2 "I used the Marquee tool to duplicate the image, flip it, and create the symmetrical mask, flattening the image afterwards and deleting the white background (10.3).

STEP 3 "I did the same thing with the illustrated dragon. I rotated them slightly and created a second identical copy, and then flattened them to one layer (10.4).

ADOBE MAGAZINE COVER
Pamela Hobbs

175

STEP 4 "I placed the paper I had collected onto the scanner and scanned it. I used Curves to adjust the CMYK levels of the colors (10.5).

STEP 5 "The objects I placed onto the scanner were 3D objects. After scanning them, I had to delete the shadows behind them using the Magic Wand tool. I was able to create separate masks and files to bring into the main mask illustration (10.6).

STEP 6 "I selected the feather and converted it to a duotone (10.7).

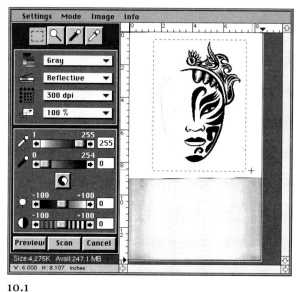

10.1

10.2

10.3

STEP 7 "I used the Pen tool to create a path around the feather, so I could use it as a selection (10.8). Then I can delete the background area and later use it as a path encase if I need to retouch the feather (10.9).

STEP 8 "After having placed in the background and scaled it to fit, I then placed the feather. I duplicated and rotated several feathers to make a 'wing.' Next, I copied that layer and flipped it to create the symmetrical right-hand wing (10.10).

10.4

10.5

10.6

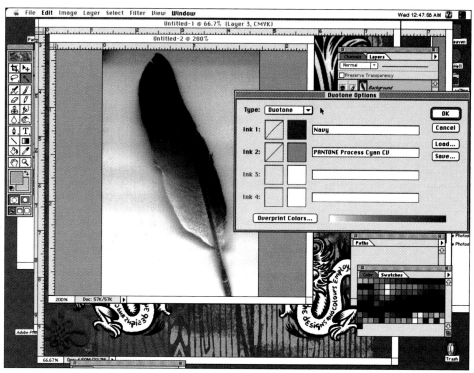

10.7

10.8

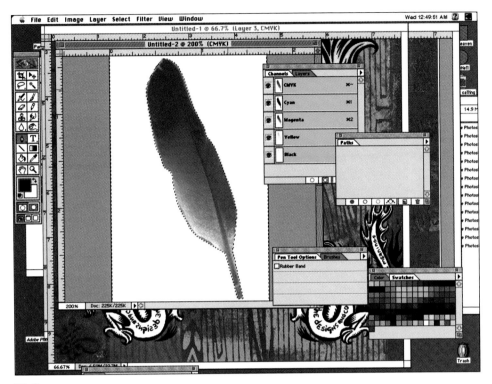

10.9

10.10

STEP 9 "The custom gradient was used to create the blend on the face through the eyes only (10.11, 10.12).

STEP 10 "Custom fills were applied using the Magic Wand and the Gradient tool. Using the Actions buttons, I was able to set up a preset fill command. This enabled me to fill various forms or areas quickly and precisely (10.13).

STEP 11 "I created an eye-reflecting shape that would radiate outwards to the edge of the paper (10.14). Using the pen tool, I created paths to give the stripped radiating color effect (10.15).

STEP 12 "Using PhotoDisc's CD-ROM of stock images, I selected the film canister, ready to place into my illustration (10.16).

STEP 13 "Using the PhotoDisc image, I applied a Quick Mask effect to it to create the faded edge effect on the canister. Using the Gradient tool with foreground black to background white, I applied a mask (10.17). After I was satisfied with the mask, I used a shortcut and dragged the layer to the trash and applied the mask.

STEP 14 "I imported other PhotoDisc images and repeated the process in Step 13 using skew, scale, and rotate to create the feeling of motion (10.18).

STEP 15 "I duplicated the dragons (10.19).

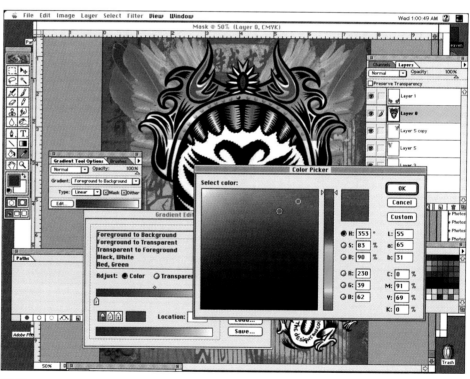

10.11

10.12

10.13

10.14

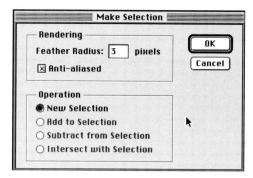

10.15

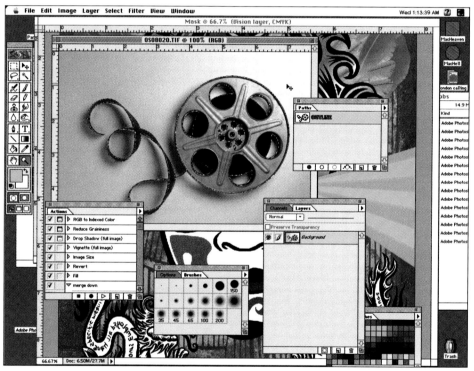

10.16

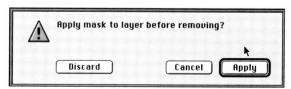

10.17

10.18

10.19

STEP 16 "I wanted to create a smoke effect, so I selected a new layer and applied a feathered fill to the duplicated shape (10.20, 10.21, 10.22).

STEP 17 "The drop shadow is a duplicate layer of the flattened prior layers. With the opacity set, it gives a precise transparent duplicate of the original layer. The Gaussian Blur filter can be also

applied to the shadow, if a softer effect is desired (10.23).

STEP 18 "After I completed the illustration, I added some final touches like the flowers behind the head. They were added using KPT Bryce 3D filters in the center and a real scanned flower" (10.24).

10.20

10.21

10.22

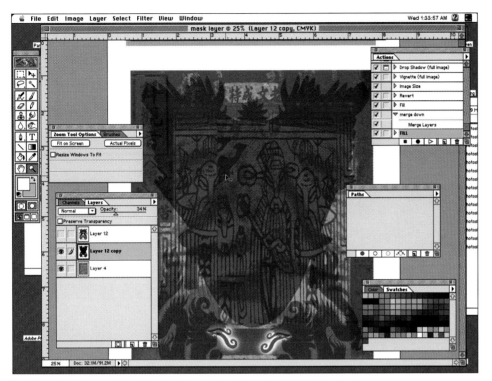

10.23

10.24

10.25

COMPUTER ARTIST MAGAZINE

Pamela Hobbs was assigned to create the cover art for *Computer Artist* magazine. The magazine was reviewing her work, so she thought of creating a sort of self-portrait for the cover (10.25).

STEP 1 "First, I hand-inked the black line art. After scanning in the line art, I used Adobe Illustrator to streamline, or trace, the image.

STEP 2 "I created some of the swirled circle backgrounds using Texture Maker by Specular International. I also used a Photoshop filter to make them swirl.

STEP 3 "With Adobe Dimensions, I created a simple cone shape. Then I wrapped the text as a texture around it to create the 3D text wrap that goes behind the logo in the top-left corner.

STEP 4 "I took screen grabs of work in progress and applied them into the screen of the computer. Using some stock images, I added the flying saucer in the left-hand side, and the coffee cup in the lower right-hand side.

STEP 5 "In Photoshop, I created my own custom blend between two colors. I used a light color in the center to create a highlight effect of metal on the arms.

STEP 6 "Using layers, I could drop in the map texture as a duotone and use a mask to create a faded background to white.

STEP 7 "I then flattened the figure layer and left the map as the background.

STEP 8 "Finally, I duplicated the top figure layer and made it into a drop shadow layer."

ADOBE MAGAZINE

Another assignment had Pamela creating a cover for *Adobe* magazine, depicting the tricks of the trade in the gaming industry (10.26). The following steps outline the process she followed:

STEP 1 "I first inked the image of the man by hand. Using Adobe Illustrator, I was able to streamline the image by tracing it and flipping it upside down, creating a mirror image.

10.26

STEP 2 "I created separate paths for the stripped background areas behind the hand by constraining the paths, holding the Shift key. I was able to get them angled correctly to the top of the page.

STEP 3 "The diamonds are created in Illustrator and duplicated on either side of the page to continue with the diamond king of the cards.

STEP 4 "I next imported the images to Photoshop. I then applied the color and texture in the suit. Using Kai's Power Tools, I was able to create some textures around the collar of the suit using 3D spheres.

STEP 5 "I duplicated the layer and brought down the Brightness and Contrast. Then I made the layer opacity 20 percent to create a drop shadow. I applied a Gaussian Blur to give it a soft edge.

STEP 6 "I touched up the image and added the 3D spheres that were previously created in Infinity D 3.0."

VCR MOVIE COVERS

ORGANIX

This cover design was created for a VCR tape. It showcases Mark J. Smith's beautiful work incorporating Photoshop, Illustrator, and various other programs (10.27).

"The jellyfish monster was created in Alias/Wave Front's PowerAnimator on the SGI platform. At the time, PowerAnimator had a new feature that enabled particle systems to be used to create hair. I used it to create the tentacles of the jellyfish beast.

"The animation of this jellyfish is quite impressive. Because the particle system was new, and not used in this way before, there were problems. Broken segments of hair and hair tentacles were passing through the body of the jellyfish beast. I used Photoshop's Smear and Rubberstamp tool to paint out some of the idiosyncrasies that were occurring. These tools in

10.27

Photoshop are invaluable. They have saved our images several times in the creation of scenes for movies. I could speak a Bible on Photoshop regarding the movies.

"The background was rendered in Bryce 2. This background was also altered in Photoshop. I put highlights into the background frame that were not in the original rendering. Finally, the jellyfish monster and background were composited in Alias Wave Front Composer 4.3. This jellyfish monster also appeared in the film remake of the 1957 classic, *Not of This Earth*."

BUSINESS LETTERS

Business letters can often be a bit boring. You can certainly liven up any letter with a jazzy logo, graphic, or altered text. Not only can letterhead benefit from this enhancing, but late notices can also be much more interesting. If your graphic on the letter catches someone's eye, they are more likely to read the contents.

ROTTEN EGG

Randy Livingston got the idea for a piece of art to use on late invoices from other such pieces he had seen. They impressed him as an effective way — decisively, yet kindly — to remind late-paying customers of their aging debt with his studio. Randy creates this image using Photoshop and Illustrator.

"After some brainstorming and sketches, I fixed on the idea of using the image of a rotten egg placed at the bottom of late invoices. I scanned the pencil

sketch shown and saved it as a grayscale TIFF at 72 dpi (10.28). This TIFF was placed in Illustrator to use as a template. I then created a second layer to begin work with the pen tool. For the most part being faithful to the sketch, I traced outlines of the basic shapes. Adjusting the paths and applying basic colors came next.

"To add dimension to the entire illustration, I used a combination of gradients and blends. First, the foreground outer eggshell half was colored with a linear gradient. The background outer eggshell half was colored with a radial gradient. I experimented with the placement of the radial gradient center point, as well as the progression of the linear gradient to get the most natural impression of light on the outer eggshell halves. The inner eggshell halves were both filled with a linear gradient (10.29).

"Eggshells being at a point of completion, I then created another layer to continue work on the egg white and egg yolk. The yolk was created with several irregular oval shapes. To get the shiny spheroid shape of the yolk, I used an oval filled with a red-yellow hue, and then copied that and scaled to about 20 percent. The smaller oval was filled with yellow, and then positioned just off-center, up and left, on top of the large red-yellow oval. Selecting these two ovals, I used the blend tool to create a 124-step blend. The blend and originating shapes were selected and grouped. Placing an extra tiny white oval shape for a highlight point and a small elongated oval shape along the bottom edge of the yolk, added the visual cues necessary to intensify the glossy quality of the yolk shape. The

10.28

10.29

egg white was built with a blend in much the same flat manner, but with a hint of thickness (10.30).

"A final layer was created to build the shadows. Experimenting with color and placement, oval-shape blends were used to create believable shadows cast on a surface by the eggshell halves. A dark shape was placed behind the egg white to create the slight shadow cast by the egg white mass. At this point, I deleted the template layer (sketch) and then selected all objects and grouped and did a final save (10.31).

"Probably the single best feature introduced in Version 6.0 of Illustrator, the ability to drag-and-drop from Illustrator into Photoshop, was used next. I grabbed the rotten-egg illustration from the Illustrator document and dragged-and-dropped on a new Photoshop document window that I created, about seven inches square, RGB, at a resolution of 300 dpi. Photoshop then parsed the Illustrator file and rasterized at the size and resolution of the Photoshop document. The Illustrator art arrives in Photoshop as an active selection where one may send it to its own layer or immediately drop it to create a 'flattened' image. In this case, I dropped it for a flat image file (10.32). I then made minor color adjustments (using Curves) and adjusted Output Levels to lighten the entire image (as I wanted the art to be somewhat screened-back on the invoice). I then applied the KPT filter, Gaussian Electrify, to the entire image.

"Still in Photoshop, I set the type 'Over 30 Days Old!' using the typeface MarkerFeltWide with a fill of deep red (10.33). While the type selection was still active, I option double-clicked Floating Selection in the layers palette to send it to its own layer. I then proceeded to duplicate the type layer (dragged the type layer onto the new layer icon at the bottom of the layers palette) and with preserve transparency checked in the layers palette, I used key combination

10.31

10.32

10.30

Shift+Option+Delete (after first changing the fore-ground color to black, such as, typing a *D*) to change the layer's type from the deep red to black. Then I unchecked preserve transparency in the layers palette and applied a Gaussian Blur with a radius of about 2 to 4 pixels. After arriving at the degree of blur that I wanted on the shadow, I offset the type shadow (of course, to the bottom and right—a classic drop-shadow effect). The shadow opacity was then less-ened with the opacity slider in the layers palette and presto! A fine classic drop shadow, the likes of which are seldom seen onscreen or in print, was created (he says with a grin) (10.34).

"I linked the type layer and the type shadow layer together by first selecting the type layer in the layers palette and then checking the box between the eye and the layer name on the type shadow layer in the layers palette. I then positioned all elements just so and, with one last save to preserve the layered Photoshop 3 file, flattened the image (choose flatten image from the layers palette drop-down menu). The image file was then converted to CMYK color mode and saved in TIFF or EPS format (with a different name so as not to write-over the layered working file) to be placed in a QuarkXPress document for final output" (10.35).

RETAIL FLYERS

Mailboxes get stuffed full of retail flyers. Design is the key to getting a flyer noticed. If you have created a colorful dramatic image, people are going to check out your advertisement. Using Photoshop to create an image and Illustrator to add the type is a beautiful blend that makes a flyer worth reading.

GOLD BOOK

Geno Coppotelli created the *Paint and Decorating Retailers Gold Book* for 1997. This happened to be their silver anniversary issue. This image uses Photoshop's channels to create the metallic look. Glen rasterizes the original logo created in Illustrator into Photoshop.

"I created a new Photoshop document. I then drew circle and lines as grommet and spine fold shapes in the background layer. I blurred the layer and dupli-cated it. Next, I used the Offset filter in each channel and used the difference blending mode on the top channel. Then the layers were flattened and inverted.

"I used a section of a TIFF image I had created to look like a silvery shadow. Next, I enlarged and blurred the section to give just general shadowy shapes. This was duplicated for use later. I used this as

10.33

10.34

a channel at 50 percent opacity and merged the two channels. I created a silver look by opening curves and drawing a zig-zag line out of curve.

"The pre-existing *Gold Book* logo was originally created in Illustrator. I copied and pasted it into Photoshop as a channel. The *Gold Book* layer was duplicated and stroked to create a fat gold layer. I duplicated the fat *Gold Book* layer to create a fatter layer and blurred it. I used an embossed blur. I then duplicated the embossed layer twice and used levels to set white point at 50 percent on one channel and black point at 50 percent on the other channel, to create highlight and shadow channels. Then the shadow layer was inverted.

"I created a gold layer and applied highlights and shadow selections. I used Curves to bring out the *Gold Book* logo. I placed the duplicate of the shadow layer over the gold layer and used the Transform command (⌘/Ctrl+T) to offset a little. I set it to multiply mode and 60 percent opacity. Then I merged the layers. I used Curves and drew a zigzag line. I loaded the channel containing the thickest stroke as a selection and dropped out background for the final image" (10.36).

BASICS COVER

The *Basics* cover, by Geno Coppotelli, was created to show a color forecast for the Paint and Decorating Retailers. Geno used Illustrator to create the type and then he rasterized the file in Photoshop for further enhancing. By tweaking the colors of a stock image, Geno completed the cover design.

"I set background type in Adobe Illustrator and rasterized the file in Photoshop. I then varied the gold blend created in Photoshop. The type layer was duplicated and loaded as selection. The selection was filled with blend at an angle. The black type logo was blurred, offset a little, and used as a shadow at 40 percent opacity. The background layer was created and blended to be used at a different angle. These layers were merged. I scanned in color swatches and deleted the background. I duplicated the swatches layer and filled it in with black. The black was blurred and set at 30 percent opacity and offset a little as shadow.

"I found chalk images on a stock PhotoDisc backgrounds and objects disc. I cut out the pieces I liked

10.35

10.36

and pasted them into the document. I then copied some pieces and used the hue and saturation filter to colorize and change color. The pieces were rotated for composition. The same is done to create shade and offset to add more depth.

"The chalkboard was created from an image from the Objects disc file of an old-fashioned wooden writing tablet. I used the Rubber stamp tool to clean up the image.

"A Rectangular marquee was created in the center, of framed wood, and filled with black. The selection was saved as a channel. After duplicating the channel, I blurred the highlight and shadow channel and loaded it into the chalkboard channel to create an illusion of recessed blackboard.

"The type on the chalkboard was created in Illustrator and pasted into Photoshop. I selected individual letters and used hue and saturation to colorize the letters. I scanned in a piece of textured paper that I rubbed chalk on. I used this scan as a channel to load into the type channel and deleted to give chalk texture to the type. I added a drop shadow to the

chalkboard and offset it to give depth. Finally, I flattened the image and saved it as a final" (10.37).

TOP TEN TIPS

The *Top Ten Tips* cover by Geno Coppotelli was created to help promote paint sales. Geno used Illustrator to create the type and the circle paint can. He rasterized the Illustrator file in Photoshop. In Photoshop, Geno took full advantage of channels to design his image.

"First, I set the type and circle for the paint can in Illustrator and drew the background lines. I used an open face type. I created a new Photoshop document. I copied the lines into Photoshop as a channel. I applied a graphic pen to add texture. The channel was colored blue. Lighting effects were used to create a spotlight with the line channel as a texture layer. I loaded the line layer as a selection and used Levels to lighten the lines in the blue channel.

"The text, *top tip* was copied into channels. I duplicated the channel and stroked the channel twice for a fat logo. I then duplicated the stroked channel and fattened it again, creating a fatter layer. The thickest stroke channel was duplicated, blurred, and embossed. I loaded [the] channel containing the thickest stroke into this channel to trim the edges. A new layer was created and made red. I added the embossed channel as a selection and used curves to create depth. I used an *S* curve. This layer was copied and I used curves to create a lighter orange version. The fat channel selection was loaded to trim its background. I merged these channels as type channel, duplicated them, and loaded it as a selection that was filled with black. A Gaussian Blur was used to soften, offset, and create a shadow layer. I used the lighting effects filter — spotlight — to add depth and variation.

"I scanned in the top of a paint can. Then I created a layer above it and made a rainbow blend. The paint can layer was copied into channels and created highlight and shadow channels. These layers were loaded as selections to create depth. I used a Circular marquee that was the same size as the inside of the can. The background was inverted and dropped out. I used a difference blending mode on the rainbow layer

10.37

and merged it with the can layer. I then put this layer behind the text layer and transformed it to place it in the circle and size. The layers were merged.

"The number ten was created in Illustrator and rasterized as a grayscale Photoshop document. I stroked and blurred the number ten and saved it as a displacement map. Next, I created a new RGB document. Specular highlights were created the same as in the silver look in the *Gold Book.* I used the number ten as the selection to cut out highlights.

"I copied a section of the top ten where the ten will reside. A displacement map was applied to that area. It was then lightened using Levels. I brought the highlight document into this new document in overlay mode. I merged and clipped away the background. I placed the top ten document where it picked up reflections from the bottom. This layer was used to create a drop shadow. I used Circle marquee as a specular highlight. The edges were feathered and placed on the top and filled with white" (10.38).

CARDS AND SCHEDULES

The natural blend of Photoshop and Illustrator comes in the form of image with type. You can create any card you want using Photoshop for the image and Illustrator for the type. Cards aren't the only area you can cover. You can also create calendars or a sports schedule for your favorite team.

VET CARD

Patricia Cheal created an image to be used as an animal sympathy card. It was made to be printed in two colors. She used Photoshop to combine the beautiful hand sketches. The file was then placed into Illustrator to add the text and print the spot color separations (10.39).

WHALERS SCHEDULE

The Whalers schedule is actually a full-sized poster. The art was created with original pencil sketches. After scanning the sketches into Photoshop on separate layers, Patricia painted the line art on its own layers. To create the guys in the background, she used MetaCreations Fractal Design Poser. In Poser, Patricia created different standing poses. Then she drew the finished sketches. After finishing the image in Photoshop, Patricia opened the file in Illustrator. In Illustrator, the headline, logo and the rest of the text were set (10.40).

10.38

10.39

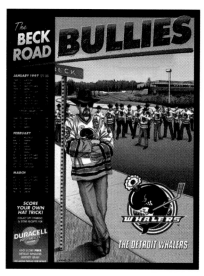

10.40

10.41

ADVERTISEMENTS

The advertising world is always showing us the newest ideas for using Photoshop and Illustrator. Any form of promotion of a product can be created in these programs. You can promote yourself, food products, toys, cars, and much more. The possibilities are endless.

BETTER HOMES AND GARDENS JUNIOR COOKBOOK COVER

Artist Wayne Vincent created the *Better Homes and Gardens Junior Cookbook* cover art (10.41). Wayne started the file in Illustrator. A sketch was approved first and used as a template to trace. After fully rendering the lines and color in Illustrator, the file was rasterized into Photoshop. He used the vector paths from the Illustrator file to create masks for the soft-edge drop shadows in Photoshop. Wayne used the same paths for masks to act as friskets, where he added touches of airbrushing and motion streaks. The whole file was saved as an EPS and placed into Illustrator for final output.

VARIOUS ADVERTISEMENTS

Wayne Vincent created these various advertisements that show creativity beyond belief (10.42). His use of Photoshop and Illustrator in creating the bag, box, and other advertising designs for various companies is seamless. Add to all this Wayne's wonderful use of color and these ads are a sure sell. Wayne explains his use of Illustrator and Photoshop together.

"First a tight line pencil sketch is created by hand. I try to resolve as many composition and design problems at the pencil stage to be able to concentrate on the painting and colorizing of the art when I begin working in Illustrator. The sketch is scanned and imported into Illustrator as a template. I use Illustrator to create an under painting, which means I block in all the basic shapes, concentrating on refining the drawing and linear problems and filling in with basic colors. I also begin to separate the drawing into sectors. (I break the drawing into layers that I will work on separately in Photoshop later.)

"When the basic drawing is completed, I import the Illustrator file into Photoshop sector by sector. A simple example would be to import a background. First, I work on that, and then I bring foreground elements on separate layers. I have Illustrator and Photoshop open at the same time and toggle back and forth between programs using the clipboard to import items from Illustrator to Photoshop. In Photoshop, I concentrate solely on colorizing and dimensions in the art. I use the Airbrush tool and various filters to add depth and texture to the art. One of the great things about the Illustrator/Photoshop way of working is the ability to bring in precise Bézier paths into Photoshop. I use those paths as friskets to fill with transparent colors and feathered edges the same way an airbrush artist would cut film friskets. In Photoshop, I work in LAB color, a three-channel mode. This keeps file size down and keeps colors true when I convert the art to CYMK on completion."

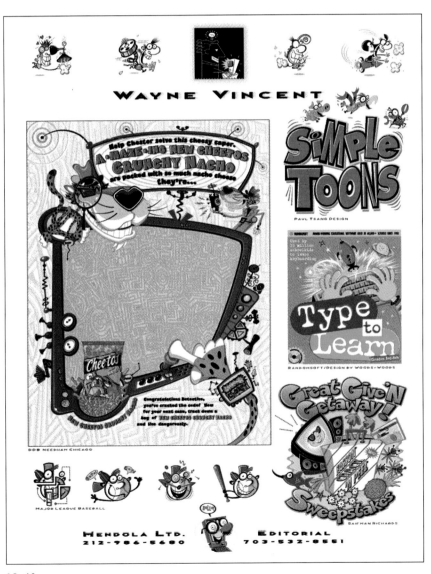

10.42

CHAPTER 11
WORKING WITH 3D EFFECTS AND TEXTURES

Most illustrations benefit from adding 3D effects or textures. An image started from a sketch or in Illustrator lacks realism and dimension. Photoshop and other image editing programs can bring out the third dimension with the use of light and shadow. This chapter consists of fantastic art that has fully used the use of light, shadow, and textures. Every piece of art you'll see has used Photoshop in some way in the transition process of creating great artistic pieces.

CREATING 3D EFFECTS

Three-dimensional effects are currently all the rage. Look at commercials, magazine ads, and billboards to see the extensive use of 3D programs. Some 3D programs create great looking pieces from a few lines, but they still need Photoshop to smooth out the banding and soften the edges or to add the background.

CREATING PERSPECTIVES

Illustrator can be used to create the base for any illustration. If you know the basics of perspective, you can easily create a grid to guide you as you create your 3D shapes. You can make the grid a pale gray, group it, and delete it when you are done.

Every day I learn something new.

ELIOT BERGMAN

The following steps outline how to create a basic room grid:

STEP 1 Draw a square.

STEP 2 Using the Direct Selection tool, click the left line of the square, hold the shift key, and click the right vertical side of the square to select both sides. Choose Edit ➢ Copy, and then Edit ➢ Paste in Front.

STEP 3 Using the Blend tool, blend the copied lines with 15 steps.

STEP 4 Delete the original square.

STEP 5 Select all the lines and double-click the Rotate tool. Enter **90** and hit the copy button (11.1).

STEP 6 Select the grid and choose Filter ➢ Distort ➢ Free Distort. Drag the top two points inward and the bottom two points outward. Click the OK button (11.2).

STEP 7 Draw a vertical line upward from the lower-left corner of the floor perspective. Draw a smaller vertical line from the upper-left corner of the floor perspective.

STEP 8 Blend between the two vertical lines with 15 steps.

STEP 9 Repeat on the other side (11.3).

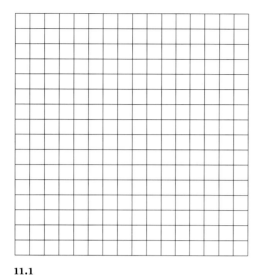

11.1

STEP 10 Copy the bottom-left angled line up to the top of the vertical line. Adjust the end point, as necessary. Select the bottom- and top-angled lines and do a 15-step blend.

STEP 11 Repeat on the other side (11.4).

STEP 12 Copy the back bottom line up to the top. Do a blend from the back bottom to the back top line with 15 steps. Change the color of the lines to 25 percent gray and .25 line weight (11.5). Lock the lines and draw your perspective room or objects on top of the grid.

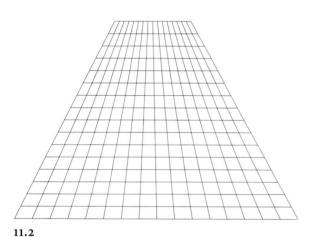

11.2

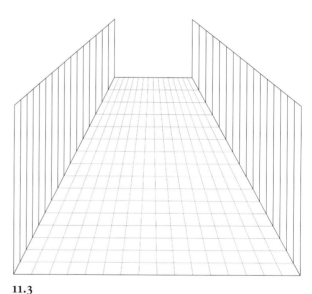

11.3

PHOTOSHOP AND THE MOVIES, MUSINGS FROM MARK J. SMITH

IN THIS SECTION, Mark explains how they completed fixing the head so it looks at the jellyfish. After fixing that task, they realized the eyes needed to be changed, as well. Again, Photoshop to the rescue!

"Two scenes later, we had a much more daunting task at hand using the same technique. Once the area had been 'replaced,' I was able to use the actor's head from the copy buffer. We rotated the head 'selection' to what we felt was the proper orientation, and then placed it down over the new background replacement. Our friend, the rubber stamp tool,

was then used to match areas of color to help the head really fit into place. We also used the blend tool to create a smoother transition between what was pasted and the background plate.

"One of the most dangerous enemies to compositing in general is lighting. An audience can pick out bad compositing all the time. They might not know what is wrong with a shot, but they know something is wrong. It now appeared that the lighting was a little off-kilter. We adjusted the lighting playing off the actor's head by adjusting the brightness.

After getting the basics of perspective down, you can move on to the different views. Some prefer the one point, two point, bird's eye view, or worm's eye view. If you prefer, you can draw the grid on tracing paper, sketch the perspective on top, and then scan in the image. Once you have scanned in an image, you can trace in Illustrator or go directly to Photoshop to add color, light, texture, and shadow.

ALLIANCE

Alliance, by Michael Tompert, began as a scan in Photoshop, taken into Illustrator for tracing, opened in Strata Vision for rendering, and back to Photoshop for light, contrast, shadow, and texture. Michael truly understands the use of 3D programs and the importance of Photoshop. As you see in the steps he followed to create the image, the effect Michael was striving for was to change the focus, so his image became much more realistic.

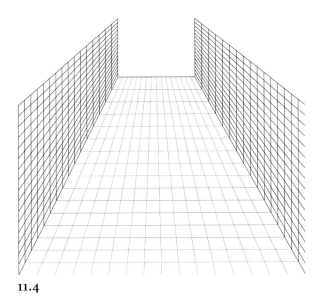

11.4

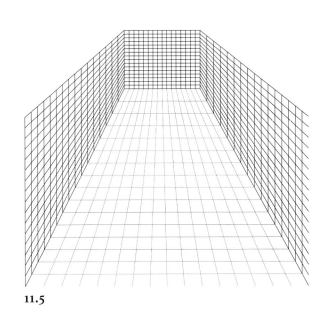

11.5

There was still something foul about what we had done. Technically it was very good work and no one would be the wiser, but....

"It then dawned on us like a slap in the face with an icy cold fish. The actor's eyes! His pupils were still oriented in the wrong fashion. By rotating the head, the line of sight had to be readjusted. It was simply wrong. The eyes are the conduit to the soul. As small as this part of our bodies is, the eyes convey an incredible amount of emotion by their position, movement, and dilation.

"Once again, I went to Photoshop to correct this problem. At the resolution at which we were working, the pupils themselves were no more than a dozen pixels across, including the dithering. I hand selected the pixels by zooming in very close and cut them into a selection buffer. I then used the rubber stamp tool to copy the whites of the eyes into the hole left by removing the pupil This was a profile shot, so I only had to deal with one eye.

"I then pasted the pupil back, and with the arrow keys, began to move the pupil

into the correct orientation. It was quite magical to see the pupil move. As it moved, the entire expression changed. The whole meaning of the scene became more clear. Initially, I had been manipulating it with the mouse.

"This quickly became tedious. Photoshop's capability to move a selection a single pixel' at a time spared me serious carpal tunnel syndrome. I was amazed to discover how much information a single pixel of pupil expressed. I found the proper orientation of the pupil and pasted it down permanently.

The creation process

STEP 1 "I started out by placing chess pieces on the flatbed scanner and then sharpening the result substantially. I saved the file out for use as a template in Illustrator (11.6).

STEP 2 "In this step, I traced the profiles of the chess figures in Adobe Illustrator and exported them to Strata Vision 3D (11.7).

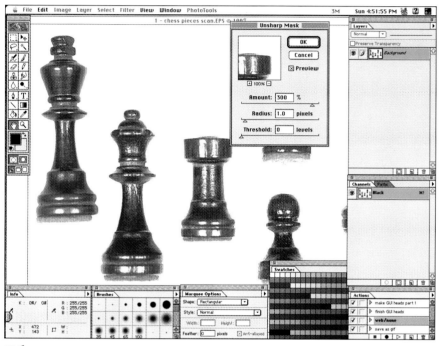

11.6

You may think, how did he do this with the guy moving? Even if he swayed a little bit, this work would have to be repeated 24 times for each second the scene lasted. Well, as luck would have it, the film crew shot several seconds for that scene.

"The saving grace was found within the low-budget nature of the production. We had instructed them, for cost concerns, to scan one single frame of the scene. This is not a good practice at all. In other words, this shot in the film could have been done with a still from a 35 mm camera. The frame was duplicated 24 times for each second the scene ran. I believe it was a four second shot. This means 24 times 4 seconds equals 96 duplicate frames of our Photoshop manipulated picture. The problem with this was the film grain. The budget was constricting and the deadline was approaching.

"We used a slight blur in Photoshop to dampen the original film grain in the shot. It was decided that between the action of the computer graphic jellyfish monster and the attempt to diffuse some of the film grain, it would not be noticed. It wasn't. Even as we looked it over many times it was quite good. We then composited the moving monster over our duplicated frames to finish the scene. Mason was now looking at the monster and not above him.

"It was a long way to travel to complete a shot that needn't have been so difficult had it been supervised properly. If we had the budget and time, the

STEP 3 "In Strata Vision, I lathed the profiles to create 3D chess pieces and then added on details, such as the crown jewels on the king and leaves on the queen (11.8).

Texture, modeling, and rendering

STEP 4 "I created seamless texture tiles and their corresponding bump maps for the grout lines in Photoshop. These were exported as PICTs for import into Strata Vision, where I made three-dimensional floor tiles from them (11.9).

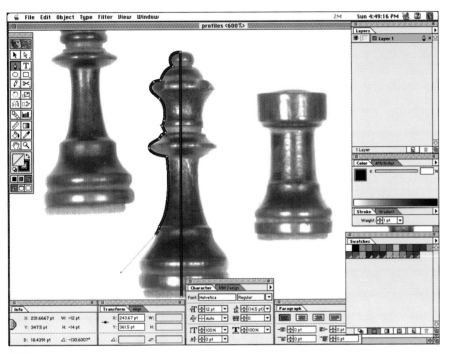

11.7

proper way to handle this would be to place animated random noise over the entire 96 frames. This would include the computer graphic monster.

"By adding film grain to the computer graphic, it would help to blend the graphic into the live action. The best trick for adding film grain is to scan some black frames of the original film stack used. This would allow the exact film grain to be used in the shot. This was not done. We do this all the time at my facility. I would not have wanted to trade this experience for anything. I learned several things. Never trust anything you see. There is often a great deal more that goes on in a scene than meets the eye, and Paintmonkeys deserve their own Academy Award. This would never have been possible at our facility without Photoshop."

STEP 5 "Now the real work started. I modeled the scene in Strata, setting up lights, applying textures, positioning cameras, and selecting interesting angles (11.10).

STEP 6 "After many low-res renderings and adjustments of the model, I finally rendered the scene to a 10MB RGB file (11.11).

Finishing touches

STEP 7 "The image didn't really come together until I thoroughly worked it in Photoshop. I adjusted contrast to work out the figures, added highlights to define shapes, added noise to simulate film grain, softened shadow edges to various degrees (note they are softer in the distance), and most important, I added depth of field. That is the biggest difference between real images and those coming from a 3D program where everything is in perfect focus (11.12).

STEP 8 "To get the final image, I converted the RGB file to CMYK and then removed any color casts. I opened up the midtones and applied a good amount of unsharp masking" (11.13).

TRAIN

Robert Forsbach created *Train* to show one common database for different aspects of the refinery business. This illustration was done primarily in Illustrator. Illustrator can create as much 3D and depth as the mind of the artist doing the drawing. As you can see in the image, Robert has an amazing gift of perspective and color for creating this "bird's eye" view of the refinery (11.14). To soften the edge of vector-based software, Robert turned to Photoshop to soften the colors and create the background (11.15).

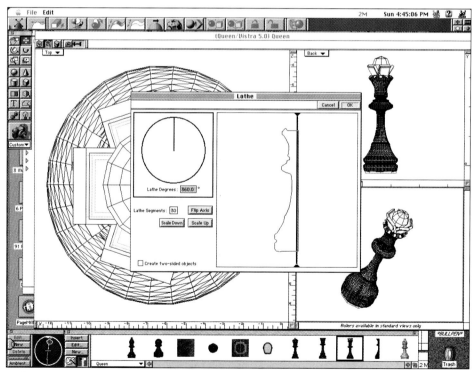

11.8

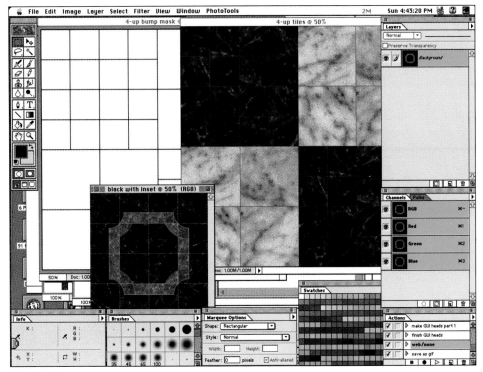

11.9

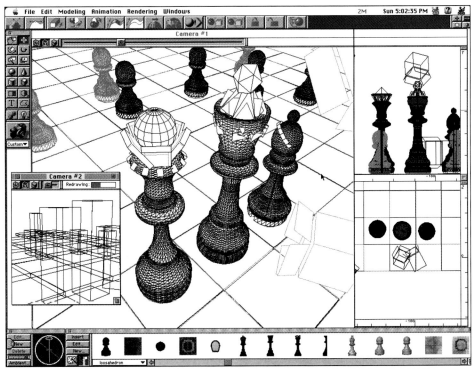

11.10

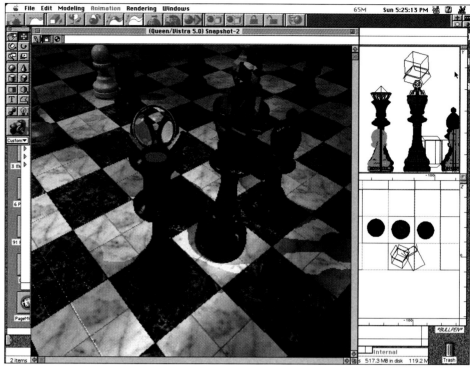

11.11

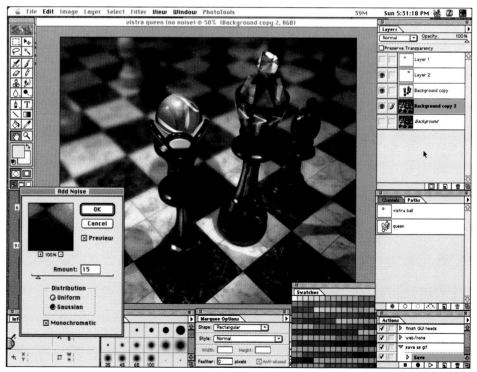

11.12

TOWN

The following steps outline the process Robert Forsbach followed to create *Town*. He broke down the image into understandable chunks to show the computer's involvement in the transfer of funds between different enterprises and services. The final image blends the use of Illustrator and Photoshop beautifully (11.16).

> **STEP 1** "The sketch was done in Illustrator and approved by the client (11.17). Then the sketch was painted, textured, and detailed entirely in Photoshop.
>
> **STEP 2** "To paint the button, I began by selecting the inside shapes with the magic wand tool. Then, using the Blend tool (Foreground to Background setting), I applied the color blend.
>
> **STEP 3** "I started at the center of the button and pulled a very short blend horizontally to the right. With the magic wand set to zero tolerance, I selected the left side of the button (11.18).

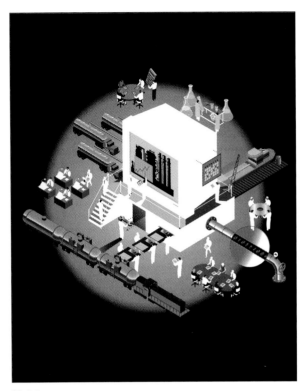

11.14

11.13

11.15

STEP 4 "Next, I pulled a long blend from the center of the button to the left. This created a nice rounded effect on the side of the button (11.19).

STEP 5 "With the paint bucket, I painted the top of the button base with a light flat color. Next, I selected the area with the magic wand tool (11.20).

STEP 6 "I deselected the part I didn't want to use for the cast shadow. Then, I filled the selected area with a flat dark color (11.21).

STEP 7 "The road was painted a medium gray, and then noise was added. Gaussian noise set to 25 and with the Monochromatic checkbox *off*, gave the road the mutlicolored speckles (11.22).

STEP 8 "I changed the shape of the cars as I painted them. I got rid of the fins and made the cars a little more streamlined. To make the speed streaks, I selected the area shown and then used the Motion blur tool (11.23).

STEP 9 "The shadows under the people are just simple oval selections I darkened using the Levels settings (11.24).

STEP 10 "I selected the area that would become a door with the Polygon lasso tool. With the Eyedropper tool, I picked up the ground color for the foreground. Using Eyedropper+Option, I picked up a much darker color for the background. Then,

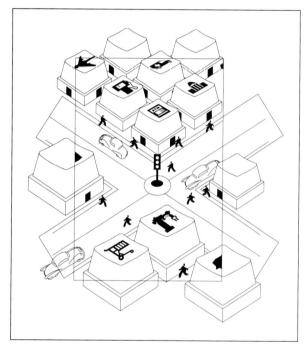

11.17

11.16

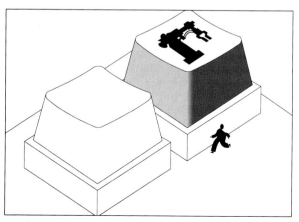

11.18

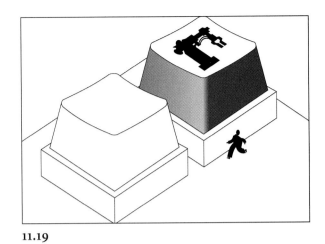

11.19

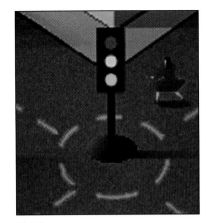

11.22

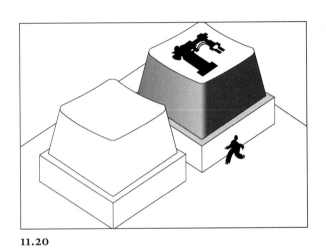

11.20

11.23

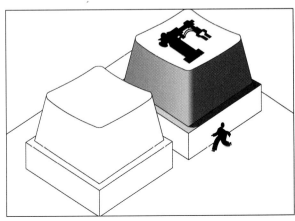

11.21

11.24

I dragged a Foreground to Background blend from the lower left to the upper right of the door. With the Rectangle selection tool, I drew the center bar shape and filled it with a light gray color (11.25). I used this technique on all the doors.

STEP 11 "The people were done with a lot of small blends and pixel-by-pixel painting" (11.26).

SONIC SCHOOLHOUSE

Eliot Bergman used Alias Sketch! for his 3D program. He also combines Fractal Design Poser, Illustrator, and Photoshop. His use of 3D is amazing as you can see with *Sonic* and *Gears*. Eliot's 3D program was Alias Sketch! and Alias RenderQ! It's fascinating to see that Illustrator was the starting ground and Photoshop the finishing step. Here, Eliot explains the steps he took to create *Sonic*.

"The first step was to create the numerals in Illustrator. I typeset the numerals, converted them to outlines, and saved them as a single file, which would serve as a plan for the 3D models I would later create. The chalkboard and walls were also created this way. The eyes were created from the profile of an eye. Sega US was unable to locate the DXF file for the character pose they wanted and, instead, furnished a render from the DXF file, which would be stripped in later.

"The second step was to create the 3D environment in Alias Sketch! I imported the plans for the walls and chalkboard and composed the set in Sketch! The numerals were extruded and a rounded bevel was applied. I revolved the profiles of the eyes I had created in Illustrator, duplicated, positioned, and grouped them with each numeral.

"The third step was to render the final image in Alias RenderQ! using ray-tracing. I opened the final render in Photoshop, placed an image (from Illustrator) for the chalk writing, applied the Diffuse filter for the chalk-like effect, and flattened the image. I opened the Sonic render, silhouetted the character using the Magic Wand and stripped it into a new layer in the file. The original render Sega provided depicted Sonic pointing at the viewer, rather than at the chalkboard, as desired. I deleted the original hand and painted a new one. The last step was to redraw the character's expression to satisfy my client's request.

"The image (and accompanying logo, which isn't shown) is an integral part of the packaging for *Sonic's Schoolhouse*, an interactive, educational CD for preschoolers" (11.27).

GEARS

Gears (11.28) was published in a special issue of *Global Sights and Logistics* magazine to illustrate supply-chain integration. Eliot describes the steps he took to create his work:

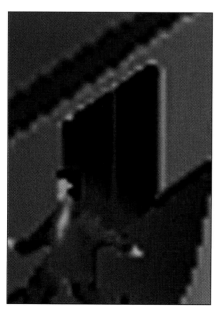

11.25

11.26

"The first step was to draft one gear in Illustrator. I drew two concentric circles, made them a compound path, and then rotated a small trapezoid around the circumference of the outer circle — at regular intervals — for the spokes. The compound path and the trapezoids were combined into one object using the Unite filter.

"The second step was to create the path the gears would follow. I made a large spiral using a plug-in, converted it to guides, and then sequentially copied, scaled, and positioned the gear following this path.

"This Illustrator artwork was imported into Alias Sketch! and extruded to create a 3D model. In Sketch!, I applied the Navigation tool to achieve the desired perspective and composition. A PICT created in Photoshop was imported and applied as the bump map, and the color of the gears was determined using the CMYK color picker in Sketch!

"I adjusted the reflectivity of the color black, assigned it to a plane I drafted in Sketch!, and positioned it below the gears to reflect them. The image was rendered in Alias RenderQ! using ray-tracing. The final step was to open the render in Photoshop, apply a Lighting Effects filter, retouch any areas that needed to be addressed, and convert the file from RGB to a CMYK TIFF file."

CREATING TEXTURES

Textures are probably the most fun use of Photoshop. Creating textures is a relatively simple process. In Photoshop, you can create anything from a solid color. Start with a basic color and you can create a background, or simply a texture, in a few minutes. I like to fill a screen with a color and use Photoshop's Noise filter to get started. After that, you can apply many effects to create any texture you want.

The following steps outline how to create a texture in Photoshop:

STEP 1 Start with a new document and fill the whole canvas with a color.

STEP 2 Choose Filter ➤ Noise ➤ Add Noise.

STEP 3 Choose Uniform and a setting of about 180. Don't check the Monochromatic button (11.29).

STEP 4 Choose Filter ➤ Pixellate ➤ Pointillize. Choose a cell size and click the OK button (11.30).

STEP 5 Choose Filter ➤ Texture ➤ Stained Glass. Set the Cell Size to 10, Border Thickness to 4, and Light Intensity to 3. Click the OK button (11.31).

11.27

11.28

STEP 6 Choose Filter ➢ Texture ➢ Texturizer. Choose Brick as the pattern. Set the size at 200 percent, the Relief at 32, and click the OK button. Isn't it amazing to think from one solid color you can create a colorful texture (11.32)?

The following steps outline how to create a sandpaper texture:

STEP 1 Start with a new document and fill the whole canvas with a tan color.

STEP 2 Choose Filter ➢ Noise ➢ Add Noise.

11.29

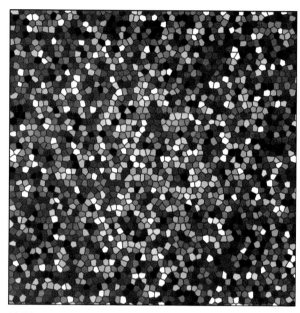

11.31

11.30

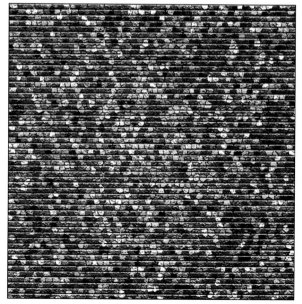

11.32

STEP 3 Choose Uniform, Monochromatic, and a setting of about 180 (11.33).

STEP 4 Finally, choose Image ➢ Adjust ➢ Levels. Set the Input Levels to 56, .24, and 204, and then click the OK button (11.34).

The sandpaper texture was easy to create, and you can use it any way you wish. One possibility is to use it as a background for type to add some interest to a page's layout.

INDIAN SUMMER

Artist Michael Tompert retains much of his original textures by scanning in actual objects. His use of the scanner to capture thistles, wood, grass, and leaves is unlike any I have seen. Photoshop and Specular Collage naturally help him finish off this imaginative touchable image.

To create *Indian Summer*, Michael followed these steps to scan and mask out found objects:

STEP 1 "I started out by collecting leaves, grass, pieces of rusted metal, weathered wood, and sundried thistles on the plains of Hollister, California, and captured them directly on my flatbed scanner (11.35).

STEP 2 "I then masked out the backgrounds using various brushes to get the edges of the masks to be from really sharp to quite soft (11.36).

STEP 3 "The central element of the collage was going to be the sun being wrapped up for winter. To create this effect, I wrapped a book with craft paper and twine, and then scanned it (11.37).

STEP 4 "Next, I used Photoshop's spherize filter and lighting effects to get the desired result (11.38). The same filters were used on the 'planets' made from scanned textures, a piece of stone, bark, or moss.

STEP 5 "Once all elements were scanned and masked, I placed them in Specular Collage and started assembling the image. I used Specular's shadow and glow capabilities extensively to create an image that seems as if it was assembled and photographed, rather than computer generated (11.39).

STEP 6 "Once all pieces were in place, I rendered a 50MB file complete with masks, which still enabled me to select individual items in Photoshop for editing (11.40).

11.33

11.34

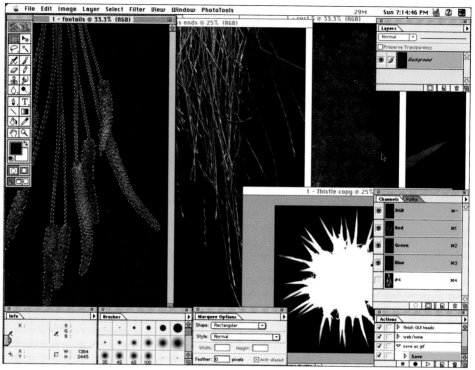

11.35

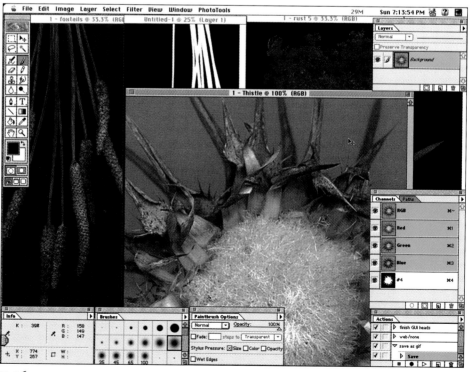

11.36

11.37

11.38

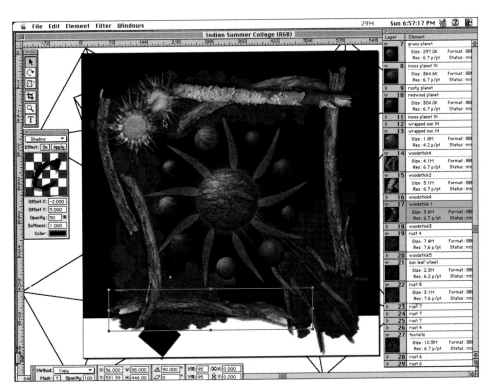

11.39

STEP 7 "Again, it took Photoshop to get the image where I really wanted it. Using Photoshop's lighting capabilities, I placed numerous spot lights throughout the image, bringing out details here and there. Most important, Photoshop enabled me to make the red glow around the sun appear as if it really was light. Notice the light reflections on

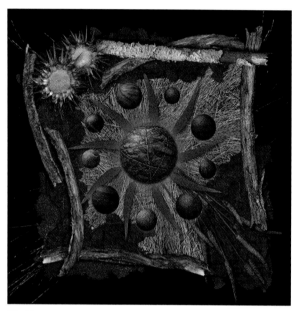

11.40

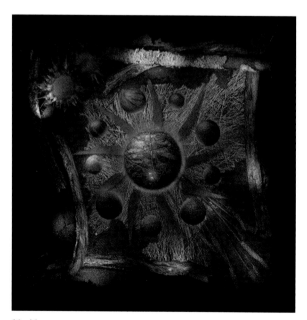

11.41

the planets in the final image compared to the Specular rendering. Finally, letting some of the sun's fire break through 'winter's wrap' completed my idea of *Indian Summer*" (11.41).

USING BRYCE 2 WITH PHOTOSHOP

Bryce 2 is a program that enables you to create fantastic landscapes. You can create real or fantasy landscapes using Bryce's 3D world. Bryce also enables you to add atmosphere to your landscapes. By combining your images from Bryce in Photoshop, you can successfully melt together your objects with a landscape background.

The Twins

The Twins, by Bill Ellsworth, was constructed with Bryce 2. The two main shapes are composed of 91 spheres. Each sphere was offset and rotated to create an organic figure. Both the figures are the same, except the one on the right is smaller. Both are covered with the same 2D PICT material (11.42), though it is mapped in different ways to achieve the different looks. One is mapped with Object Space; the other is mapped with Parametric. Remember, you are looking at a collection of spheres of which only a tiny piece of each is visible, so you are seeing a small piece of the 2D PICT on each sphere. These small sections create an interesting pattern for the surface of the major figures (11.43).

11.42

USING PHOTOSHOP AND KPT 3.0 PLUG-INS

Kai's Power Tools 3.0 is chock-full of cool plug-ins. You can create bubbles, textures, gradients, and much more. Using Photoshop alone or with a third-party plug-in, you can create textures and light to your image. Artist Bill Ellsworth uses KPT Bryce to start some of his images and goes to Photoshop to finish the images.

Buried Dreams

Buried Dreams, by Bill Ellsworth, began by collaging together Bryce images. The resulting image was lacking excitement, so Bill applied KPT3's Spheroid Designer and Vortex Tiling to the entire surface. The two sphere-like objects were created by floating an oval selection and applying KPT3's Gradient Designer in various apply modes (11.44).

Contact

Contact, also by artist Bill Ellsworth, is a collage of low-resolution Bryce images. The overall composition and feel of the image comes directly from the low-resolution Bryce source image. To make it look good at a higher resolution, Bill applied Photoshop's Lighting Effects filter to a slightly blurred copy of the image. Then he applied that to the scaled-up original, effectively removing the pixelation and creating a new, interesting texture. Several other Bryce images were added via various apply modes using the same process (11.45).

Sphere Sunset and Orange Sunset Sphere

The textures used to create the two versions of *Sunset Sphere* and *Orange Sunset Sphere,* by George Hazelwood, were created using Kai's Power Tools 3. Once George had the texture created in Kai's Power Tools 3, he used Photoshop's Wave and the Ripple filters to adjust the texture further. Finally, Photoshop Variations were used to create the panes of glass (11.46). These panes of glass were then imported into the materials composer in Bryce 2.

After importing the glass by loading them into each section of the materials composer in 3D Textures, B Textures, C Textures, and D Textures, George used custom settings in the other dialogs. Diffusion, Ambiance, Specularity, Transparency, Reflection, Bump Height, Diffuse Color, Ambient Color, Specular Color, and Transparent Color were all adjusted for just the right effect.

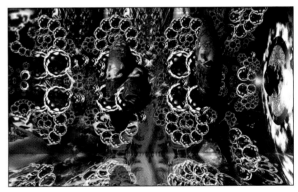

11.44

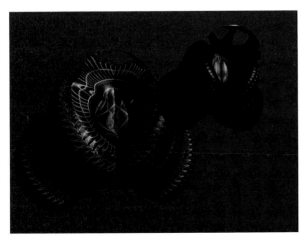

11.43

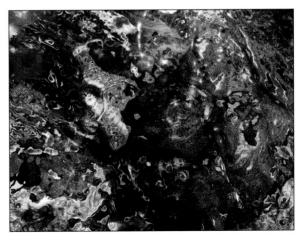

11.45

There are five spheres with the colors contained in one large sphere on the table. Each of the five internal spheres has an internal light source projecting the light out through the assigned PICT textures. These light sources, combined with the almost transparent main sphere, give a unique look to the images *Orange Sunset Sphere* (11.47) and *Sunset Sphere* (11.48).

11.46

11.47

11.48

CREATING BACKGROUNDS

An image usually isn't complete until the background is done. Some artists prefer Photoshop to Illustrator to create a background mainly because of Photoshop's capability to produce smooth backgrounds. Many gradients or blends in Illustrator tend to have a banded effect. Artist Mark J. Smith, for example, has created eye-popping objects with unobtrusive backgrounds and light effects.

ROSE BIG

Artist Mark J. Smith explains his thoughts in creating his image, *Rose Big* (11.49):

"I created this object in Alias Power Animator 7.5. The image was exported into Bryce where I used it in a scene. Bryce lost a great deal of the polygons in the object. The terrain and object were filled with black unrendered triangular polygons. I liked the image, but the black triangles had to go. Photoshop was used to paint out the triangles. Using the Rubberstamp tool, I cloned the good areas into the bad ones. The Burn tool placed shadows and negative highlights in the image."

Mark's secret to his success is the use of Photoshop's Rubberstamp tool. He says: "The Rubberstamp tool is the most used tool in Photoshop. The mistakes that have been fixed with this tool alone are worth the price of Photoshop. Filmgoers are none the wiser."

11.49

SPINEY

Spiney (11.50), created by Mark J. Smith, was started in Bryce and enhanced in Photoshop.

"The black-and-white height map used in Bryce was modified in Photoshop. The final rendering was touched up in subtle ways with Photoshop. I finish off everything, with the exception of animation, through Photoshop," Mark said.

11.50

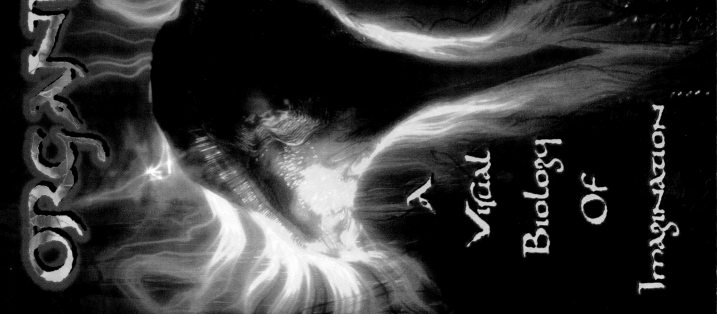

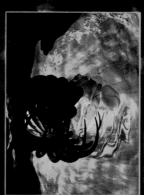

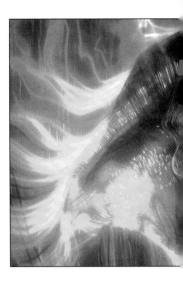

CHAPTER 12
FINISHING TOUCHES

Any image you create needs to be finished off in some way to feel complete. Photoshop and Illustrator work nicely together to finish off any image. Even if you use other programs, such as Bryce 2 or any 3D program, you'll still return to Photoshop to soften and complete your image. Photoshop enables you to add light, shadow, and texture.

I remember when pixels were monochrome and the size of postage stamps. Only the imagination rivals how far we have come in computer graphics.

MARK J. SMITH

ADDING FINISHING BACKGROUNDS AND TEXTURES

Many artists go back and forth between multiple programs to achieve the look they want. Photoshop and Illustrator are always in the mix. Illustrator creates lines like no other program, while Photoshop softens and adds depth, light, and texture like no other program. Many images begun in Illustrator are finished in Photoshop because of Photoshop's capability to create backgrounds and textures with ease.

NORTHERN CLIPPER

Glen Reigel created *Northern Clipper* (12.1) using multiple programs. Glen goes into detail on how each step was created and which programs he uses. In the following steps, Glen explains the process in his own words.

The creation process

STEP 1 "The inspiration for *Northern Clipper* was twofold. First, it is an extension of a previous work that was of the same street-side scene, albeit a summer version. I liked the mental image of this

12.1

little neighborhood so much I decided it would be interesting to see what it would look like as a winterized version. As a resident of Pennsylvania, I can harken back to a childhood filled with images and memories of sledding down hills and pushing through snow several inches, if not several feet, deep. Using memory as a guide, I set out to fill the landscape with an accumulation of snow.

Using Bryce 2

STEP 2 "The image is modeled and rendered in Bryce 2 by MetaCreations. I used a Macintosh PowerPC 8500/132. By nature, one of the ways in which Bryce functions is to take grayscale PICT files to create grayscale-to-height maps. Although Bryce does include a grayscale paint-style editor, it is not practical to create maps or 'terrains' that include the complexity required for this work. As a result, Photoshop becomes my tool of choice. In this particular instance, even the tools in Photoshop were not all I needed. As a result, this bit of work also involved the use of Adobe Illustrator to make the project complete.

STEP 3 "As with any modeling project, the image started by assembling the main models and then working down to details. Because the thrust here is to discuss the use of Photoshop and Illustrator, little will be stated about the creation of the main scene components if there was no involvement from Illustrator or Photoshop.

STEP 4 "In *Northern Clipper,* areas stand out for their use of Photoshop and Illustrator. The chief object created using Photoshop and Illustrator to augment Bryce's ability is the focal point of the image: the sled. To create the sled, a number of parts had to be created in Photoshop and Illustrator to complete the model.

Illustrator creates great paths

STEP 5 "The primary involvement of Photoshop was to create the 'wooden' body of the sled. To create the boards, I needed an outline of the basic sled body shape. Recognizing that Photoshop has a competent Bézier/pen tool, I chose to do the outline creation in Illustrator. Illustrator is just easier to work with paths and who can beat the number of levels of undo?

STEP 6 "First, the outline of half the sled body was created using the pen tool. Just a straightforward open path demonstrating some simple Bézier curves (12.2). After the path was created, the path was copied and the copy was reflected, so there were now two paths facing each other. The paths were positioned to form the whole sled body. After selecting both paths, the Object ➢ Pathfinder ➢ Unite command was used. The two paths became one closed path (12.3). The steering bar at the front of the sled was constructed in a similar manner. This file was saved as an Illustrator file for import into Photoshop.

Photoshop for texture

STEP 7 "In Photoshop, a new file was created in grayscale mode. The Illustrator file was imported into the image and used to create the outline of the sled body. A selection was saved based upon the Illustrator outline. KPT Bryce uses a PICT image format to create a terrain; therefore, the image was saved as a PICT (12.4).

STEP 8 "Now that the form or the sled body had been established, it was time to create a texture for the final sled image. Creation of the 2D texture that would wrap onto the grayscale sled body would begin by converting the saved grayscale file of the sled to an RGB file and saving it as a new

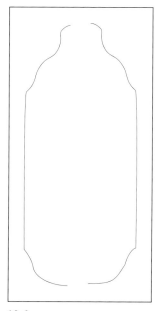

12.2

file. Converting the file was necessary for three reasons: (1) because the texture file would need to be in color, (2) the file needed to be saved with the alpha channel selection intact (this would be lost if it was Saved as... in grayscale format), and (3) that alpha channel selection of the sled body was needed once it was imported into KPT Bryce.

STEP 9 "In previsualization, the texture that wrapped onto the sled would have to have a worn, weathered look . . . more a feeling of use and exposure to the melted snow, and summer days spent drying out in some storage shed or garage . . . but not so worn out as to look old.

KPT 3.0 plug-in for Texture

STEP 10 "With a new color file created at the same resolution and dimension as the sled file, I opened KPT Power Tools Texture Explorer 3.0 and proceeded to experiment with a combination based upon a preset, but that was modified to taste. The custom texture was then applied to the new color file. Back in Photoshop, I used a combination of applying noise (to create a more grainy effect), blur, and Hue/Saturation to produce the weathered sled body. From this stock texture,

a square selection was copied and defined as a pattern (12.5).

STEP 11 "The RGB file of the sled body image map was then opened, the selection loaded of the body, and filled as a Pattern. This was then saved. The next step was to put some artwork/graphics on the sled — the trim painting and lettering. For that process, it was time to go back to Illustrator.

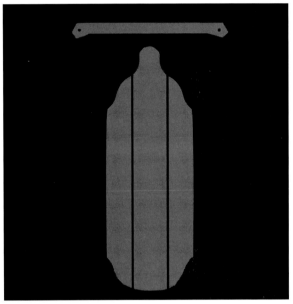

12.4

12.3

12.5

Illustrator used to create sled trim and arrowheads

STEP 12 "Using the sled outline previously created, I used a new layer in Illustrator to make a new set of paths that described the paint trim on the sled body. Once again, I created one side of the sled trim as a path, copied it, and reflected it, so it had both left and right facing trim (12.6).

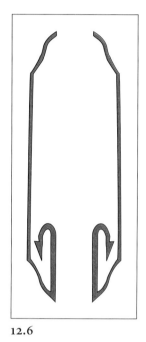

12.6

12.7

STEP 13 "The arrow graphic was easy enough to create within Illustrator because Filter ➤ Stylize ➤ Add Arrowheads seems to have been made for such occasions. After creating a line segment of suitable length, the desired arrow point and fletching were applied. The arrow was then rotated and scaled to its final state.

Photoshop adds shadow and depth

STEP 14 "The graphics were imported into Photoshop and saved as separate layers for ease of handling. All the text effects were handled directly in Photoshop. For final prep toward being used in KPT Bryce, the RGB file was flattened and converted to PICT format.

STEP 15 "The grayscale image of the sled body was imported into Bryce using Bryce's terrain editor — the resolution for the terrain was set high to give best quality. The base of the terrain was clipped off in the terrain editor, so only the sled body appeared (12.7).

STEP 16 "The RGB PICT file was applied to the terrain of the sled with the 2D PICT manager in Bryce control within the Materials Composer. The image was assigned within the image library. So that only the image of the sled appeared, the alpha channel mentioned earlier was applied to mask out the black portion of the PICT image. Using the Diffuse, Ambient, and Specular settings assured the proper appearance of the sled body" (12.8).

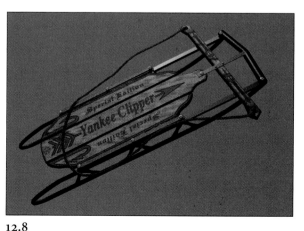

12.8

ARGON ZARK! (PAGES 40 AND 41)

Argon Zark! presents two pages from Charley Parker's online virtual comic book (Pages 40 and 41) at www.zark.com (12.9, 12.10). On Page 40, Argon, his companion Zeta Fairlight, and Cybert (Argon's personal digital assistant), are attempting to find the mysterious Badnasty Jumpjump by using an Internet search engine that appears to be without power. On

12.9

12.10

Page 41, the search engine has been powered up. Charley used Photoshop 4, Painter 4, KPT Bryce 2, Kai's Power Tools 3, and ProJPEG 2.1 to create these pages. He used a Power Mac 7500/132 with 128MB RAM, and a Wacom ArtZ 6 × 8 pressure-sensitive tablet.

The following steps outline the process Charley followed to create these pages of *Argon Zark!*:

Starting With KPT Bryce 2.0

STEP 1 "The search engine was constructed and rendered in KPT Bryce 2.0. I constructed the 'light' version for Page 41 first (12.11). I started with a cylinder. In edit mode, I used the Rotate control to make it horizontal (using the Shift key to restrain the movement to 45-degree increments), duplicated it (⌘/Ctrl+D), and used the Resize control to shrink it to fit inside the original. I aligned them on center with the Align Objects control (Align XYZ center). I was working quickly, so all the textures I used were stock Bryce 2 textures. I assigned the inner cylinder a mechanical texture with the appearance of lighted machinery, and I assigned the outer cylinder an open lattice that would let the inner cylinder show.

STEP 2 "This was capped with two toroids assigned mechanical lighted textures. I then created a sphere, placed it partially below the ground plane, elongated it on the vertical *Y* axis with the Resize tool and gave it the Guilded Cage texture. This was duplicated and the duplicates moved an

equidistant number of Bryce Units along the *Z* axis by using the arrow keys on an extended keyboard. Using the arrow keys, rather than the move control, enables more precise control of position and spacing. The large sphere was similarly set part way below the ground plane and given the Alien Disco Ball texture for the look of a shimmer of energy. Two smaller, flattened spheres with mechanical textures and a ground plane with the Tyrell Building texture completed the scene (12.12). The scene was then quick-rendered (using the quick render option to the left of the main render button) from several angles until I got the look I wanted for the scene.

STEP 3 "I then used Save as to prepare a new file using the same wire frames, to which I applied different textures for the darker 'off' version of the scene (12.13). Because I was pressed for time, I didn't render the files at a resolution to match my comic page file (6 × 4.5 inches at 300 dpi). Instead, I chose the quick-and-dirty solution: both files were rendered out at 768 × 512 and then interpolated up in Photoshop (Image ➤ Image Size) and sharpened (Filter ➤ Sharpen ➤ Unsharp Mask: 200,1,0).

Using Photoshop to put it together

STEP 4 "The PICT image of the 'off' version from Bryce was opened in Photoshop and made the background of a new document. It was fit into my page leaving a half inch at the bottom to allow for Zeta's hand to extend beyond the image.

12.11

STEP 5 "In preparation for bringing the file into Painter, I created three layers and filled them with white (with white as the foreground color, choose ⌘/Ctrl+A to select all, and then Option/Alt+Del to fill). I saved the file in Photoshop format and opened it in Painter.

Painting your pixels with MetaCreations Painter 4.0

STEP 6 "The white layers are a substitute for Painter's Tracing Paper feature, which is limited to 50 percent opacity. I turned off the top two white layers, which were now interpreted as Painter 'Floaters,' by clicking the visibility icons in the Floaters palette. I selected the remaining white layer and adjusted its opacity to 80 percent with the slider in the Controls palette. Using a Wacom pressure sensitive tablet, I sketched the figures of Argon, Zeta, and Cybert in over the background with a variant of the 2B Pencil, which I have reduced to 10 percent opacity and saved as a 2H Pencil (Brush ➤ Variant ➤ Save Variant).

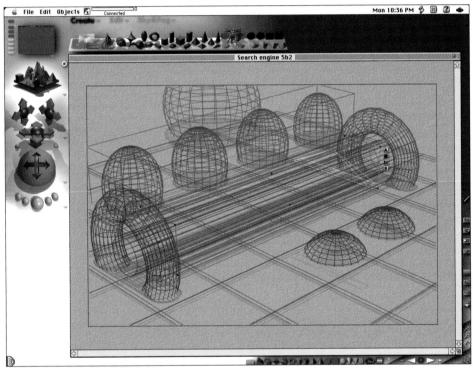

12.12

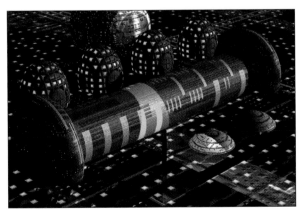

12.13

STEP 7 "With the pencil sketch complete, I returned its floater to 100 percent opacity, turned on the visibility icon of the second floater, and reduced the opacity of that floater to 80 percent. Using a custom variant of the Pens ➤ Scratchboard tool (Size: 2.4, +/– Size: 2.00, Size Step: 1 percent), I carefully drew the finished 'ink' lines for Argon and Zeta over my pencil sketch, leaving Cybert (the robot) for work in Photoshop.

STEP 8 "Back in the pencil layer, I erased and resketched the variations of hands and faces needed for the second page. These were 'inked' separately in the topmost white layer.

STEP 9 "Returning all three layers to 100 percent opacity (more important when moving layers from Photoshop to Painter than vice versa), I used Save as to save the file in Photoshop format, making sure I had enough disk space available because Painter doesn't compress files it saves in Photoshop format. This can catch you by surprise if you're moving a big file back and forth between the two applications. I also unchecked the Save mask layer box. Painter adds a mask layer to all files and will save it by default unless you tell it not to, adding further to the file size.

12.14

Using Photoshop to add inked lines

STEP 10 "Because I'm more comfortable with Photoshop's Bézier pen tools, I opened the image in Photoshop and finished the ink drawing of the robot with Bézier curves stroked with the paintbrush as a 2 or 3 pixel hard brush (12.14). (With the path active in the Paths palette, use B to select the brush tool and the Enter key to produce the stroke. A double tap of the delete key will delete the path.) With the ink drawing complete, I deleted the pencil sketch layer.

STEP 11 "In the layer containing the figures, I drew a temporary black line along the bottom of the figures where they would meet the edge of the underlying Bryce image. Because all the lines were carefully 'closed' at this point, I was able to select the white area around the figures with the Magic Wand. This area was then deleted and the layer returned to 100 percent opacity, leaving the black-and-white figures isolated above the Bryce image. I repeated this process with the layer containing the face and hand variations.

STEP 12 "Because of the feel and response to the pressure sensitive tablet, I tend to move freely between Photoshop and Painter when coloring. In this case, I was in Photoshop, so I began my coloring there. I selected areas of the figures with the Magic Wand and, where necessary, adjusted or altered those selections in Quick mask mode. I used the gradient tool to fill the selected areas with gradients, and then refined the modeling with the soft brush set to a low opacity and Darken mode.

STEP 13 "I made a point of saving the selection of Argon's vest by clicking the Mask icon in the Channels palette while the selection was active.

KPT Texture Explorer
enables you to add textures in Photoshop

STEP 14 "Argon's vest is filled with a texture from Kai's Power Tools Texture Explorer. This is usually modeled a bit with the Dodge and Burn tools. I also occasionally touch up the shading on the figures and the robot with Dodge and Burn.

Adding Light and Shadows with Photoshop

STEP 15 "To make the shadow under Zeta's arm where it apparently hangs out of the frame

(12.15), I first added a layer and used the rectangular marquee tool to select an area under the arm and fill it with white. In the layer containing the figures, I loosely selected around her arm with the lasso tool, and then snapped the selection to the shape of her arm by clicking inside the selection (but outside of her arm) with the magic wand, while holding the option key down, which subtracts from the selection.

STEP 16 "With the layer containing the white rectangle active, I distorted the selection using Layer ➢ Transform ➢ Distort so it was offset under her arm, and filled it with a dark gray to light gray gradient. This layer was then merged with the layer containing the figures (with the figures layer active, ⌘/Ctrl+E to merge down).

STEP 17 "To make the image for the 'on' version, I duplicated the entire layer with the figures by dragging its name into the new layer icon in the Layers palette, turned off the visibility icon of the original layer, and turned on the layer containing the variation of the heads and hands that I had drawn in Painter. With the new figures layer active, I erased the areas of the original figures that would be replaced and then merged these two layers. I colored the new faces and hands and used the saved selection of Argon's vest (by dragging its name in the channels palette into the Marching ants icon at the bottom of the palette) to fill it with a different KPT Texture Explorer selection. (To

give the impression that Argon's vest is constantly changing, I give it a different Texture Explorer texture in every panel of the comic.) I repeated the process just described to make a new shadow for her hand and again flattened those two layers.

STEP 18 "I then turned this layer off and reactivated the original figures layer (for the dark version). To give the impression they were in the dark, but that Zeta was partially lit by a source outside the panel (12.16), I made a selection using the lasso tool excluding her lower torso and arms. I then chose Layer ➢ New ➢ Adjustment Layer and chose Type: Hue & Saturation from the dialog box. I used the darkness slider to darken the selected area and boosted the saturation a tiny bit to keep the colors rich.

STEP 19 "To make the word balloons, I created a new layer filled with white and reduced its opacity to 80 percent, so I could still see the background, but so black text placed above it would be easy to see. As I created each block of text, Photoshop created a new layer for it. I merged these into one text layer using ⌘/Ctrl+E to merge them down as I went.

STEP 20 "On the lowered opacity white layer underneath the text, I created word balloons by using the oval marquee selection tool, stroking the selections, and adding 'tails' with stroked paths. Cybert's straight-edged balloon is all one path.

12.15

12.16

Following the procedure I had used to isolate the figures, I selected the area outside the closed balloons with the magic wand and deleted it, leaving the balloons isolated above the image. I returned the balloon layer to full opacity, turned off the text layer, and entered the text variations for the other page on a new layer.

ProJPEG software

STEP 21 "With the appropriate layers visible for the dark version, I chose Image ➤ Duplicate, checked Merged Layers Only in the dialog box, and named it *az40.jpeg*. To prepare this image for the Web, I reduced its resolution to 72 dpi, deleted all alpha channels, and saved it as a JPEG using Boxtop Software's ProJPEG plug-in. This has the advantage of a very intuitive interface and a preview feature that enables you to see a good approximation of the image quality and file size as you adjust the compression level slider before committing to your compression level.

Back to Photoshop

STEP 22 "Back in the Photoshop file, I finally imported the PICT image of the second 'on' Bryce image and placed its layer just above the other Bryce image in an identical position. I then turned on visibility for the appropriate layers for the text and figures and repeated the previous procedure to make the 'on' version of the image.

Images loading into Netscape Navigator

STEP 23 "I now had two identically sized JPEG images. The first (dark) image was placed in its own HTML page and made into Page 40. The 'button' was a separate image, placed in the page, and given a link to the next page. On Page 41, I took advantage of an unofficial Netscape HTML enhancement using this tag: <IMG LOWSRC= "az40.jpeg" SRC="az41.jpeg">. Navigator reads this by first loading the lowsource image, in this case, az40.jpeg. This image is already in the browser's cache if the user has just been to Page 40 and, therefore, loads almost instantly. Navigator then loads the second or source image over the top of it. Unless you have a lightning-fast Internet connection, this gives the impression the search

engine is 'lighting up' as the bright image gradually loads over the dark image" (12.17).

USING LIGHT AND SOFTENING EFFECTS IN PHOTOSHOP

Many 3D programs can bring depth to your objects, yet you still need Photoshop to add light and to soften the images. Simple and complex Photoshop techniques can both be applied to any image to finish your creation. From feathering to altering channels, you can achieve effects by combining the program's strengths.

ADDING LIGHT

One of the easiest ways to create the illusion of light in Photoshop is to use feathering. By selecting an object and creating a soft framed feather around that object, you can create the illusion of light. Eliot Bergman gave the 3D light bulbs he created in *Bulbs* (12.18) a soft, fuzzy, brighter appearance by simply using feathering around some of the brighter bulbs.

Matt Hoffman certainly has the gist of adding light in Photoshop. In *Stairs* (12.19), you can see the use of light coming down the stairs. By combining levels and contrast/brightness settings, Matt created a light streaming through the opening. In *Outlook* (12.20), Matt took a Bryce image into Photoshop to enhance the light effects. He used a bubble effect to simulate the light hitting the camera lens.

ADD TEXTURE

Creating texture is essential in Photoshop. Many images look fine when brought into Photoshop, but they lack texture and depth. Photoshop has many different effects you can use to create texture on an image. *Chalk* by Matt Hoffman (12.21) shows how the wood frame on the chalkboard has a definite wooden quality and feeling, thanks to Photoshop. Many 3D programs can do an amazing job, but still need Photoshop to enhance certain areas further.

Sjoerd Smit uses texture to enhance a vector-based image. In *Football* (12.22), the Illustrator file of a football player and background was brought into Photoshop. Using the Adobe Gallery Effects on

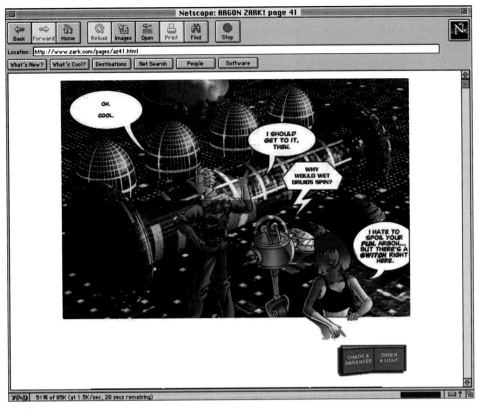

12.17

12.18

different settings, he texturized the different parts of the image with Note Paper. Several selections were saved and used to play around with color to get the right combinations of color. Using KPT Gradient Designer and Texture Explorer, Sjoerd further enhanced the background. After adding shadows, the image was complete.

BLASTING CHIP

Glen Reigel created *Blasting Chip* (12.23), of a chip blasting off, using Photoshop, KPT Bryce 2.0, and KPT 3.0 plug-ins for Photoshop. This image shows many uses for creating a background. Bryce creates wonderful backgrounds to start with and using Photoshop to combine layers finishes off the whole piece. Glen's words describe his thoughts about creating this image.

Starting in 3D

STEP 1 "The image of the processor chip blowing its way into space was created for a commercial product that has yet to be released. The entire premise revolved around the desire to show this chip 'cooking off' due to its indicated tremendous speed.

STEP 2 "Most of the image work was completed as a 3D project handled in KPT Bryce. Bryce did need a little help in polishing the final image, however. Namely, the effect that lots of light and other energies were being expanded could only be shown to a certain level in Bryce. To round off the effects, I opened the image in Photoshop.

12.19

12.20

12.21

12.22

Using Photoshop to add light

STEP 3 "Four main areas of concern were the overall effect of the 'blast' under the chip. The appearance was that energy was flying out in all directions from the main blast effect, the need for a light source or star included in the void of space, and the ambient light reflections created by the blast. This figure demonstrates the image without Photoshop enhancement (12.24).

STEP 4 "First, a mask was created for the chip itself (12.25). A blast pattern was added to the mask, which was then converted to a selection. The selection was feathered slightly (12.26).

STEP 5 "The outer edge of the actual chip mask was then altered using a ragged selection and again feathered. This was completed within the alpha channel for the mask.

© 1997 Glenn Riegel

12.23

© 1997 Glenn Riegel

12.24

Gradients in Photoshop

STEP 6　"In the composite view of the image, the chip was selected, copied, and pasted into a new layer. Underneath the new chip, another new layer was created; this was the target layer for the blast effect. The blast mask was loaded and, using a number of applications of the radial gradient tool,

the final blast was achieved. These figures show the effect without the chip layer for comparison (12.27, 12.28).

STEP 7　"Another big aftereffect was the energy burst. Because layers had already been created for the chip and blast, it was now possible to place another layer under the chip to give the ray effect.

STEP 8　"The first step was to create rays of light. Creating a file the same size as the final image, I opened KPT 3.0 Gradient Designer. Experimentation had led to the use of a custom gradient based on a ray burst pattern (12.29). The trick was to use the lighter values of the burst without showing the darker values of the image.

STEP 9　"Using the Layer Option palette, I clipped the darker values out using the slider control for the Overlay, while holding down the Option key. The burst image was copied and flipped to create the lower portion of the effect (12.30).

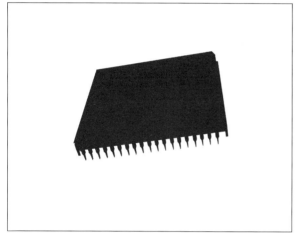

12.25

12.26

12.27

Altering the Opacity in Photoshop

STEP 10 "To create a more subdued effect, the opacity of the rayburst layer was reduced by 15 percent (12.31).

STEP 11 "The next step was to add a virtual source of the lighting in the scene. This was fairly simple with the Filters ➢ Render ➢ Lens Flare.

12.28

12.29

12.30

Layer Options

Name: Layer 1   OK

Options

Opacity: 100 %   Mode: Normal ▼   Cancel

☐ Group With Previous Layer   ☒ Preview

Blend If: Gray ▼

This Layer: 38 / 177   255

Underlying: 0   255

12.31

Photoshop finished off with light

STEP 12 "Similarly, the ambient light effect that would be present in objects with proximity to the blast energy needed to be strengthened. By creating very select lassoed and feathered areas, the Filters ➤ Render ➤ Light Effects was applied numerous times" (12.32).

12.32

PART III
APPENDIXES

ABOUT THE CD-ROM

The CD-ROM in the back of this book is compatible with both Macintosh and Windows platforms. It contains a slide show of the art, free plug-ins, and the following items:

- All the art in the book in a convenient slide show
- Free Photoshop plug-ins from Extensis
- Free copy of Extensis' Fetch that you can upgrade (for a mere $49) to Portfolio (Mac only)
- Tryout version of Photoshop 4
- Tryout version of Illustrator 7
- Demo versions of all Extensis software
- Demo version of Painter 5 (Mac only)
- Demo version of Alien Skin's Eye Candy (Mac only)
- Adobe Acrobat Reader 3.0

EXTENSIS' PHOTOTOOLS AND INTELLIHANCE SPECIAL EDITIONS

Included on the CD-ROM are free, special edition filters. You get three PhotoTools effects: PhotoShadow, PhotoGlow, and PhotoTips. You also get a special version of Intellihance that enables you to enhance any RGB image in one click.

SLIDE SHOW

You'll find all the images used in *Photoshop and Illustrator Synergy Studio Secrets* in a handy slide show on the CD-ROM. You can view the images at your leisure. Following this appendix you'll find the Artists Index, which gives you contact information for each artist. If you like what you see, drop the artists a note or send them some work.

DEMO VERSIONS OF PRODUCTS

You'll find many demo versions of various products on the CD-ROM. Included are demo versions of Adobe Photoshop 4.0, Adobe Illustrator 7.0, MetaCreations Painter 5.0, Extensis' PhotoTools, QX-Tools, CyberPress, Intellihance, Mask Pro, PageTools, Portfolio, PreFlight Pro, QX-Effects, VectorTools, and Alien Skin's Eye Candy.

MACINTOSH SYSTEM REQUIREMENTS

To run the CD-ROM and the files it contains, you need a PowerPC Macintosh with a math coprocessor or a 68040 processor, Macintosh OS 7.1 or higher, a CD-ROM drive, a color display, and at least 8MB of RAM. (QuickTime 2.0 or above is needed for some applications on the CD-ROM.)

WINDOWS SYSTEM REQUIREMENTS

To run the CD-ROM on a Windows system, you need a 486 or a Pentium PC using Windows 3.1, Windows NT, or Windows 95, a CD-ROM drive, at least 8MB of RAM, and a color display. (QuickTime 2.0 or above is needed for some applications on the CD-ROM.)

For information about how to run the programs on the CD-ROM, see the "CD-ROM Installation Instructions" in the back of the book.

ARTIST INDEX

JENNIFER ALSPACH
E-mail: jen@bezier.com

Jennifer Alspach is a nationally renowned artist and author whose artwork has appeared in a wide variety of publications. She is the author of several books and articles on computer graphics, including *Illustrator 7 Complete*. Jennifer is one of the owners of Bezier, Inc., located somewhere in the middle of Arizona. She has six cats, a dog, a horse, a husband, and a Gage.

FEATURED IMAGES: *Studio Secrets* (Chapter 2), *Bird Banner* (Chapter 2), and many various untitled images throughout this book

TED ALSPACH
E-mail: ted@bezier.com

Ted Alspach is the author of several books on computer-based drawing and graphics applications, including *Official Kai's PowerTools Studio Secrets* and *Illustrator 7 Studio Secrets*. He offered a few of his insightful images for *Photoshop and Illustrator Synergy Studio Secrets*. When Ted isn't creating art for books, he writes just to see his name in print. (Ted has written teeny books, like the 1,000-page *Illustrator 7 Bible* for IDG Books Worldwide.) On rare occasions, Ted can be pulled away from writing to play whatever games are on his PC hard drive.

FEATURED IMAGES: PageMaker 6.5 Visual QuickStart Guide (Chapter 6), Adobe PhotoDeluxe 2.0 Visual QuickStart Guide (Chapter 6), *Lucy Ann* (Chapter 7)

ELIOT BERGMAN
Phone: 888.COOLPIX
Voice: 212.645.0414
Fax: 212.645.0751
E-mail: ebergman@emedia.net
URL: www.ebergman.com

FEATURED IMAGES: *The Computer* (Chapter 2), *Blocks* (Chapter 6), *Fish* (Chapter 6), *Column* (Chapter 8), *Shoji* (Chapter 9), Balance (Chapter 9), *Duracell* (Chapter 9), *Sonic* (Chapter 11), *Gears* (Chapter 11), *Bulbs* (Chapter 12)

GERARD CHATEAUVIEUX
E-mail: ngchateauvieux@macromedia.com
URL: www.macromedia.com, www.joesplanet.com/gerard

Gerard Chateauvieux's interest in visual arts led him to an education in architecture and fine arts, specializing in painting and sculpture. When 3D and paint applications became available on computers, this seemed a natural transition to digital art. As an in-house artist at Macromedia, Gerard leverages his background in fine arts to create beautiful images and animations. In this capacity, he provides software development teams with a living example of how an artist's process is changed and augmented by using creative tools on the computer.

Specializing in Photoshop and 3D applications, Gerard has attracted attention from users around the world. He has contributed to magazine articles and lectured at user conferences where his 3D expertise is desired.

Gerard also has a special passion for Japanese cultural arts and British sports cars, influences that are evidenced in his artwork. He lives with his wife and three children in San Francisco, California.

FEATURED IMAGE: Mueller Beer logo (Chapter 8)

PATRICIA CHEAL
Patricia Cheal
Illustrator/Designer
940 Sugden Road
White Lake, MI 48386
Phone: 248.360.8452
Fax: 248.360.8462
E-mail: kitzel@earthlink.net

In 1988, I quit my job as a staff illustrator for a small agency where I had been doing automotive technical art, heavy on the airbrushing. So, after abandoning the security of regular paychecks, what did I do? Why, I borrowed money, of course! $8,500 to set myself up with a nifty, then top-of-the-line Mac IICX with 8, count 'em, 8MB RAM and a gargantuan 40MB hard drive! And the best part was, I didn't have a clue how to use the darn thing.

But learn it I did, and I haven't looked back. No more clouds of overspray, no more paper cuts, and the freedom to try almost anything without fear, thanks to multiple undos! I've been freelancing as an illustrator and designer ever since.

As I consider how the print/ad business has changed, I'm grateful I trusted my instincts and was able to take my blind leap of faith. I love this techno stuff, and I can't wait to see what the next ten years will bring. Long live Apple, Adobe, Wacom, and MetaTools!

FEATURED IMAGES: *Atlanta '96* (Chapter 1), *Bullseye* (Chapter 3 and Chapter 8), *Storm Watcher* (Chapter 6), *Africa Shirt* (Chapter 7), *Vet Card* (Chapter 10), *Whalers Schedule* (Chapter 10)

VICTOR CLAUDIO
Phone: 813.891.6188
E-mail: Madcirq@aol.com

Victor Claudio is a Pratt Institute graduate; worked as art director for Norman, Craig & Kummel. He was creative graphic director for Grey Advertising in Puerto Rico, and is presently creative director for AAA Auto Club South's marketing department in Tampa, Florida. Victor has been illustrating on the Mac since 1988. His painting background strongly influences his illustrations, which incorporate a wide range of techniques.

FEATURED IMAGES: *Camel Magic* (Chapter 9), *Volcanic Dali* (Chapter 9), *Hera's Surprise* (Chapter 9)

SANDEE COHEN
Phone: 212.677.7763
E-mail: sandeec@aol.com

FEATURED IMAGE: *Test Tubes* (Chapter 9)

GENO COPPOTELLI
Phone: 314.727.4252
E-mail: Gcoppo@aol.com

FEATURED IMAGES: *Primer Toon* (Chapter 5), *The Fish* (Chapter 7), *Gold Book* (Chapter 10), *Basics Cover* (Chapter 10), *Top Ten Tips* (Chapter 10)

BILL ELLSWORTH
E-mail: Loa9@aol.com
URL: http://members.aol.com/Loa9/ellsworth.html

I am deeply interested in the ability to create art that expresses and inspires abstract thought, and I have pursued this ability through a few means throughout my life. Most recently, computers have availed themselves of my peculiar vision and I am most grateful. Through the agency of the computer and, more specifically, through the software I tend to use — Adobe Photoshop and MetaCreations' Bryce — I have been able to create a very satisfying language of color and form. The range and flexibility of this language make me think I will only have scratched the surface of its possibilities after many more years of work.

FEATURED IMAGES: BIOTA Advertisement (Chapter 6), *Buried Dreams* (Chapter 6 and Chapter 11), *Contact* (Chapter 6 and Chapter 11), *Into the Labyrinth* (Chapter 6), *Spheroid Invader* (Chapter 6), *The Twins* (Chapter 11)

ROSS EASON
Ross Eason Photography
7 Possumwood Place
Buderim, Queensland 4556
Australia
Phone: (07) 5445 6855
Fax: (07) 5445 6855

Ross has won a variety of Australian photographic awards and handles projects from Sydney through to the Sunshine Coast where he now lives. Ross has embraced digital photographic retouching, using traditional techniques and an eye for detail to bring the best results.

FEATURED IMAGE: *The Ride* (Chapter 9)

ANDREW FAW
Phone: 212.633.9063
E-mail: afaw@crl.com
URL: http://www.crl.com/~afaw

Andrew Faw is happily at home in New York City — his base of operation since 1996. "I only miss Denver when I go outside!" Andrew spends about 12 hours a day using Photoshop, Illustrator, Live Picture, and miscellaneous filters trying to capture impossible images in his artwork. "I love all the goodies you have at your fingertips while using these software packages, but I try not to create artwork that screams a specific effect. I try to use these tools to enhance/change/build/composite images that end up saying more than the 'parts.'" Andrew's work has been used for advertising, software packaging, Web site development, fashion prints, and T-shirts for clients, including Disney, Warner Brothers, and Nickelodeon.

FEATURED IMAGES: *Common Desktop Environment* (Chapter 6), *D[AI]sy* (Chapter 8)

PHIL FREE
Phone: 205.257.1494
E-mail: philfree@aol.com

Phil works in "The Cave," a small, forgotten closet in the bowels of an electric utility building. From there, he creates illustrations, presentations, multimedia titles, and Internet sites for the corporation and its customers. For his personal friends and clients, Phil works in "The Basement," a small, hidden room under the floors of his home. Phil's easy to spot: he's the one with the pale skin and large white eyes.

FEATURED IMAGES: *Wheeling* (Chapter 9), *Lumina* (Chapter 9), *Curtain of Confusion* (Chapter 9)

ROBERT FORSBACH
Phone: 972.222.5402
Fax: 972.222.5403
E-mail: forsbach@flash.net

FEATURED IMAGES: *Bugs* (Chapter 2), *Trojan Horse* (Chapter 2), *Nokia* (Chapter 9), *Bridge* (Chapter 9), *Train* (Chapter 11), *Town* (Chapter 11)

LAURIE GRACE
Phone: 212.678.5435
E-mail: LGrace@aol.com or lgrace@interport.net

FEATURED IMAGE: *Decade Piece* (Chapter 8)

GEORGE HAZELWOOD
Phone: 303.683.8096
E-mail: GeorgeH521@aol.com

George Hazelwood owns GH Designs, a Denver-based design firm, specializing in digital imagery and multimedia projects. He is always looking for freelance projects. George has used the Macintosh since its beginning to create, illuminate, and teach. He holds three degrees from colleges and universities in business, advertising, and computer graphics. George has contributed images to the Kai's Power Tools CD-ROM and he helps in the test development of various companies' software tools, as well as graphic and multimedia design. George is also a regular contributor to AOL graphic forums. He lives on the outskirts of Denver with his wife and daughter.

FEATURED IMAGE: *Sunset Sphere* and *Orange Sunset Sphere* (Chapter 11)

PAMELA HOBBS
Fax: 415.550.8899
E-mail: xrau4u@aol.com
URL: www.pamorama.com

Her wrought-iron work ethic, combined with her dedication to cool, have made Pamela Hobbs wildly successful internationally. When she isn't off to Tokyo serving her Japanese clients, Pamela churns out work in her tiny studio in San Francisco's Mission District for sexy accounts like Absolut Vodka and Bill Graham Presents.

FEATURED IMAGES: *Digi Hong Kong* (Chapter 8), *Creative Black Book* (Chapter 10), *Computer Artist* magazine cover (Chapter 10), *Adobe* magazine cover (Chapter 10)

MATT HOFFMAN
E-mail: shoqman@hotmail.com
URL: http://members.aol.com/shoqwave

Matt Hoffman is a freelance graphic designer and musician who currently resides in Orem, Utah.

FEATURED IMAGES: *Cannon* (Chapter 9), *Stairs* (Chapter 12), *Outlook* (Chapter 12), *Chalk* (Chapter 12)

LANCE JACKSON
Phone: 510.253.3131
Fax: 510.253.3191
E-mail: lsd@ccnet.com
URL: http://www.ccnet.com/~lsd or
http://www.theispot.com/artist/ljackson

FEATURED IMAGES: *Workbook* ad (Chapter 2), *Macworld Expo* sign (Chapter 8), *Fast Track* (Chapter 8), *Alt Pick* (Chapter 9), *Java Happy* (Chapter 9)

JOE JONES
Art Works Studio
802 Poplar Street
Denver, CO 80220
Phone: 303.377.7745
E-mail: Duja Ve@aol.com

A Denver native with a foundation in fine art, Joe Jones has been a professional graphic artist since 1983. Over eight of those years were spent as vice president and art director of his own production screen printing shop, Cotton Grafix. In 1987, Joe was recognized for his work and featured in a five-page article in the industry publication, *Printwear* magazine. In 1994, Joe earned his degree in computer graphics and was awarded highest honors. In early 1995, the concept of Art Works Studio made the leap from the drawing board to reality. Since then, Joe's art work has been displayed in various publications, including *The Offical Kai's Power Tools Studio Secrets*, *Illustrator Complete*, *Illustrator 7 Studio Secrets*, and *Macworld Illustrator 7.0 Bible*. Joe took on one of his toughest assignments in September 1996 as a Digital Prepress instructor at Platt College in Denver.

Involved in various groups, Joe is an advisory board member at the Career Education Center. He also is a long-time member of a five-piece rock band known as *Duja Ve*.

FEATURED IMAGES: Precision Logo (Chapter 2), Stone Cliff Vineyard & Winery Logo (Chapter 2), *TV World* (Chapter 7), *Borg* (Chapter 8)

RANDY LIVINGSTON
Randy Livingston
Bona Fide Illustration & Design
206 Ernest Street
Washington, IL 61571-2017
Phone: 309.745.1126
E-mail: randy@bradley.edu
URL: http://bradley.edu/~randy/fatboy.htm
or
Randy Livingston
Assistant Professor/Graphic Design
Department of Art, Bradley University
202C Heuser Art Center
Peoria, IL 61625-0001
Phone: 309.677.3332
Fax: 309.677.3642
E-mail: randy@bradley.edu
URL: http://gcc.bradley.edu/art or
http://bradley.edu/~randy/fatboy.htm

Randy Livingston is assistant professor of art at Bradley University in Peoria, Illinois. He received his B.F.A. from Middle Tennessee State University and his M.F.A. from the University of Georgia. Both degrees are in drawing and painting. Responsible for Bradley's graphic design program, Randy blends digital work with fine art foundations. As a painter, Randy has exhibited his work at Cheekwood Museum, LaGrange Museum, The Georgia Museum of Art, and in other exhibitions, competitions, and galleries throughout the southeast. As an illustrator and designer, he has performed work for Ingram Micro, Ingram Book Company, Read USA, Island Lake Press, ESPN, ABC, The Museum of Modern Art, Nashville Now (TNN), and Major League Baseball. Randy has taught classes in illustration, graphic design, color theory, and art history at Middle Tennessee State University, the University of Georgia, and Dynamic Graphics Educational Foundation in Peoria. Randy and his wife, Dawn, work with various clients through the studio, Bona Fide Illustration & Design.

FEATURED IMAGE: *Rotten Egg* (Chapter 10)

BRIAN MCNULTY
Phone: 703.494.7713
E-mail: ShckByte@aol.com

Brian E. W. McNulty is cofounder of Shark Byte Productions, a digital-design firm, based outside our nation's capital.

FEATURED IMAGES: *Wrecking Ball* (Chapter 7), *Wrestler* (Chapter 7), *Lounge Lizard* (Chapter 7)

THOMAS-BRADLEY ILLUSTRATION & DESIGN
Thomas-Bradley Illustration & Design
411 Center Street
P.O. Box 249
Gridley, IL 61744
URL: www.thomas-bradley.com

FEATURED IMAGES: *Bag* (Chapter 9), *Car Interior* (Chapter 9)

CHARLEY PARKER
E-mail: cparker@zark.com

Charley Parker is a freelance Web designer, illustrator, and cartoonist, living in the Philadelphia area. His online "virtual comic book," *Argon Zark!*, at www.zark.com, has received numerous Internet awards since its inception in 1995. The site has also been featured in articles in the *Philadelphia Inquirer*, the *Houston Chronicle*, the *Richmond Times-Dispatch*, and *Internet Underground* magazine, as well as a number of computer graphics books including *Official Kai's Power Tools Studio Secrets*, by Ted Alspach and Steven Frank (IDG Books Worldwide), *Designing Digital Media* by Nick Iuppa, and *Painter 5 Studio Secrets* by Adele Droblas Greenberg and Seth Greenberg (IDG Books Worldwide).

   Argon Zark!, the "dead-tree" version of the comic, will be released in December 1997 from ArcLight Publishing.

   When not glued to his Wacom tablet, Charley likes to use pieces of compressed graphite encased in wood to make marks on sheets of dried tree pulp.

FEATURED IMAGE: *Argon Zark!* (Chapter 12)

GLENN RIEGEL
E-mail: glimage@aol.com
URL: http://users.nbn.net/~glimage/

Glenn Riegel has been a photographer for 15 years. During his tenure with two local advertising studios, Glenn photographed and processed images including anything from semiconductors to Mac trucks. For the past nine years, Glenn's profession has been as a state-certified commercial photoimaging instructor at the Berks Career & Technology Center, teaching tenth- through twelfth-grade high school students.

   Glenn's experience with computer technology spans back to 1988 when he discovered the Mac GUI. Since then, he has become proficient in using Photoshop, PageMaker, Illustrator, most MetaCreations products (Bryce is a favorite), and other applications too numerous to mention. His work currently appears on the KPT Bryce 2.1 CD. Choice works have been printed in *Official Kai's Power Tools Studio Secrets*, by Ted Alspach and Steven Frank (IDG Books Worldwide) and *Real World Bryce*, by Susan Kitchens.

FEATURED IMAGES: *Northern Clipper* (Chapter 2 and Chapter 12), *Blasting Chip* (Chapter 12)

MARK CHALON SMITH
E-mail: SmithMC1@aol.com

Mark Chalon Smith is an internationally award-winning digital artist specializing in Photoshop and Painter. He runs an online minigallery, AartJones, at http://members.aol.com/smithMC1/AartJones.html. When Mark isn't doing personal or freelance graphics, he writes about movies and theater for the *Los Angeles Times*. Mark has also written books; his latest is *bodyPRIDE*, focusing on the issue of teen self-esteem and fitness.

FEATURED IMAGE: *Jamal* (Part Openers)

MARK J. SMITH
URL: http://home.earthlink.net/~digitaldrama

Mark Smith has been a professional digital artist and animator for the past 13 years and involved in the field for about 20 years. He considers himself an original *paintmonkey*, a term he coined, which found its way into *Wired* magazine and, hopefully, into the popular vernacular. Mark's obsession with the digital realm has led him to a wide array of medium, including film, video, television, books, software, and magazines. Along with consulting, Mark writes computer graphics hardware and software reviews, for any magazine that will listen. His company, Digital Drama, is responsible for visual FX for such companies as MCA/Universal, HBO, Showtime, Fox Home Entertainment, SABAN, Trimark Pictures, Gramercy Pictures, Concorde/New Horizons, and others. Mark hopes to finance a computer-generated, 40-minute short called *Organix* in the future. He lives nestled amongst the foothills of Livingston, New Jersey with his wife Nella, and their children, Franco, Kathy, and Marco.

FEATURED IMAGES: *Digital Drama* (Chapter 8), *Shiny Turkey* (Chapter 9), *Random Veg* (Chapter 9), *Bjorkland* (Chapter 9), *Organix* (Chapter 10), *Rose Big* (Chapter 11), *Spiney* (Chapter 11)

SJOERD SMIT

Sjoerd Smit is a graphic designer/digital illustrator living and working in the Cincinnati, Ohio area. He was born and raised in The Netherlands, where he worked as a freelance designer and musician. In 1991, Sjoerd moved to the U.S. and started his own design studio, Swan Designs. Photoshop and Illustrator are his "brothers in arms" in his digital toolbox. He is currently working as creative director and graphic artist at Silver Hammer Workshops, Inc., an environmental awareness company located in Cincinnati.

FEATURED IMAGES: *Hmmm ...* (Chapter 2), *Football* (Chapter 12)

DARREN SPROTT
Darren Sprott
Design Solutions Australia Pty Ltd.
70 Beach Parade, Maroochydore
Queensland 4558
Australia
Phone: (07) 5479 6000
Fax: (07) 5479 6100
E-mail: eshop@squirrel.com.au

Darren is the creative director of Design Solutions Australia, a small boutique advertising agency specializing in producing high-quality work that delivers a strong marketing message.

FEATURED IMAGE: *The Ride* (Chapter 9)

CLARKE TATE
Tate Studio
P.O. Box 339
Gridley, IL 61744
Phone: 309.747.3388
Fax: 309.747.3008
E-mail: TATESTUDIO@aol.com
URL: http://members.aol.com/TATESTUDIO

FEATURED IMAGE: *Surf's Up* (Chapter 2)

MICHAEL TOMPERT
URL: www.tompert.com

Michael Tompert manages to earn a living as a graphic designer in Palo Alto, California, together with his wife Claudia and a couple of Macs. Together, they design and produce digital illustrations, logos, Web sites, graphical user interfaces, and packaging. Originally from Germany, Michael came to the U.S. as a journeyman typesetter and worked with Connie at Swan until the advent of desktop publishing forced him to let go of type and pursue a B.F.A. in graphic design at the Academy of Art College in San Francisco.

FEATURED IMAGES: *Alliance* (Chapter 6), *Indian Summer* (Chapter 11)

WAYNE VINCENT
Wayne Vincent & Associates
957 North Livingston Street
Arlington, VA 22205
Phone: 703.532.8551
Fax: 703.532.1808
E-mail: wvassoc@aol.com

Wayne Vincent was born on November 27, 1953, in Hartford Connecticut. He graduated from the Corcoran School of Art in Washington D.C. and has been working as an illustrator in the Washington area for the past 17 years. Trained as an airbrush illustrator, Wayne began working with Macintosh computers 11 years ago and now works exclusively in digital media. Wayne lives in Arlington, Virginia with his wife, Tori, and his two daughters, Allie, seven years old, and Charlotte, two years old, and their three- year-old greyhound, Willi.

FEATURED IMAGES: *Family PC* (Chapter 8), *Better Homes and Gardens Children's Cookbook* (Chapter 10), *Restaurant* (Chapter 8)

BRIAN WARCHESIK
11113 East Alemeda Avenue
Aurora, CO 80012
Phone: 303.360.9883

Brian Warchesik began his career as an artist in 1991 when he attended the Savannah College of Art and Design on a portfolio scholarship. Although he majored in illustration, Brian focused mainly on the art of painting. From there, Brian worked as a graphic designer and continued his education at Platt College in Colorado. This is where Brian learned the computer skills he now uses to produce artwork. One of Brian's teachers at Platt was Joe Jones, who is also the owner of Art Works Studio. Brian now works with Joe as a designer and illustrator.

FEATURED IMAGE: *Icarus* (Chapter 4 and Chapter 7)

INDEX

(continued)

(continued)

(continued)

ABOUT THE AUTHOR

Jennifer Alspach is the author of other books on computer-related subjects, including *Illustrator 7 Complete* and *PhotoDeluxe 2.0 Visual Quickstart Guide.* She is a professional illustrator who has illustrated the *Macworld Illustrator 5.0/5.5 Bible, Macworld Illustrator 6 Bible,* and *Illustrator Filter Finesse.* Jennifer's illustrations have appeared in various publications, including *Adobe* magazine. In addition, Jennifer regularly speaks at various seminars, Macworld Expos, and user groups all over the country. She also teaches Photoshop and Illustrator for business and everyday users.

COLOPHON

This book was produced electronically in Foster City, California. Microsoft Word Version 7.0 was used for word processing; design and layout were produced with QuarkXPress 3.32 on a Power Macintosh 8500/120. The typeface families used are Myriad Multiple Master, Minion, and Trajan.

Acquisitions Editor: Michael Roney
Development Editor: Katharine Dvorak
Technical Editor: Susan Glinert
Copy Editors: Marcia Baker, Michael D. Welch
Production Coordinator: Tom Debolski
Book Design: Margery Cantor
Graphics and Production Specialists:
  Renée Dunn, Linda Marousek, Andreas F. Schueller, Elsie Yim
Quality Control Specialist: Mark Schumann
Proofreader: Sarah Fraser
Cover Design: Deborah Reinerio
Indexer: Ann Norcross
Cover Art: Gerard Chateauvieux

IDG BOOKS WORLDWIDE, INC.
END-USER LICENSE AGREEMENT

READ THIS. You should carefully read these terms and conditions before opening the software packet(s) included with this book ("Book"). This is a license agreement ("Agreement") between you and IDG Books Worldwide, Inc. ("IDGB"). By opening the accompanying software packet(s), you acknowledge that you have read and accept the following terms and conditions. If you do not agree and do not want to be bound by such terms and conditions, promptly return the Book and the unopened software packet(s) to the place you obtained them for a full refund.

1. License Grant. IDGB grants to you (either an individual or entity) a nonexclusive license to use one copy of the enclosed software program(s) (collectively, the "Software") solely for your own personal or business purposes on a single computer (whether a standard computer or a workstation component of a multiuser network). The Software is in use on a computer when it is loaded into temporary memory (RAM) or installed into permanent memory (hard disk, CD-ROM, or other storage device). IDGB reserves all rights not expressly granted herein.

2. Ownership. IDGB is the owner of all right, title, and interest, including copyright, in and to the compilation of the Software recorded on the disk(s) or CD-ROM ("Software Media"). Copyright to the individual programs recorded on the Software Media is owned by the author or other authorized copyright owner of each program. Ownership of the Software and all proprietary rights relating thereto remain with IDGB and its licensers.

3. Restrictions on Use and Transfer.

(a) You may only (i) make one copy of the Software for backup or archival purposes, or (ii) transfer the Software to a single hard disk, provided that you keep the original for backup or archival purposes. You may not (i) rent or lease the Software, (ii) copy or reproduce the Software through a LAN or other network system or through any computer subscriber system or bulletin-board system, or (iii) modify, adapt, or create derivative works based on the Software.

(b) You may not reverse engineer, decompile, or disassemble the Software. You may transfer the Software and user documentation on a permanent basis, provided that the transferee agrees to accept the terms and conditions of this Agreement and you retain no copies. If the Software is an update or has been updated, any transfer must include the most recent update and all prior versions.

4. Restrictions on Use of Individual Programs. You must follow the individual requirements and restrictions detailed for each individual program in the Appendix, "About the CD-ROM," in this Book. These limitations are also contained in the individual license agreements recorded on the Software Media. These limitations may include a requirement that after using the program for a specified period of time, the user must pay a registration fee or discontinue use. By opening the Software packet(s), you will be agreeing to abide by the licenses and restrictions for these individual programs that are detailed in the Appendix, "About the CD-ROM," and on the Software Media. None of the material on this Software Media or listed in this Book may ever be redistributed, in original or modified form, for commercial purposes.

5. Limited Warranty.

(a) IDGB warrants that the Software and Software Media are free from defects in materials and workmanship under normal use for a period of sixty (60) days from the date of purchase of this Book. If IDGB receives notification within the warranty period of defects in materials or workmanship, IDGB will replace the defective Software Media.

(b) IDGB AND THE AUTHOR OF THE BOOK DISCLAIM ALL OTHER WARRANTIES, EXPRESS OR IMPLIED, INCLUDING WITHOUT LIMITATION IMPLIED WARRANTIES OF MERCHANTABILITY AND FITNESS FOR A PARTICULAR PURPOSE, WITH RESPECT TO THE SOFTWARE, THE PROGRAMS, THE SOURCE CODE CONTAINED THEREIN, AND/OR THE TECHNIQUES DESCRIBED IN THIS BOOK. IDGB DOES NOT WARRANT THAT THE FUNCTIONS CONTAINED IN THE SOFTWARE WILL MEET YOUR REQUIREMENTS OR THAT THE OPERATION OF THE SOFTWARE WILL BE ERROR FREE.

(c) This limited warranty gives you specific legal rights, and you may have other rights that vary from jurisdiction to jurisdiction.

6. Remedies.

(a) IDGB's entire liability and your exclusive remedy for defects in materials and workmanship shall be limited to replacement of the Software Media, which may be returned to IDGB with a copy of your receipt at the following address: Software Media Fulfillment Department, Attn: *Photoshop and Illustrator Synergy Studio Secrets,* IDG Books Worldwide, Inc., 7260 Shadeland Station, Ste. 100, Indianapolis, IN 46256, or call 1-800-762-2974. Please allow three to four weeks for delivery. This Limited Warranty is void if failure of the Software Media has resulted from accident, abuse, or misapplication. Any replacement Software Media will be warranted for the remainder of the original warranty period or thirty (30) days, whichever is longer.

(b) In no event shall IDGB or the author be liable for any damages whatsoever (including without limitation damages for loss of business profits, business interruption, loss of business information, or any other pecuniary loss) arising from the use of or inability to use the Book or the Software, even if IDGB has been advised of the possibility of such damages.

(c) Because some jurisdictions do not allow the exclusion or limitation of liability for consequential or incidental damages, the above limitation or exclusion may not apply to you.

7. U.S. Government Restricted Rights. Use, duplication, or disclosure of the Software by the U.S. Government is subject to restrictions stated in paragraph (c)(1)(ii) of the Rights in Technical Data and Computer Software clause of DFARS 252.227-7013, and in subparagraphs (a) through (d) of the Commercial Computer—Restricted Rights clause at FAR 52.227-19, and in similar clauses in the NASA FAR supplement, when applicable.

8. General. This Agreement constitutes the entire understanding of the parties and revokes and supersedes all prior agreements, oral or written, between them and may not be modified or amended except in a writing signed by both parties hereto that specifically refers to this Agreement. This Agreement shall take precedence over any other documents that may be in conflict herewith. If any one or more provisions contained in this Agreement are held by any court or tribunal to be invalid, illegal, or otherwise unenforceable, each and every other provision shall remain in full force and effect.

Publish

THE MAGAZINE FOR ELECTRONIC PUBLISHING PROFESSIONALS

FREE 101 Tips Book!

Pixel-Perfect Scans

Managing Color: Get Consistent Results From Start To Finish

The Next Generation of Publishing Software

Affordable Big-Screen Monitors

Top Products of the Year

Choose The Right Paper For Dramatic Effect

Can You Trust Onscreen Proofing?

Just an hour a month with *Publish*

gives you the edge in mastering your electronic publishing tools— from design to → print → web screen → or CD-ROM!

With today's explosion of new electronic publishing technologies, you have more options than ever before. To keep up, you need the magazine that pioneered the digital publishing revolution... and still sets the pace for graphics professionals.

It's *PUBLISH.* Month after month, *PUBLISH* improves your skills at every step in the electronic publishing process.

PUBLISH provides the ongoing education you need to save time and money in today's competitive world of electronic publishing. Our experts not only discuss new digital technologies, they show you how to use design and imaging tools to achieve spectacular results.

my2cents.idgbooks.com

Register This Book — And Win!

Visit http://my2cents.idgbooks.com to register this book and we'll automatically enter you in our fantastic monthly prize giveaway. It's also your opportunity to give us feedback: let us know what you thought of this book and how you would like to see other topics covered.

Discover IDG Books Online!

The IDG Books Online Web site is your online resource for tackling technology — at home and at the office. Frequently updated, the IDG Books Online Web site features exclusive software, insider information, online books, and live events!

10 Productive & Career-Enhancing Things You Can Do at www.idgbooks.com

- Nab source code for your own programming projects.

- Download software.

- Read Web exclusives: special articles and book excerpts by IDG Books Worldwide authors.

- Take advantage of resources to help you advance your career as a Novell or Microsoft professional.

- Buy IDG Books Worldwide titles or find a convenient bookstore that carries them.

- Register your book and win a prize.

- Chat live online with authors.

- Sign up for regular e-mail updates about our latest books.

- Suggest a book you'd like to read or write.

- Give us your 2¢ about our books and about our Web site.

You say you're not on the Web yet? It's easy to get started with IDG Books' *Discover the Internet*, available at local retailers everywhere.

CD-ROM INSTALLATION INSTRUCTIONS

To install the *Photoshop and Illustrator Synergy Studio Secrets* CD-ROM, insert the disk· in the CD-ROM drive. On a Macintosh, double-click the CD-ROM icon that appears on your desktop. On a Windows system, double-click My Computer, then double-click the CD-ROM drive icon (usually drive D).

To install the demo versions of products, open the folder of the demo you wish to install and double-click the installer icon. Follow the onscreen prompts. For demos that contain more than one installer icon, start with the installer in the Install Disk 1 folder. Double-click the installer icon and follow the onscreen prompts. (For more information see the Readme.txt file included with the demo.)

To play the *Photoshop and Illustrator Synergy Studio Secrets* (PAISSS) Slide Show, double-click the file, "PAISSS Slide Show Program," located in the PAISSS Slide Show folder (in the main window of the *Photoshop and Illustrator Synergy Studio Secrets* CD-ROM). To play the CD-ROM Slide Show, you must have the following:

- A Mac with 5MB of application RAM (more is better)
- Color 13-inch or larger monitor
- A Mac with at least a 68040 (PPC is preferable)
- Adobe Acrobat Reader 3.0 installed (Version 3.0 is provided on the PAISSS CD-ROM)

If you have trouble, do the following:

- Give more memory to the "PAISSS Slide Show Program" (the more the better) and leave about 200K for your system, if possible.
- Copy the PAISSS folder and its contents to your hard drive. Double-click the PAISSS Slide Show Program.
- Quit any other applications.

There are no incompatibilities with RAMDoubler, though don't allocate more than your physical RAM to "PAISSS Slide Show."

If you have comments about the *Photoshop and Illustrator Synergy Studio Secrets* CD-ROM or book, or if you are interested in having artwork appear in a future edition of *Photoshop and Illustrator Synergy Studio Secrets*, send a note to jen@bezier.com. Depending on the volume of responses, I may not be able to reply, but I will do my best to write *something* back to everyone who offers suggestions, tips, praise, and so on.